African Rural-Urban Migration

BY THE SAME AUTHOR

Population Growth and Family Change in Africa: the New Urban Elite in Ghana, Australian National University Press, Canberra, 1968

(Ed., with Chukuka Okonjo) *The Population of Tropical Africa,* Longmans, Green, London, and Columbia University Press, New York, 1968

African Rural-Urban Migration

The Movement to Ghana's Towns

John C. Caldwell

Columbia University Press
New York
1969

Published in Australia by
Australian National University Press 1969

Library of Congress Catalog Card number: 69-17496

Printed in Australia

Acknowledgments

This is the second of two books to arise directly out of the 1962-4 Population Council demography program at the University of Ghana. Inevitably the pattern of acknowledgments and gratitude expressed here must bear a strong resemblance to that already testified in the writer's *Population Growth and Family Change in Africa: the New Urban Elite in Ghana*, Australian National University Press, Canberra, 1968.

Thanks and gratitude must be expressed to the Population Council, which financed both the general program and the specific research projects, and to its individual employees, especially Dudley Kirk, now Professor of Demography at Stanford University who took a personal, professional interest in this project.

The project was assisted in many ways by the staff and students of the University of Ghana, many of the Ghanaian members of which were rural-urban migrants with a resultant interest in this phenomenon. Particular thanks go to the University's Sociology Department, which, under K. E. de Graft-Johnson and N. Elias, proved a happy home for the project.

In an undertaking of this kind one shares much of the labour and interest for a long period with the field workers. In this work they were drawn largely from the University of Ghana and the majority had taken the writer's demography courses. Thanks for their contribution, which was very great, must be expressed here unstintingly. Many of them have already begun work measuring and charting other social and economic changes which are accompanying the transformation of their country.

Much of the analysis and the writing up of this work has been carried out in the Demography Department of the Australian National University. For this, and for other help over a considerable number of years, the writer's deep thanks and appreciation go to the head of the Department, W. D. Borrie.

J.C.C.

Contents

Tables

Introduction

Since independence in 1957, Ghana has, for reasons of self-interest and of social and economic planning, taken a good deal of interest in the size, characteristics, and behaviour of its population. The most prominent manifestation of this was the taking of an elaborate census in 1960 and the subsequent publication of a series of volumes recording its findings.

Another manifestation, coupled partly with the interest in the census and related to what was felt to be its needs, was the establishment of a demography program in the Sociology Department of the University of Ghana. This began in the 1959-60 academic year and has continued and expanded until it now forms a complete Demographic Unit, staffed by three of the program's first students. During the whole period the Population Council has financed the program, and, when approached, its members have acted as consultants.

During the writer's tenure of office in 1962-4, there was a considerable demand for demographic research and analysis and for the publication of results. The demand arose in two ways. Firstly, Ghanaians in the University who were interested in the development of their disciplines, such as K. E. de Graft-Johnson who headed the Sociology Department when the writer arrived, felt that continued efforts should be made to increase the Ghanaian content of the demography and sociology courses, a view with which the writer concurred. Secondly, the government was concerned that university research workers should take an interest in the analysis of the 1960 census and that supplementary work should be done to illuminate some of its findings. In order to provide material which could be employed by government, the Ghana Academy of Sciences organised a series of studies, which have been published as Walter Birmingham, I. Neustadt, and E. N. Omaboe (editors), *A Study of Contemporary Ghana*, Allen and Unwin, London, and Northwestern University Press, Chicago. Some of the general findings of the research described in this book, as well as related research, were described in Vol. II, *Some Aspects of Social Structure*, 1967.

It was important that effort in the demographic field should not be duplicated and that it should be put to the best use by designing studies for which the findings could be integrated. It was important also that initial concern should focus on matters of real importance about which information was urgently needed.

One such topic was rural-urban migration and urbanisation. The census had sought data which could be used for the analysis of internal migration; and the subsequent post-enumeration survey had made migration one of its chief fields of inquiry. Between the two, they should provide an invaluable description of movements within the country.

But a full understanding of social phenomena depends on various types of inquiry. In this case it was felt that the rural-urban migration stream could be better understood if many detailed questions could be asked of migrants and non-migrants in rural emigrant and urban immigrant areas. Investigations of population samples in depth, and the asking of many intimate questions, can often be more easily undertaken in unofficial inquiries of this kind than by government.

It is hoped that the two approaches will illuminate each other. By the time this study was in a position to be written the main census tabulations had been published, and their findings have been incorporated in this book. The material on migration from the post-enumeration survey is not yet available. It is anticipated that, when it does appear, the findings presented here will fit meaningfully into its larger framework.

Certain comments on usages and practices adopted within the book should be made.

The term 'Ghana' has been employed to describe the area at present covered by the country, usually even for historical references, where 'Gold Coast' or 'Mandated Togoland' would have been strictly correct.

Three different regional systems have been employed; if these should prove confusing, reference should be made to the map in Appendix 1 where they are delineated together with survey sites. Part of the problem is that the administrative regions of the country had experienced some change between the 1960 census, to the tabulations of which we frequently refer, and the time of the 1963 survey. The other aspect of the problem is that even the administrative regions of 1960 were too many for meaningful migration analysis. Analysis elsewhere (Caldwell 1967a: 121-5) has shown that, using 1960 nomenclature, there were, excluding the Accra Capital District, four distinct groupings of region by migration behaviour. These were two predominantly emigrant areas, which were too different in socio-economic characteristics for aggregation, the Northern Region and the Volta Region; two predominantly immigrant areas which could be aggregated, the Ashanti and Brong-Ahafo Regions; and two areas, of near equality in immigration and emigration, which could also be aggregated, the Eastern and Western Regions. They were too large to be described as 'districts' and conformed too much with the existing administrative boundaries to be lamely described as 'areas'. Thus the term 'region' was retained and they have been described as 'major migration regions'. Where statistical tests are employed in analysing the survey these regions are employed exclusively and are entitled either 'South Major Migration Region' or just 'South'. However, when referring to census or other official data, the administrative regions are frequently employed, as the 'Eastern Region'. Sometimes all regions except those now known as the 'Upper Region' and the 'Northern Region' are collectively called the 'southern regions of the country' or just the 'more southern part of the country'.

In order to prevent endless repetition of the terms 'urban' and 'rural', 'town' and 'village' are often employed as synonyms. Thus 'village' and 'villager' refer to the whole rural population, even though some of the population in the far north of the country come from more dispersed populations described elsewhere as 'compound farming areas'. However, even the migrants from these areas regard themselves as coming from a certain populated locality, and the 1960 census (Vol. I, Summary Table B) succeeded in dividing the Northern Region into localities so that only 17 per cent of the people were found in localities with fewer than 200 inhabitants and only 7 per cent in ones with fewer than 100 inhabitants. Some of the respondents also employed the term 'bush' to mean either rural areas or the more backward parts of the rural areas.

The terms employed in describing migrants have caused some concern. In countries where there is a clear distinction between the inward movements of people from foreign countries and those of local residents into the towns or other areas, the former have been termed 'immigrants' irrespective of their destination and the latter 'in-migrants'; conversely the terms 'emigrants' and 'out-migrants' are also employed. In West Africa the division is not so easy, although ultimately it should no doubt be adopted. At the present stage of terminology it has been thought clearer here to describe, in a study confined almost entirely to Ghanaians moving internally, all persons moving out of any area as 'emigrants', into any area as 'immigrants', and between two areas as 'migrants'. Occasionally it has been necessary to specify that some persons moved wholly within the country, in which case the process has been described as 'internal migration', or that persons came from foreign countries, in which case the terms 'external immigration' or 'foreign immigration' have been employed.

Originally it was intended to differentiate in statistical tests of the significance of association between those associations significant at 0·1 per cent, 1 per cent, and 5 per cent. However, the size of the four subsections of the rural sample, on which most of the tests were carried out, together with the fact that there are striking differences in many respects between them, meant that most associations were significant at the 0·1 per cent level. Hence, if it is stated without qualification that an association was statistically significant, it is meant that this was so at the 0·1 per cent level. In all other cases the level is stated. Where it is said that no significant association could be shown, it is meant that it could not be shown even at the 5 per cent level.

In order to save readers from constant reference to the Appendix, the interviewing schedule questions, apart from the migration classification and personal data schedule, have been set out in full above the tables. The questionnaire can be reassembled by the addition of these questions. It is also felt that this method of presentation, while giving some appearance of rigidity and of repetition of table form, has scientific validity in that the responses can be compared with the exact questions and not with a generalised caption of doubtful accuracy.

This study was part of a broader, interrelated investigation into certain population phenomena which seemed to affect social and economic change and to be affected by them. Thus, inevitably, some reference had to be made to other reports on these investigations, most of which appear under the writer's name in the bibliography. However, many references to population trends are not specifically noted. The more general ones often refer to material discussed in *A Study of Contemporary Ghana,* Vol. II, *Some Aspects of Social Structure*, or to *The Population of Tropical Africa*; references to change amongst the urban elite to *Population Growth and Family Change in Africa: The New Urban Elite in Ghana* or to *Fertility Differentials as Evidence of Incipient Fertility Decline in a Developing Country: the Case of Ghana*; references to the effect of education to *Extended Family Obligations and Education: A Study of an Aspect of Demographic Transition amongst Ghanaian University Students* or to *The Erosion of the Family: A Study of the Fate of the Family in Ghana*; references to regional differences in the value of the large family and certain related matters to *Fertility Attitudes in Three Economically Contrasting Regions of Ghana*; and references to propensity to migrate to 'The Determinants of Rural-urban Migration in Ghana'.

1

The Movement to the Towns

The present century has witnessed a dramatic change in the way of life of a great many Africans. One of the most interesting experiences which can befall a visitor to tropical Africa is to talk to an old man, especially one who migrated in his youth from the countryside to one of the small towns of that period, and to hear him talk of the days before cash crops, railways, roads and mammy lorries, cinemas and secondary schools. Describing economic life at the turn of the century, Kimble pointed out that 'Before the present century, almost every sub-Saharan African earned his living by gathering food (including hunting and fishing), by cultivating crops or by herding, or by a combination of these activities' (Kimble 1962: Vol. I, 21-38).

The growth of towns

In the last century the number of people in African cities with 100,000 or more inhabitants has grown from under one-third of a million to eleven millions, so that one person in twenty lived in such centres by the middle of the twentieth century. Almost twice as many were to be found in all centres with populations over 20,000 (E.C.A. 1965: 33-4). Such proportions of townsmen were still lower than those of any other continent, but, nevertheless, they did indicate that many Africans were no longer experiencing a traditional village-centred, agrarian way of life. Furthermore the rate of increase of urban population had been very high, effecting a forty-one-fold growth in a century compared with a multiplication during the same period of nine times in Asia and twice in Europe. A continuing growth rate of 4 per cent per year in urban population meant that much of the increase was undoubtedly attributable to rural-urban migration and that many of the inhabitants of the towns had been born in villages.

In West Africa Ghana's level of urbanisation was third only to Senegal and Nigeria, and the proportion of her people found in cities of 100,000 or more inhabitants nearly doubled in the twelve years preceding 1960 to a point where almost a ninth of all her people were found in them. During those years, urban population had been exploding at over 10 per cent per year compared with a growth of rural population of only a little over 3 per cent (E.C.A. 1965: 52-4).

The *1960 Population Census of Ghana* provided the most detailed measurements yet available of urbanisation in the country. It showed that almost a quarter of the population lived in urban centres, defined as those with more than 5,000 inhabitants, a dividing line which rather neatly separated the centres where less than half the workforce were engaged in farming from those where more than half were. In a country with less than seven million people, over three-quarters of a million were to be found in three large towns, Accra-Tema, Kumasi and Sekondi-Takoradi, and another quarter of a million were in five other municipalities or urban council areas with 50,000 or more inhabitants, Tamale, Cape Coast, New Juaben (Koforidua), Oda-Swedru, and Tarkwa-Aboso. As only four-ninths of the million or so persons found in the eight towns were enumerated as having been born in the locality, and as most of these were children, there was evidence of massive movement to the larger urban centres.

Migration studies

A formidable bibliography can be compiled of African migration studies, but very few are strictly studies of rural-urban movement. There are great numbers of works dating back over half a century and further which are indexed in such bibliographies as 'movements of labour' but most are essentially concerned with the transfer of adult male workers. Such analyses no longer cover all or even most of the movement in Ghana. For instance, fewer than two-fifths of the Ghanaians enumerated by the 1960 census outside the regions of their birth were 15-54-year-old males. Just under one-third were children and almost four-ninths were females (Gil and Omaboe 1963: Appendix). In the eight towns, slightly more than four-ninths of the inter-regional migrants were females (Census 1960: Vol. II).

There is also a rapidly growing body of work on urban population and urbanisation as studied from the town end of the process. These works are of great importance when examining rural-urban migration, but they do not cover all migrants who have ever set out from the villages for the towns. Nor do the retrospective reasons given by migrants for leaving the farming areas necessarily coincide with their feelings about the matter at the actual time of their departure or the feelings of those now departing.

At the time the present study was planned, few strictly demographic works bore on the question of the West African rural-urban migrant. There were some suggestive leads in two collections of conference papers published in 1960 (Lorimer and Karp 1960; I.U.S.S.P. 1960) and in Lorimer's survey of *Demographic Information on Tropical Africa* (1961). During the early field stage of the study the Economic Commission for Africa produced an assessment of 'Demographic Factors related to Social and Economic Development in Africa' (E.C.A. 1962) and in a late stage of the analysis its estimates of 'Recent Demographic Levels and Trends in Africa'

(E.C.A. 1965). This was supplemented a year later by a paper on 'The Demographic Situation in Western Africa' (E.C.A. 1966).

When the study was planned some of the more relevant observations on labour migration were to be found in Hailey's *African Survey* (1957), Church's *West Africa* (1957), Elkan's article on 'Migrant Labour in West Africa: An Economist's Approach' (1959) and in the important I.L.O. study, *Why Labour Leaves the Land: A Comparative Study of the Movement of Labour out of Agriculture* (I.L.O. 1960). In the latter the view was expressed that

> Large-scale periodic migration between subsistence agriculture and industrial employment is a chronic condition of the employment market in African countries south of the Sahara. It is certainly not a transient phase in development, for in South Africa it has been continuing for nearly three-quarters of a century and its volume is on the increase. (p. 165)

Most of the evidence was drawn from southern and central Africa where the influence of mining economies is very marked; the kind of adult-child and male-female ratios which can be obtained from the inter-regional migrants enumerated in the 1960 Ghana census leads one to suppose that such a phase was in Ghana transient and has already begun to decline in terms at least of internal migration.

International migration is beyond the scope of this book, but it should be noted here that the I.L.O. description of migratory labour streams applies much more to movements which cross the Ghanaian borders, especially those movements from the north. This has been brought out in the work of Rouch (1954; 1956; 1961a; 1961b), Gil (1965), and Hoyt (1962). The 1960 census had enumerated over three times as many males as females who had been born in the sudanic countries to the north (Census 1960: *Advance Report*, Table 10). Hoyt pointed out that mobility of labour has been a factor of production in West Africa, but he also drew the conclusion that, although over half a million workers still migrate each year in West Africa, this pattern is, with the achievement of independence by most West African peoples, now passing.

Some labour-migration studies are in a special class in that they do provide information on the rural end of the migratory process. Of particular value to the present study was the work of Rouch, and that of Prothero (1957; 1965; 1968). Unfortunately the concentration was, because of the way of life of the groups studied, on rural-rural migration. In Rouch's work Ghana is essentially an area that receives migrants, and the emigration of Ghanaians from rural areas of the country is not a major theme. An article by Skinner on 'Labour Migration and its Relationship to Socio-cultural Change in Mossi Society' (1960) did suggest some hypotheses during the planning stage of the present study, especially when examining migration from northern Ghana.

Of specific interest to Ghana are a number of studies of labour movements within Ghana, for, even where the emphasis is on movements to cocoa-growing areas or the mines, we are dealing with that fraction of the same people who chose such destinations instead of the towns. Two studies by Davison examine the country before independence (1955; 1957), while Polly Hill's work is a long-term study of the movement of families and sections of families during the establishment of the cocoa belt of southern Ghana (1961; 1963). Killick, writing more recently (1966: 131) and drawing on work by Gil and Omaboe (1966), concluded that 'There cannot be many countries in the world in which migrant labour is as important as it is in the Ghanaian economy'. Rouch pointed out that part of the explanation for such mobility is that the dry season in the north coincides with the maximum demand for labour for the cocoa crop in the south (1961b: 300).

But the immediate foundation for the present work was that which had already been done on urbanisation. Although comparatively few studies have been undertaken in tropical Africa, and although the levels of urbanisation are still the world's lowest, the growth of towns has for a number of reasons excited considerable interest. Davis and Golden (1954-5: 20) wrote, somewhat overstating the case in so far as it applies to modern Ghana, that:

> the flow of migrants from countryside to city in Africa corresponds to a rapid transition telescoping several millennia into a short span. The social disorganization to which it gives rise is probably greater than that ever before experienced by urban populations. The native coming to the city cannot immediately divest himself of his tribal customs and allegiances, his superstitions and taboos; yet these are fantastically inappropriate to a modern urban milieu. Nor can he acquire suddenly the knowledge and habitudes necessary to make city life easy and workable. The result is a weird and chaotic mixture which gives to the average African city an unreal, tense, jangling quality.
>
> Yet urbanization is probably going ahead faster in this region than anywhere else in the world.

As early as 1956 the International African Institute produced *Social Implications of Industrialization and Urbanization in Africa South of the Sahara*. From around that date onwards appeared such works as McCall's 'Dynamics of Urbanization in Africa' (1955), Little's 'The Role of Voluntary Associations in West African Urbanization' (1957), Aldous's 'Urbanization, the Extended Family, and Kinship Ties in West Africa' (1962), and Bascom's 'Some Aspects of Yoruba Urbanism' (1962). Meanwhile in Ghana Ioné Acquah had published her *Accra Survey* (1958).

But these were essentially studies of towns and town life. And town life was being embraced by more people only because fundamental changes were occurring in African society. Okigbo (1956: 424-5) pointed to some of these shifts in his 'Social Consequences of Economic Development in West Africa', when he wrote:

> If we were asked what has been the most significant change in West African society in the twentieth century, the answer would readily be found in the individualization of activity which seems to have taken firm root in most sections of African society. The production and consumption units in West Africa have traditionally been much wider than the European concept of family would suggest. In the fifty-five years of this century, the social unit in West Africa has been shrinking because of emergent individualism, a shrinkage revealed in production and consumption no less than in marriage and other social relationships.

The United Nations (1957: 145-6) reported on 'Urbanization in Africa South of the Sahara' and on the causes of migration to cities.

> While, in general, the causes of migrations to cities are similar to those found elsewhere, certain factors can be considered to have special importance in various parts of Africa: the desire or necessity to obtain money income for such purposes as the payment of taxes, the purchase of certain highly valued consumers' goods or implements, or the payment of bride price; pressure of population on the land, which is not generally found in Africa in the form of a shortage of land area per capita, but which, in many regions, results rather from a recurring threat of famine or crop failure (owing largely to inadequate equipment and faulty methods of utilization and cultivation of land); the desire to break away from the monotony and strict controls of tribal life; the attraction of the town and its real or imagined opportunities for personal advancement and independence, as well as improved material welfare; the desire to join one or more members of the family already in the town; the social prestige associated in certain tribes with a period of residence in the town; and, finally, the pressure of labour-recruiting agents, administrators and chiefs, which has been in the past, and still sometimes remains, an important factor in movement to the cities. There is also evidence that education affects the tendency towards migration. . . .

A recent important contribution to the literature on rural-urban movement in West Africa has been Little's *West African Urbanization* (1965), and especially its first chapter, 'The Lure of the Town'. He strongly emphasised the effect of social and economic change, commenting, 'In the main, however, Western contact having created needs and aspirations impossible to satisfy in the countryside, migration means a flight from the land' (p. 9). He noted that the 'most primary need was cash, and that in many areas the town was the obvious place to earn it'. He also noted the relation between bridewealth and cash and went on to write,

> More generally, a person requires money in order to live in a 'civilized' way, to buy good clothes, manufactured products, and acquire modern housing. It is also needed for taxes, to pay dues to local associations, to educate oneself or one's children, and so on. (p. 10)

Little (1965: 11) rather strikingly emphasised the lure of the town, especially as it affects the young rural-urban migrant:

> Also, closely coupled with these rural practical considerations is the idea of the town being a centre of civilization. Its modern amenities like electric lighting, large stores and shops, cinemas, bars and dance halls have a particularly strong appeal for individuals whose mental horizon has hitherto been bounded by the bush enclosing their village. Even an upcountry trading station may be impressive, and his first visit to a small town on the railway line connecting Freetown with the interior prompted a young migrant to say, 'I became a sort of idiot as we moved along, for I stood to gaze at whatever English-made articles I have ever seen before, for example, cycles, motor-cycles and cars. I took a very keen interest in gazing at two-storey buildings, I admired people moving in them, and I often asked my little brother whether they would not fall from there'. For such a person the novel experience of meeting and moving among strangers and the new things he sees have been expressed in the songs of migrants to Ghana. 'Qui n'a pas été à Kumasi, n'ira pas au Paradis', is the refrain. Doubtless it conveys very truly rustic reactions to the relative whirl and bustle of the Ashanti capital.

He also pointed out (p. 14) that,

> Since, however, the flight from the land seldom involves whole families it is much easier to speak about the lure of the town than to assess the precise significance of migration as a whole. For one thing, migration is often within the same territory and of a stable reciprocal nature.

This brief, selective summary of the literature gives an impression of the studies available, or the ideas being aired in the cases where the studies had not yet been written, on rural-urban migration, at the time when the present survey work was being planned in 1962 and 1963. No large-scale quantitative attempt had been made to test some of the hypotheses; and no attempt had been made to quantify the effects on rural society of rural-urban and urban-rural movements. Many of the questions asked of respondents in this work were suggested by experience in the field, but the origin of others can be detected in some of the material quoted above.*

* Two other books became available only when this study was already in manuscript. Hilda Kuper (1965) edited the papers presented to a 1962 conference which contained a paper by Wallerstein (1965) categorising in a thought-provoking manner types of migration over historical time and three papers which had something to say on the impact of rural emigration on the residual community and presented findings which in essentials agree with those given here (Berg 1965; Miner 1965; Skinner 1965). Brokensha's study (1966) of a transitional town in southern Ghana, Larteh, demonstrated how close were the contacts between centres of this type and the nearby cities, for one investigation showed one-third of the population visiting Accra at least once a month (p. 59). Amongst the schoolchildren, two-thirds of the fathers or guardians who were in any sense rural-urban migrants were to be found in the large towns defined in the present study.

In addition a specific contribution to the study of the population mechanics of town growth in Ghana was Addo's paper, 'Demographic Aspects of Urban Development in Ghana in the Twentieth Century', presented to the First African Population Conference held in Ibadan in 1966.

The position in Ghana

When the present study was being planned in 1962 no official data were available later than the 1948 census. The 1960 census had already been taken but no results had been made public other than the information that the total population enumerated was almost two-thirds greater than that claimed twelve years earlier.

While the work was in progress three census publications became available which did provide valuable and detailed information (Census 1960: Vol. I, Vol. II, *Advance Report*). They permitted two forms of analysis of rural-urban change: longitudinal analysis in cases where 1960 data could be compared with those provided by earlier censuses, and a more detailed analysis of the situation in 1960 where the census of that date yielded more information than did its predecessors.

The summary tables in Vol. I, from which selections are shown in Table 1:1, confirmed the assumptions upon which the survey was based, namely that the larger towns were increasing in population much more rapidly than the country as a whole, indeed apparently so rapidly that a great deal of the growth could not be explained merely in terms of urban natural increase.

Table 1:1 Population change in the largest towns and the whole country, Ghana, 1948-60

	1948 population (thousands)	1960 population (thousands)	1948-60 increase (percentage)
Ghana	4,118	6,727	63
Large towns:[a]			
Accra-Tema	148	416	181
Kumasi	82	218	167
Sekondi-Takoradi	51	123	140
Tamale	32	58	83
Koforidua	34	54	59
Cape Coast	30	57	91
Oda-Swedru	26	53	105
Tarkwa-Aboso	30	49	63

[a] Towns defined by Municipal Council or Urban Council areas; Koforidua is the New Juaben Urban Council.

Source: Census 1960: Vol. I, Summary Table 1.

The 1948-60 population increase for the whole country appeared to be 63 per cent. The explanation was not natural increase alone; for even though that had undoubtedly been great, immigration from other parts of West Africa and some undercounting in 1948 were also part of the picture. Nevertheless, the growth of town population was very much greater. It was most marked in the largest centres, Accra and Kumasi having gone far towards trebling their size in the twelve years.

Such expansion could have occurred only if massive rural-urban migration had been under way. The release of Census Vol. II confirmed that this must have been the case in so far as it provided the birthplace statistics shown in Table 1:2. These actually understate the effect of rural-urban migration for a large proportion of the locally born are children, born in the towns in the years preceding 1960 to immigrant parents from the countryside or farther afield.

Table 1:2 Population by birthplace, largest towns, and whole country, Ghana, 1960 (percentage distribution[a])

	This Locality[b]	Another Locality in the same Region	Another Region in Ghana	Another African country	Country outside Africa
Ghana	58	21	12	8	0
Large towns:					
Accra-Tema	46	4	33	15	2
Kumasi	39	19	30	12	1
Sekondi-Takoradi	31	35	18	14	1
Tamale	59	19	16	6	0
Koforidua	44	24	21	10	0
Cape Coast	65	16	14	5	0
Oda-Swedru	60	12	18	11	0
Tarkwa-Aboso	22	41	21	15	0

[a] Percentages do not always add to 100 owing to rounding.

[b] Localities are nucleated settlements, but the towns above consist usually of one large locality plus some smaller peripheral localities; regions are those at the time of the census (i.e. before the division into two of the Northern and Western Regions).

Source: Census 1960: Vol. II, Summary Tables 2 and 3.

The large towns differ distinctly from the whole country in the way that their populations are made up. In the three largest towns fewer than half the population was born in the locality. In fact a large proportion were born far away. In Accra half the inhabitants were born either in another region of Ghana or another country. The proportion in Kumasi is four-ninths and in Sekondi-Takoradi one-third, still well above the proportion in the country as a whole.

The history of urbanisation in Ghana and a discussion of the measurable differences between rural and urban life can be found elsewhere (Caldwell 1967a), but some of the conclusions should be noted here.

The rate of growth of urban population has been greater than that of rural population since the end of World War I, when Ghana secured its present boundaries. In the forty years preceding the 1960 census the proportion of town population (i.e. those in centres with more than 5,000 inhabitants) rose from less than one-eighth to just under one-quarter. The actual numbers in the towns multiplied almost nine-fold and had passed one-and-a-half millions by 1960. Between 1948 and 1960, urban population increased at an average annual rate of over 9 per cent compared with 3 per cent for rural population, and the towns absorbed about two-fifths of the intercensal population increase in the country. The marked growth was in the larger centres.

An analysis of urbanisation between 1948 and 1960, with various assumptions about the accuracy of censuses and the increase of various sectors of the population, suggested that the natural increase of the 1948 urban population accounted for no more than one-quarter of town growth during the succeeding twelve years. One-fifth was probably explained by foreign immigrants, mostly from Nigeria, Togo, and Upper Volta, and their natural increase. But over half the growth must be attributed to Ghanaians who moved from the countryside to the town, and to the children subsequently born to them in the towns. Included in this latter group are some who merely stayed at home while their villages grew in size to towns, but even in this case there was undoubtedly some change in environment and way of life. Probably rural-urban migration reduced rural population growth between the censuses by between one-quarter and one-third.

Two other points should be noted about Ghana's towns: first their location and second their distinctive characteristics.

For those from northern Ghana, moving to the town means, except for the few heading for Tamale, travelling to the south. By every index of economic development and cultural change southern Ghana is furthest in transition from what was traditional society. In the south an area, in size less than one-quarter of the whole country, contains three-fifths of the population and in or adjacent to it an overwhelming preponderance of the towns: all towns with more than 100,000 inhabitants, 32 out of the 36 towns with over 10,000 inhabitants, and 87 of the total 94 urban centres.

Ghana's towns, like those of most developing countries, are very different from the countryside. In Ghana the large towns are markedly cosmopolitan. They house far more foreign immigrants and many more people from distant and somewhat strange parts of the country than do the villages. They attract more males than females; in the three largest towns there are one-and-a-half times as many adult males as females. They permit more education and attract more of the educated. Only half as many adults in the three largest towns have never been to school as in the country as a whole. Above all, and this to the rural-urban immigrant is often the key point, the economy is different. Only 3 per cent of Accra's workforce is employed in agriculture, compared with 62 per cent of that of the whole country. The wealth, for those who can secure it, is greater. Income per head, as measured by gross value added, was computed for 1960 to be £176 sterling in the Accra Capital District, four times as much as in the Volta Region, which contains none of the large towns listed in Tables 1:1 and 1:2, and six times as large as in the Northern Region (Szereszewski 1966: 92).

The first three census publications (Census 1960: Vol. I, Vol. II, *Ad-*

vance Report) also contained valuable material on the inter-regional flows of the Ghana-born since birth. While these statistics cannot be equated with rural-urban migration they are suggestive. For instance the greatest losses of native-born to other regions, in all cases over 100,000 persons, have been experienced by the Northern Region (now Northern and Upper Regions) with Ashanti as the most important single destination, by the Eastern Region particularly to the Accra Capital District, by the Western Region (now Western and Central Regions), and by the Volta Region especially to the Eastern Region and Accra. In terms of net flows Northern Ghana and the Volta Region are the two great exporters of men, with net losses of enumerated native-born of 157,000 and 95,000 respectively, while Ashanti, the Accra Capital District, and Brong-Ahafo have each imported almost 100,000.

At the time of the 1960 census the eight largest towns contained not only between one-sixth and one-fifth of all population and two-thirds of the urban population, but over one-fifth of all persons enumerated outside the localities of their birth. They may well have housed more of the real internal migrants than this, for many of the rural migrants who have been returned in the census as living in the regions of their births but in different localities have merely moved short distances to settlements associated with those of their births or have participated in some general shift of all the people of the original centre. Thus it is important to note that the eight towns alone contained in 1960 one-third of the Ghanaian population enumerated as outside the region of birth. While it is probably true that rural-urban migration streams tend to persist over longer distances than rural-rural ones, it is likely that when all urban population is taken into account, the theme of this book applied to around one-third of all migrations in existence in 1960, a fraction that was almost certainly increasing rather rapidly at that time. The importance of rural-urban migration is relatively greater than this, not only because of the amount of money it generates and social change it spreads, but because some of the rural-rural migrants at the time of the 1960 census had already participated in migration to the towns and even more were likely to do so in the future.

The later volumes of the census did not add greatly to our knowledge of rural-urban migration, but the forthcoming Report on the post-enumeration survey should do so. However, a volume on town statistics (Census 1960: *Special Report A*) has yielded an impressive amount of data, which with further analysis will tell us much more about the nature of the towns and indirectly suggest motives for migration and assess the effect of migration on the nature of the urban areas.

The two most important recent sources of data on migration have been a paper by Gil on foreign immigration (1965) and one by Gil and Omaboe on internal migration (1966), both making available previously unpublished census tabulations. Some of the findings in the latter study will be compared later with the findings of the rural-urban survey. Care must be taken when interpreting such comparisons. For instance, many inter-regional migrants are not migrating to towns; some might be migrating from them. More importantly, much rural-urban migration occurs within a single region, a position which would be even more the case in the published data only for the separation of the Accra Capital District as a separate region for administrative and statistical purposes.

Gil and Omaboe showed that in 1960 the incidence of inter-regional migration was greatest amongst 15-24-year-olds, when one-fifth were outside the region of their birth. Furthermore, the figures suggested a change in the pattern of such migration, for 45 per cent of the migrants aged 15-24 were females, compared with only 37 per cent of 25-54-year-old migrants. In the Accra Capital District 15-24-year-old and 25-54-year-old in-migrants amounted to 85 and 69 per cent respectively of the enumerated populations of that age born in the district. They showed that the in-migrants to the Accra Capital District were particularly important as labourers and service workers, important in transport and 'white collar' occupations, but less inclined than the locally born to become sales workers (i.e. largely petty trading). They also demonstrated that the volume of migration, as a proportion of the base population, tends to increase with the income differential between the sending and receiving areas and decrease with greater distance.

Surveying rural-urban migration

In 1962 the Demography Unit attached to the University of Ghana decided that the obvious importance of rural-urban migration, and of the resulting complex relationship between the villages and towns, warranted the use of a major part of its resources in studying the phenomenon.

Several decisions were made at an early stage. Firstly, it was agreed that the important decisions about migration must occur at the rural end of the process; even if the major motive for migration is the 'pull' of the town, that pull is only important as it is felt in the countryside and in the perhaps transmuted form in which it is felt there. Therefore the chief effort should be put into an examination of the sending area. Nevertheless, a smaller and nearly identical survey should be held in one or more of the receiving towns so as to check on the main survey and perhaps to gauge the sea-change which occurs to the outlook of the migrant. It was felt that the work should be sharply focused on rural-urban migration, and that nothing could be more dangerous than the attempt to collect supplementary information on all mobile population.

Secondly, it was felt that the unit was of a type, and could command sufficient resources, to work on a large enough scale to obtain a quantitative picture of the exodus from the village and in particular of the resultant effect on rural population. Thus questions should dichotomise population according to residence in towns or in rural areas, when examining both the position at the time of the survey and the record of past movements, and should not divide rural population according to location at household of origin or elsewhere in rural areas.

Thirdly, it was decided that the information should aim at supplementing the 1960 population census and post-enumeration survey. Thus the data to be gathered were to be either the intricate quantitative data which censuses cannot handle *en masse* or the questions of opinion and experience which they wisely choose not to handle.

Fourthly, it was found after some trials that the fact that comparatively few families ever migrate in their entirety would allow the survey to conduct a kind of census of all household 'members', whether living at the time in the village or away in the town.

The core of survey workers, some of whom participated in the previous phases of the project from April 1962 until April 1964, was drawn from second and third year undergraduate, together with a few graduate, students of sociology who were being trained in demography as part of the Population Council demography program at the University of Ghana. They took part in planning, testing, training, surveying, and analysing. Their numbers were supplemented by other students and some outsiders, especially for work in areas from which few or no students were drawn and where there were consequently problems of local knowledge and linguistic difficulties.

Much of 1962 was spent in drawing up and testing the questionnaire, the rural and urban versions coinciding in most questions. The first tests in the more remote areas, especially those carried out in the north, disclosed a fundamental problem, the overcoming of which served to shape the whole inquiry. In a great number of households there was going to be no question of interviewing each member of the household separately. The family interview was going to be a mass affair and the number of family spokesmen was going to be few, in many cases one dominant old man as head of the household. It would certainly be possible to obtain a range of factual information about each member of the household, although the details would often be provided only as a product of family consultation. It was, therefore, possible to construct a kind of schedule within each household questionnaire linking each individual's migrant classification with such characteristics as sex, age, position in household, conjugal condition, education, literacy, and occupation.

With the main body of questions somewhat different tactics had to be employed. In many households it was found impossible to use anything but a common household questionnaire, so in the end that was what was used. But different parts of the questionnaire obviously refer to different members of the household: at times to those about to set off for the town, at other times to those wishing to do so, or definitely remaining in the village, or on temporary return from the town, or permanently returned, and so on. All such persons had been identified during the construction of the individual schedules. When questions referred specifically to them the first attempt was made to interview them individually on these points. If this proved to be impossible, because the head of the household kept on taking over the conversation, the interviewer then asked his permission to put the questions through him to the members of the family concerned. This usually proved to be an acceptable alternative. However, in some cases, the head of the household merely quoted what he believed to be the position with regard to other members of the family.

The questions were concerned mainly with identifying where respondents fitted into the various migrant classifications, determining the various push and pull factors exerted by both village and town, discovering which kinds of migration were favoured by the family, detecting the interrelation between village and town, studying the mechanism of the actual migration, plumbing the reactions to the urban environment, checking on the flows of money, and asking about ultimate satisfactions. The initial body of questions was built up in several ways, from the migration literature, by preliminary small-scale surveys involving at first the recording of general discussions on migration and later the reactions to open-ended questions, by setting migrant students essays on their own experiences, by scanning the newspapers for migrants' complaints and observations, by conducting classroom discussions with university students, and through private discussions and in more formal seminars with Ghanaian members of the university staff and others. Subsequently questions were modified, deleted, or added as a result of field testing.

A major problem was that of language. Rural interviewing at least was almost invariably carried out in Ghanaian languages. In the great majority of cases in the rural survey, interviewers were working in their own areas of origin using their first language. But translators, sometimes supplied by the chief, were needed at times. In urban migrant areas teams of interviewers were sometimes needed before all the questions were clearly understood.

But the main problem was the translation of the questionnaire itself. Originally it was intended that the schedule should be reproduced in as many languages as were needed and the answers should be entered on schedules of the same language type as the survey had been conducted in. However, the number threatened to become rather large. Furthermore, various colleagues quoted experiences tending to prove that less error was likely to occur if all schedules could finally be compared on the same basis, with questions in the same wording so that it could be clearly understood that the answers were those to identical questions; this meant a basic schedule in English. Initial experiments in translation showed that two students from the same area could translate a question from English, only to find that, when it was translated back into English by two more students, the emphases had not only changed from the original but also differed one from the other. In the end translation classes were set up in each distinctive language or dialect (there were, for instance, three separate Ashanti classes). Every student likely to undertake interviewing in that language attended the class and prepared his own master questionnaire in the language as a result of group debate which ultimately translated each question, and often each word, into a form which was held by consensus to have the right meaning. Each meeting had a chairman; the writer occasionally acted as chairman and found he could help to resolve debates, after having listened to argument from all sides, without knowing the language concerned. Subsequently each interviewer made multiple copies of the agreed-on master sheet. The main advantage of the translation classes lay not so much in the achievement of an adequate schedule in a local language but in introducing the interviewers to the problems of translation. Many of them developed an interest in the field in the finer points of conveying meaning across the language barrier and in securing and recording the replies intended by respondents.

Partly because of problems of this kind, partly because the writer was directing work in a society other than his own, and partly because the Ghanaians in the team were undertaking work of an unusual type in their society and often working with social groups with attitudes differing from their own, fixed choice questions were found in trials to be peculiarly dangerous. Thus only free choice questions were employed. Although a very great deal of time was subsequently consumed in taking trial runs through large samples of the schedules and in organising groups to debate the classifications which had to be created to fit the answers and to debate how well those answers fitted the classifications, the very complexity of the operation, even after a full survey, revealed the many pitfalls which any restriction of possible answers would have produced. In any case the main danger of fixed answers with an unsophisticated sample, necessarily being interviewed by more sophisticated interviewers from outside the village, was that of leading the respondents.

Finally, before going into the field, interviewers tested schedules in villages near the university and in mock interviews within the university.

The choice of rural survey areas presented some problems. When areas were being chosen in 1962 we possessed the census map of local authorities but not the large-scale maps of enumeration areas which were later published nor the population figures for enumeration areas. We did have regional population totals, and these, together with the Local Authority Areas, determined the spread of the survey work.

It was decided that the sample was not large enough to attempt a scientifically balanced national sample, but that survey areas would be allocated so that the main areas with distinct migration characteristics would be approximately represented by a number of interviews in proportion to their population. For this purpose we divided Ghana, excluding the Accra

Capital District, into four migrant areas. These areas largely coincided, accidentally from our point of view but somewhat meaningfully in terms of history, with the old colonial divisions, the Colony, Ashanti, British Togoland, and the Northern Territories.

The first two are not emigrant areas, but their migration patterns might well differ. The *South* (see map in Appendix 1), consisting of the Western and Eastern Regions in 1960, and the Western, Central, and Eastern Regions now, is the area with the longest commercial traditions and the greatest number of towns. In it and the enclave formed by the Accra Capital District are found six of the eight towns listed in Tables 1:1 and 1:2. *Ashanti,* defined in this study as the Ashanti and Brong-Ahafo Regions, is a major immigrant area, especially for people from the north, but the migrants are mostly headed for the cocoa farms and other rural work places. However, it should be noted that the one town in Tables 1:1 and 1:2 found in the area, Kumasi, is an important magnet for rural-urban migrants from the north. Its fame has long been almost legendary in much of savannah West Africa. *Volta,* identical with the Volta Region, contains no towns as large as any listed, and had by 1960 suffered a net loss of almost 100,000 native-born Ghanaians to other parts of the country. However, many of its emigrants remain in close contact with their home villages and frequently visit them, for most of the region's population live within a hundred miles of Accra. The position is very different in the other emigrant area, the *North,* the Northern Region in 1960 but now the Northern and Upper Regions, for, although it contains one of the listed towns, Tamale, an administrative centre, the great majority of its emigrants pour southward. Many of the rural-urban migrants go to Kumasi, over 300 miles from the most densely settled parts of the North, or to Accra and Takoradi, a further 200 miles by road. By 1960 almost 200,000 of its native-born, a seventh of the total, were to be found further south. Its peoples have more reason than those found elsewhere for seasonal migration, for its dry season is acute and in its later stages is often accompanied by widespread hunger.

It was not certain at the time of surveying what rural populations the 1960 census had enumerated in each of the survey areas, but it was estimated that the survey would be on a large enough scale if it included details of close to 15,000 persons, so subdivided that about 6,000 would be from the South, 3,600 from Ashanti, 3,200 from the North and 2,000 from Volta. It was further estimated that this could be achieved if fifteen, nine, and five locations were surveyed in the South, Ashanti, and Volta respectively, each survey obtaining information on about 400 persons, and sixteen in the North each seeking details on 200 persons. The smaller quota in each centre in the North was selected after initial investigation had shown that the nature of many compound farming settlements in the area would make it difficult to reach the higher quota used elsewhere in many districts.

The attempt was made in all areas to have population represented in general accord with its distribution by size of inhabited centre. In 1948 two-fifths of the country's people lived in localities with fewer than 500 inhabitants and in 1960 a third did so. In order to include them, while retaining the 400-person quota, which was necessary so that our efforts would not be too uneconomically dispersed, in various districts adjacent small settlements had to be linked for survey purposes. In Appendix 1 they are sometimes described by the name of a nearer larger centre, but in such cases they should not be confused with that centre as described in the census.

A difficult decision, but one fundamental to the investigation, was the defining of 'rural' and 'urban'. The problem is more one of setting limits than of establishing meaningful categories. If certain characteristics are identified with town life, or even found to be associated with it, one can speak of one settlement being more urban than another. There is, however, no clear break, but rather a kind of rural-urban continuum. In Ghana, the census division line of 5,000 inhabitants separated on average at the time of the 1960 census those centres where the majority of employed persons were engaged in non-agricultural pursuits from those where farming predominated. But, employing this occupational definition alone there were centres of a few hundred people in the mining regions which were urban and others elsewhere that were rural with populations well over 5,000.

When analysing rural-urban migration, it is probably logical to speak of 'more urban' and 'less urban' than of 'urban' and 'rural', and to classify rural-urban migration as that migration which is motivated by the desire to seek a residence with more urban characteristics than the emigrant locality. However, when ascertaining attitudes towards such 'urban' characteristics, there is less chance of misunderstanding if discussion centres on the characteristics of the larger towns, for it is usually the intensification of one or more of these aspects of the residential locality that the migrant is seeking.

It was decided that when asking questions about the pull of the town an urban attraction could not definitely be said to be exerted on all potential migrants studied by any centre smaller than the eight listed in Tables 1:1 and 1:2, all of which probably contained over 50,000 inhabitants at the time of the survey. A good argument could be put for limiting the 'towns' to Accra-Tema, Kumasi, and Sekondi-Takoradi. In fact, when putting such questions as those asking about the good or bad aspects of town life, respondents in doubt about the kinds of centres referred to were cited only these three centres so as to secure their views on the type of life most contrasting with their own. But, in the original construction of the rural-urban migration schedule, movement to any of the eight towns was considered from the earliest planning stage to be of this type. However, in preliminary trials it was found that for the purposes of the schedule, the definition had to be modified. If the family insisted that one of its members had gone to a centre to secure an urban type of job, as distinct, for instance, from working on a cocoa farm, then he had to be counted as a rural-urban migrant even if he had gone only to a town like Ho with 14,000 inhabitants or even to Axim with 5,000. Clearly such movements could not be seriously regarded as rural-rural movements.

On the other hand, such a decision did raise the question whether movement from, for instance, Keta, with almost 30,000 persons in the Urban Council Area, to Koforidua, or from Winneba, with over 25,000 inhabitants, to Cape Coast was rural-urban migration. Ultimately it was decided to include no centre in the rural survey unless its population was less than 15,000, an upper limit which was still well above that of 5,000 set by the 1960 census, but which was justifiable because it was found that persons do move from towns of 5,000-15,000 inhabitants to larger centres for precisely the same reasons as they move from tiny hamlets. Thus the survey examined migration from Bawku but not from Obuasi. The total number of centres excluded by these definitions from being definitely either sending or receiving areas in terms of the examination of rural-urban migration was surprisingly small, and probably amounted to little more than 1 per cent of the country's population at the time of the survey. In theory the survey could have been faced with awkward problems of persons transferring from one small town to another. In practice the problem rarely arose; movement was either to an obviously larger town or to one very much more in the modernised sector of the economy. For instance, movement from subsistence farming on the outskirts of Bawku to marketing in Suhum was counted as rural-urban migration even though the latter centre is smaller than the former.

The focus of the investigation was on those members of the rural population who had transferred to more urbanised centres for one or more periods and their reasons for doing so. Thus, although considerable attention was paid to first migrations and how they were achieved, it was not taken to be of any great moment for analysis purposes that migrants had later moved directly to another town or that they had chosen another town as the destination of a later migration from the village. It is obvious, but not of crucial analytical concern, that some of the migrants may have held concepts of urban areas which were compounded of experiences in several towns and that some village households may have received their impressions of urban migration from the experience of a single member in various towns or of several members in different towns. It is sometimes difficult to distinguish sharply between the somewhat haphazard trying out of luck in various towns and the more systematic *step migration* where there is some orderly progress in moving on to successively larger towns or in a constant direction to a final geographical goal. The evidence (which will at a later date be examined more exhaustively and published elsewhere) suggests that the latter type of movement has not been of great importance, particularly in recent times, in the Ghanaian rural-urban migration movement.*

One complexity was provided by those absent seasonal migrants who were essentially rural-rural migrants but whose families anticipated that they would seek employment for a period in a town either on their outward or return journeys. Such persons were classified as rural-urban migrants, since they did fall into this category as well as others.

Local Authority Areas were chosen for survey purposes so that, in circumstances of somewhat limited manpower, advantage could be taken of local knowledge and skills. Thus some Areas were surveyed because our team contained one or more persons from within the Area. Nevertheless, a random choice of nearby districts and centres within the districts was made, and in general we approved of interviewers working in places where they understood the general culture rather than in places where they were personally recognised. Such an approach used alone might well have resulted in an over-representation of Areas with above average educational levels. So other Local Authority Areas were chosen in order to give a balance and efforts were made to recruit suitable interviewers. For parts of our work, some of it outside the scope of this volume, we wished to examine the movements into Accra and Kumasi from within one hundred miles of each and the general movement from the north, especially that from the densely settled far north. For comparative purposes two areas were selected in the southwest on the grounds that they might have a closer relation with Takoradi than with either Accra or Kumasi. Thus the survey could not be described as a national sample, but, as Table 1:3 shows, it did give approximately proportional representation to each of the four migration areas. Its coverage is least satisfactory in the new Western Region, largely because of design aimed at conserving limited human resources, and in the Anlo area of Volta, because a planned survey was unable to take place.

In the individual survey districts we lacked adequate maps and sampling frames. In the event the districts were sketched and routes were plotted so as to give each household an even chance of selection. A sampling fraction was chosen for a systematic survey, after the data collected while sketch-mapping the centre had been assessed to give an estimate of the average number of persons per Ghanaian household, both present and absent, and the total number of houses. Subsequently the sampling ratios were adhered to strictly. This is the reason that the average number of persons per location as shown in Table 1:3 is slightly at variance with the target numbers.

* In a random sample of 2,700 women, 15-49 years of age, studied by D. I. Pool in Accra in 1966, 60 per cent had moved into Accra since they had turned 15, and of these two-fifths had participated in more than one movement since that age. These movements include successive limited-term migrations to Accra, step migration to larger urban areas, random migration to various urban areas, rural-rural movements followed by rural-urban migration, as well as urban-urban and probably some preliminary urban-rural movement (Pool 1968).

The rural survey was confined to families of Ghanaian origin, for members of other households had already participated in a migration and any subsequent movement would form part of a much more complex migratory movement than the relatively simple movements we were examining.

Table 1:3 Comparison of surveyed rural population in four migration divisions of Ghana, 1963, with census population distributions, 1960

Migration Division[a]	Locations		Individuals surveyed		1960 census population percentage distribution	
	Number	Average No. of persons	Number	Percentage distribution	Total population	Rural population
South	15	385	5,769	42	44	38
Ashanti	9	377	3,397	25	25	26
Volta	5	414	2,069	15	12	13
North	16	159	2,541	18	19	23
Total				100	100	100

[a] The divisions were as follows in 1960 and 1963:
South: 1960 = Western Region, Eastern Region;
1963 = Western Region, Central Region, Eastern Region.
Ashanti: 1960 and 1963 = Ashanti Region, Brong-Ahafo Region.
Volta: 1960 and 1963 = Volta Region.
North: 1960 = Northern Region;
1963 = Northern Region; Upper Region.

The household was defined by common cooking arrangements and residence, except that where separate residence of spouses was normal the definition was confined to the cooking arrangements. Absent persons were regarded as part of the immediate household if they were so regarded by household members, and if they had been born in the household to those who were heads of the household at the time of the survey or alternatively had been reared by them in the household or usually lived there but were temporarily absent at the time.

The urban survey was something very different. Many researchers have already worked on tropical African towns and a great number more will do so. We wanted a limited survey, carried out in the same country and at the same time as the rural survey to serve as a check on the latter and to determine if the picture painted of town living by those in rural areas approximated to the impressions of those who had arrived in the towns. One-fifth as many individuals were to be surveyed in urban areas as in rural ones, namely about 3,000. Most were to be done in Accra, which was close to the university and in many ways the prototype of the developing urban areas, but approximately one-tenth were to be carried out in each of Kumasi, Sekondi-Takoradi, and Cape Coast to serve as a check on the Accra findings. In all areas the surveys were confined to predominantly immigrant areas, as explained in Chapter 2. But within these districts all African population, Ghanaian as well as non-Ghanaian, was surveyed. In Accra-Tema survey areas were distributed so that various types of suburbs could be examined, and an intensive examination, again partly for purposes beyond the scope of this book, was made of the newly developing port and industrial area, Tema. Within each survey area, houses were sampled along the same lines as had been done in rural areas. The actual distribution of urban respondents is shown in Table 1:4.

Table 1:4 Surveyed urban population, 1963

Urban area	Individuals surveyed	
	Number	Percentage distribution
Accra-Tema	2,148	68
Kumasi	328	10
Sekondi-Takoradi	349	11
Cape Coast	342	11

The total surveyed population is shown in Table 1:5. In all 2,367 households were examined and details of 16,943 individuals were collected. These figures for average household size cannot be compared with the census averages for houses, for frequently such houses contained two or more households. In fact the census found an average of 10·4 persons per residence for the whole country and 12·7 in the Accra Capital District. Neither can they be compared with census-type household figures, for the survey households include persons absent in the towns at the time of the count.

The field survey took place in March and April 1963, following a year of planning and testing. The rural survey met with astonishingly few difficulties, largely presumably because of the care taken in the prior contacting of the areas to be surveyed.

Table 1:5 Total surveyed persons and households, 1963

Survey	Persons	Households	Persons per household[a]
Rural	13,776	1,782	7·7
Urban	3,167	585	5·4
Rural and urban	16,943	2,367	—

[a] Includes persons absent in the towns or other rural areas.

Several months before the field work began, the main survey worker in that centre arranged to visit the Chief. On the visit he took with him a present from the writer, as organiser, together with various documents explaining the undertaking, which were read and discussed. It was found necessary to emphasise that the replies would remain confidential and would not be given to government officials. Throughout the whole survey we found, with one or two exceptions, that we had to work through traditional organisations, and that too much contact with District Commissioners or Convention Peoples' Party officials could jeopardise the success of the survey. Before the survey, during it, or both, the writer visited the Chief, received presents or drinks, and helped to strengthen confidence. Before the survey we usually paid to have the village *gong-gong* rung, thus calling a public meeting at which the Chief introduced the survey worker. The latter then emphasised the importance of the survey, asked for co-operation, and often read and explained the entire schedule. The Chief usually also spoke urging co-operation.

The usual survey worker's report spoke of co-operation, although the following extract is more glowing than most:

> I found no difficulty with my research after having presented myself to the Chief with the customary gift followed by the beating of the gong-gong. I paid a courtesy call on the Local District Commissioner who gave me invaluable assistance in my work.

In rural areas the following report describes reactions that fortunately were relatively rare:

> It must be pointed out that in spite of the customary gifts presented and the gong-gong which was caused to beating, I found it very difficult to extract information from the people for what they called intrusion upon their private affairs . . . Others also thought they were going to be taxed as a result and a lot of other stories. Others also insisted on my writing their needs to the Government. But, by and large, it was most interesting fishing for what was required. At one point, I had to stand up against insults for not paying a courtesy call on the Local Party Chairman after seeing the Chief!

In one sense the prior knowledge of the questionnaire did reduce the spontaneity of replies. But it certainly prevented suspicion from spreading. It may have permitted discussion, but it also meant that both questions and replies had been thought about—a very important matter when presenting what in many ways are necessarily sophisticated questions to an audience which in this regard is unsophisticated. With such thought often came increasing enthusiasm. In a surprising number of cases respondents said to interviewers or Chiefs said to the writer some variant of the observation, 'This is the first time anyone has ever asked us about a really important matter'. For it is true that migration of all kinds, and increasingly rural-urban migration, is a matter of fundamental importance to everyone living in rural Ghana.

Perhaps because of the method of approach, and perhaps because of the co-operation of the Chiefs, refusal to answer the questionnaire was almost unknown. So was the absence of the respondents, because the household questionnaire was of a type that could be answered even if there were some members of the household who were out; but usually they were not, or they returned, for the progress of the survey through the village, and forewarning about the next household to be interviewed, became part of the village entertainment and way of life. Methods for recalls and substitution had been worked out but they were very rarely used.

The position in the town was somewhat different. There was often suspicion in immigrant areas, and in squatter settlements rumours were easily aroused that our survey was part of an official investigation which would ultimately lead to eviction. The writer had often to quell such fears and repeatedly we emphasised the neutral position of the university. In the end the argument that won the day was that better housing and other improved living conditions could come only from the community knowing of the immigrants' problems and learning more about why they came to town. In Nima, Accra, success came only after the interviewers arranged a meeting lasting several hours and involving much translation between the interviewers and the writer on one hand and twenty-five elective-type Chiefs on the other in the grounds of the mosque. The other major source of urban difficulty was with some of the better-off groups who were either very busy or a little worried about too much probing into their way of life and background. Sometimes they were genuinely very busy. If a survey could not be undertaken at first visit, interviewers called back a second and even a third time; if that failed they substituted the next household in the same or adjoining house; on the rare occasions where that also failed they substituted the previous household.

The survey did not take the form of a national sample; and as such its results cannot be held to define the national population in the sense that the 1960 census findings can. Indeed, the essence of the survey is not to determine the nation-wide pattern, but instead to search for patterns in the various communities studied. It seeks to correlate information by asking of each, for instance, what the relative proportions of long-term and seasonal migrants were; whether the educated showed a stronger propensity to migrate than those without education; how prospective migrants regarded the attractions and dangers of the far-off city.

Yet reassurance and guidance both come from a knowledge that data gathered are reasonably representative of the community as a whole. A comparison of survey and census data is made easier by the fact that the 1960 census was held in March and the survey three years later in March and April. These months fall late in the dry season and the cocoa season, and, although the trek back home of seasonal migrants has at that time begun, large numbers are still away from home. Our impression from talking to Chiefs, Elders, and others was that the census attracted considerable numbers of rural-urban migrants home, especially in the South where distances are comparatively short, while the survey, of course, did nothing of the kind.

The rural survey findings cannot be compared directly with those of the census, for the survey included as 'rural' many centres described by the census as 'urban', and included many persons actually in urban areas at the time of the survey. In fact it included all population except those born in the large towns. However, some comparisons are possible.

Because of the household method of survey, the survey should be compared with census-enumerated population by region of birth. Such data are now available (Gil and Omaboe 1966: Appendix), and closely approximate the total numbers of respondents in the migration schedules for each of the 'migration areas'.

A comparison of the age and sex structure of the survey population with that of the population of Ghanaian origin enumerated at the 1960 census reveals general agreement, but those divergences that do occur are part of the nature of the survey and should be noted for guidance in the interpretation of survey results. The sex ratio in the survey was just under 103 males per 100 females, which falls between the census figures of 104 for the total population and 98 for the population of both Ghanaian ethnic origin and birth. In fact the sex ratios of the latter group, who were, when born in rural areas, the rural survey universe, coincide with the survey ratios up to 30 years of age. After that, the greater tendency for females who have married out of the household, especially if resident elsewhere, to be regarded as being essentially not part of the household than for males in a similar position (a point discussed in Chapter 2) leads to a relative rise in the survey sex ratios. Thus the rural survey enumerated 5 per cent fewer females altogether, and 12 per cent fewer females over 30 years of age, than might have been expected if the census distribution had been followed. In fact the discrepancy points to a very real fact of the rural household. The second point, and one largely anticipated, was that a smaller fraction of the survey population was under 15 years of age than the census population. This arose partly from the fact that the defined household population included most adult rural-urban migrants but not most of their town-born children. But the survey proportion of persons of this age, one-third compared with the census four-ninths, was somewhat lower than was expected. A check revealed that the reason lay in the 5 per cent of survey population for whom age was neither given nor estimated. The survey workers attempted to estimate age when the family failed to provide it or disagreed on the matter, but, in a migrant survey, many apparently felt that an estimate was of no great importance in the case of the very young, and so this group forms a large fraction of the age-unknown group.

Both survey and census yielded an average number of wives per husband of 1·4 (E.C.A. 1966: 32).

Size of locality presents some analysis difficulties, for, although the survey attempted to distribute survey centres according to expected 1960 distribution, the locations were classified for rural-urban migration analysis purposes, as is explained in Chapter 3, by the largest centre in the survey area. Nevertheless, the analysis does suggest that the survey did not include as many of the very small centres as the census indicates would give completely balanced representation, partly because the maps available at the time of the survey did not show such locations. This suspicion is strengthened by the fact that 50 per cent of the male survey population over 15 years were farmers, compared with 57 per cent in the census, and is further strengthened by a somewhat lower proportion of 'never at school' in the survey than census. On the other hand, probably because of slight variations in definition, the survey counted more adult females giving 'farming' as their primary occupation than did the census.

Finally, a rough comparison is possible between the inter-regional migration analysis of Gil and Omaboe (1966) and the survey analysis. Strict comparison is impossible because much migration, either rural-rural or rural-urban, is not inter-regional. However, two points should be noted. Firstly, the adult age patterns of the two types of migration as shown by the two investigations are identical. The question of child migration is taken up in Chapter 2. Secondly, the proportion of rural-urban migrants absent from the rural areas at the time of the survey was for all but the South smaller in number than the native-born enumerated in other regions at the time of the census, the proportion of the former ranging between one-and-a-half and three-quarters of that of the latter. In the South, where the major towns are found, the proportion of rural-urban migrants was slightly above that of inter-regional migrants. None of these data suggest that the two studies are incompatible, for not all inter-regional movements are rural-urban in nature, and much rural-urban movement is intra-regional.

The preliminary analysis was carried out at the University of Ghana, where such important processes as the preliminary classification of answers were carried out largely by the survey workers. The detailed coding and computing has been undertaken at the Australian National University.

2

The Pattern of Rural-Urban Migration

Rural-urban and rural-rural contrasts

One of the continuing truths of life for most Ghanaians is the contrast between rural and urban residence. To many, the former represents the traditional life, while the town presents the new possibilities. The countryside can be equated with the family and family duties, while the town represents the break from these things. The former offers only farming while the latter seems to promise the possibility of work indoors.

Most of these contrasts are only half true. To a very great extent in southern Ghana, and to a lesser degree in the north, traditional rural society has been undergoing transformation for generations. Any social research in the villages reveals a culture which owes much to the missions as well as to indigenous ancestry. A genuine Ghanaian blend has been produced which is at the same time fairly satisfying but far from being either stable or stationary. No longer do the vast majority of people live in very small villages made up entirely of huts of traditional construction. In the Eastern, Western, and Ashanti Regions over one-eighth of the population living outside the large towns listed in Tables 1:1 and 1:2 now live in centres with over 5,000 inhabitants and many more again are found in large villages of 2,000-5,000 persons. In many of these centres a considerable proportion of the houses are not constructed of the traditional earth (*swish*) walls and palm-thatch roofs but of material which includes at least some cement topped by galvanised iron. The main street may well be bitumen surfaced and be bordered by some electric lights. The houses in the larger centres frequently have electricity, surprisingly often produced by home generating units. Migration to the town may reduce family ties; it rarely removes them, and few Ghanaians would desire it to do so. Chain migration to the towns plus his own marrying and reproduction may soon surround the village-born townsman with a surprising number and range of relatives. Furthermore his connections with his own village are likely to remain strong, cemented by obligations and frequent visits. But towns do offer an escape from farming, especially the traditional cultivation of locally eaten foodstuffs. The 1960 census showed that nine-tenths of the employed population in the rural northern parts of the country still work in this way, but the proportion falls to one-third in rural areas outside the north, for cash crops and non-farming activities become more important, to one-thirteenth in all urban areas, and to one in every 150 in the urban areas of the Accra Capital District (Census 1960: *Advance Report*, Table 33).

One way in which these contrasts were impressed upon the writer in the course of the research described here were through the conversation and written reports of the survey workers. Almost without exception the rural interviewers were rural-urban migrants from the same general area which they surveyed. They were 'successful' migrants coming back to look with trained eyes at the society they had almost certainly left for ever. Yet their remarks, though more sophisticated and copious, were often strangely reflected in the words which came from the villagers' lips. For this reason, some space will be devoted to selections from the students' reports on the areas in which they worked.

It was reacquaintance with the north that often produced the strongest response:

> Western civilisation has not yet been fully appreciated and accepted by the people of Lambussie;* and as a result some primitive customs are still practised—customs heavily laden with superstitious beliefs . . . it is generally accepted that anyone who commits adultery with the wife of a hunter of a certain grade must be whipped, while naked, with thorny branches, and must, in addition to other things, give up live flies, a one-eyed cat and cowrie shells to sacrifice. The Roman Catholic Church has converted a few of the people into Christians. Christianity, however, is taboo for most of the families because it was believed by their ancestors that the *White Fathers* had tails and ate dead bodies. This belief does not exist now, since a few local people have become *Fathers*, but the taboo exists and is observed rather instinctively than intentionally . . . The people of Lambussie are a contented people and very hospitable. They say they have a glorious past and strive hard to discipline their children according to traditional customary standards and protect themselves against certain trends of modern civilization, which, they feel, tend to destroy what they call 'good breeding'.

There was considerable stress on changes in both religion and clothing as signs of general social change. It was said of one village in the far north-west:

> These people, especially the *Lobis*, are not advanced in any way though they are quite near an advanced town. The actual citizens of this village have Moslems amongst them, and, as a result, are fast learning the use of cloth. The *Lobis* who do not belong to any religion still do not know the use of cloth.

*Lambussie and Suggo were surveyed with Tongo, twenty miles away, and listed as 'Tongo' in the survey.

It was reported of another:

> The amount of Western civilization assimilated in Suggo is little. The principle assimilation is the change from leaf and skin dresses to clothing. No organized religion exists at Suggo; ancestor and heathen worship are prevalent.

This is a different world from the rural areas of the south described in the reports, underlining the fact that the 'rural' component in rural-urban migration studies must not be treated as too homogeneous a quantity. A report of a village in Brong-Ahafo, depicting many of the stresses of transitional cultures, read:

> Gradually the traditional ways of doing things are giving way to Western ones chiefly through the work of the churches and through the influence of the so-called educated slice of the population. The Methodist, Presbyterian, Roman Catholic, Seventh Day Adventist, Mosamo Disco Christo churches, to mention a few, are doing everything they can to debar their members from taking part in native dances, drumming, festivals and traditional funeral rites. The churches think all these things incompatible with Christianity. And the Moslems too are leaving no stone unturned in injecting Arabic ways of life into the social fabric. What is giving this change a greater momentum is the fact that the small number of people who can read and write simple letters think it unscholarly to take part in the traditional social activities. They go to the extent of refusing to sing funeral dirges at funerals. It is not surprising, therefore, to see two groups of mourners at any funeral celebration, those who mourn in the 'Western' way (i.e. singing hymns) and those who mourn in the traditional way (i.e. singing the traditional funeral dirges). In addition the Moslems mourn in the Arabic way (i.e. singing their Arabic songs to the accompaniment of a snail's pace marching on the streets to the grave yard). It is not at funeral celebrations alone that the people divide themselves into groups, but they also do so at all social gatherings.

Such matters were not the main concern of those describing social change in the towns. The following extract from a report on Labadi, Accra, is fairly typical:

> Most of the buildings there are native or private owned or built, though of late a cinema house, some petrol filling stations and the proposed Holiday Resort promise to change the monotonous and purely native atmosphere and scene.

Amongst the interviewers, as amongst their respondents, more attention was paid to contrasts in entertainment facilities than to any other topic, the contrasts in this respect seeming to epitomise the rural-urban choice. Traditional forms of entertainment were certainly under-stressed by the young survey workers. In the North comments were generally of the type:

> Although the people of Kubin* live quite near each other they have no

* Examined in work centring on Chiana Asunia.

> social organization which brings them together. Normal social intercourse as goes on between neighbours generally prevails.
>
> There are no social activities in this locality. Members go to Chiana Asunia to enjoy the market days.

On the southern boundary of the North, it was said of Yeji:*

> There are no night club pubs or any big beer bars in the town where people could go and while away their time. On moonlight nights, the youths of the 'real' Yeji people play a modern form of traditional drumming. The Gonjas and the Hausas play traditional drumming on festive and religious occasions.

In the closer settled villages further south the position is different.

> Although there are no night clubs or beer bars in the village where they could go to enjoy themselves in the evenings, they travel to distant larger villages weekly to attend dances and dramatic plays.

Even in the larger villages,

> Apart from the music of a few beer bars, the town is quiet. There isn't any form of organized recreation for the townsfolk. Children, however, enjoy playing on the streets in the evening.

In contrast is Sekondi-Takoradi,

> Where in the traditional way families used to keep indoors most of the time, the tendency here is to go out and enjoy themselves in any of the numerous night clubs, among which are the 'Sphynx' and the 'Zenith', which will be superseded by the 'Atlantic Hotel', a government-owned enterprise now under construction. Cinema goers are extraordinarily numerous.

Of Osu, Accra, it was said, 'Here night clubs, cinema houses, football parks and other amenities abound, because the immigrant workers usually patronize them more than the natives of Osu or Labadi'. It was reported of Ashanti New Town, Kumasi, that

> In the evenings, houses are full of people, especially women and children. Beer bars are crowded. Those who do not go out stay at home and play records. Streets are full of people and cars. On Sundays many people dress up in expensive clothes and go down to their churches, either in their own cars or in taxi-cabs. On the whole, the average woman in this locality has a reasonable amount of income, earned mostly by trading.

These descriptions are obviously strongly orientated towards middle-class expenditure patterns, but this does not prevent very similar descriptions from exciting distant and restless villagers. The other side of the urban picture is provided by the following accounts of two of Kumasi's poorest suburbs:

> Most of the people are related by blood or marriage and the area swarms with people who are related to one another. In the evening

* From a report on the area around Salaga compiled during the survey of the Salaga district just over twenty miles to the north.

> children from different houses gather together and entertain themselves. The people here are not so well off. A whole family (man, wife and three children) may live in one room. There is very little in the form of entertainment, but free film shows are very common and on most nights one can hear the singing of a Hausa wedding procession.

The second most common type of comment was excited by the presence or absence of educational facilities. But in this case the relative lack of schools in rural areas was often noted while observations were made about current changes in the position. It was said of one village in the North: 'There is now a primary school. Education of girls is not popular. The school was put up only recently, and its first pupils have not yet completed middle school education'. But it was remarked of the failings of another small village in the area that it had, apparently in order of deprivation, '(1) no school; (2) no market'. The position has, however, changed rapidly, especially in the larger centres, so that absence of schools is no longer such a pressing reason for taking children to the distant south.

> Bawku has not been left behind in Ghana's educational revolution. It has six primary schools, two middle schools and one secondary school. The extra-mural courses offered by the University of Ghana are very popular there.

In the south, schools are not a particularly recent innovation even in the rural areas, as many of the effects of schooling are plainly visible. A student said of the centre in Ashanti on which he was working:

> A large number of the youths are ex-middle school scholars. There are no higher educated people beyond the middle schools, however. But the large number of ex-middle school scholars in the town gives the population an outlook of enlightenment.

A rural-urban contrast also exists in both the provision of medical facilities and the readiness to use them. In the north, 'There is neither a hospital, dispensary nor clinic at Suggo. People depend on herbalists for cure. They also believe in charms'. Even where there is a hospital, 'Some families taboo attendance at the hospital when ill'.

Underlying some of these contrasts are very different forms of economic activity. In the north the following is a typical description of a village economy:

> The people of the area are almost all farmers. Crops cultivated include rice, yam, cassava, groundnuts, beans, potatoes, maize, millet, guinea corn and tobacco. Whatever is reaped is kept for household consumption and extras are sold only when it is absolutely necessary. It is believed that if grains are sold there would be a poor yield next season. However, a popular occupation of the men is selling shea butter. There is only a very small market and as a result people have to carry goods either by cycle or on foot to larger markets. Lorries to the markets are scarce.

The north, even more than the south, is dominated by the year's two seasons. One survey worker wrote of a village in the far northeast:

> The year is marked into the wet and dry seasons. This means that for six months of the rainy season the people engage in grain-growing and farming as well as rearing their cattle, sheep and goats. In the other half of the year, the dry season, the people engage in gardening and various forms of handicraft, such as basket-weaving, straw-hat-weaving, cloth-weaving, pottery, fishing and hunting. However, their agricultural produce, such as millet, corn and rice, are mainly for home consumption, though small quantities of rice are exported down south to Kumasi and Accra.

A very different description is that of the economy of one of the surveyed centres in the cash-cropping cocoa part of the rural south:

> The major occupation of the people is cocoa-farming with an off-cocoa season resort to the growing of corn, chiefly for marketing further south where the corn is more or less a staple food. Groundnuts and onions are grown on a small scale for consumption. Kola is grown wild, cultivation being only on a small scale. The Kola nuts are sold to the Mossi people from Upper Volta. The staple food is coco-yam and plantain. A fair number of the young men are drivers who carry petty traders to and from Kumasi where they get most of their consumer goods, salt, kerosene, soap, cloths etc. Artisans include a few carpenters, smiths, both silver and gold, masons, fitters and electricians, all of whom are self-employed. Local craftsmen include mortar carvers and pot-makers who supply the palm wine tappers with pots. There are no commercial stores. The petty traders include Nigerians and a few natives. There is no fixed market day. People from the farmsteads in the neighbourhood can come to the market any day of the week to get their salt, kerosene, candles, smoked fish etc.

Yet another world is that of Ashanti New Town, Kumasi:

> There are not many people about during the daytime. Most of the women go to market to buy or sell goods. The men go to work and the children go to school. If one happens to visit a house between 8 a.m. and 4 p.m., he will see only very few people.

Sometimes the comments bore more directly upon the problems of rural-urban migration or its effects. It was pointed out by a survey worker in the northeast that by lorry from 'Bawku to Tamale is a seven-hour journey, and to Kumasi, all being well, not more than thirty hours; to travel from Bawku to Tamale will cost you 8/- to 12/-, while to Kumasi £1 is the most in normal weather'. Such migration may leave its mark. It was said of an Ashanti village that 'the general outlook of the people was "progressive" and "enlightened" (in the popular meaning of the terms) and this may be due to their frequent long visits to Kumasi'. Such movements were not always welcomed. Another survey worker not far away reported:

> The exodus of a large number of the young people to Sunyani, the Regional Headquarters, and to Bui, about 60 miles away where the

Russians are building a dam, in search of jobs is worth mentioning because it is feared that such an exodus will very soon arrest the growth of the town.

These then are the contrasts, not only between bush and town but between north and south. On the whole rural areas have fewer commercial entertainments, few schools and hospitals, and a greater shortage of jobs. The comments quoted later from respondents will not essentially change the picture drawn by the interviewers. But rural Ghana is not itself homogeneous. The south, especially the cash-cropping areas of Ashanti and the South (as they are defined in this study) have more of the facilities of the towns and more of the possibilities of earning money incomes than the North. The Volta Region is, as far as income-earning possibilities go, in an intermediate position. The north has a fearful dry season, which is a strong inducement to at least seasonal migration, while the seasons are less starkly contrasted elsewhere. On the other hand traditional society is more completely preserved in the north and migration from there to the towns must present strains such as the southerner never has to face.

There has been some point in prefacing a systematic study of rural-urban migration by these quotations. They make various points which will help in an understanding of the tables about to be presented. These points are not essentially different from those which would be made by less literate Ghanaians if they had equal facility of expression. The quotations do show the belief in social change and even advancement which saturates Ghanaian society at every level of literacy, although to a lesser degree in the north than further south. Finally, and rather importantly, the quotations introduce the reader to the Ghanaian survey workers who carried out the interviewing. If one wishes to understand responses to questions, it is often advisable to know something about those asking the question as well as those answering them. In this case each interviewer was of a very special type; essentially he represented a successful case of rural-urban migration from the area.

Finally, it should be emphasised that the questions were taken seriously. Rural-urban migration is a very important feature of contemporary Ghanaian life. Again and again respondents told interviewers, 'This is the first time anyone has asked me what I think about such an important matter'.

The pattern of movement from the rural areas—its validity

The method of sampling used ensures a balanced picture of the population found in the various rural centres at the time of the survey. The real worry is about those who were absent at the time of the survey.

Absence from the village can affect any of the categories. Because the survey was focused solely on rural-urban migration, persons were classified according to their rural-urban migration classification as long as they were still in the countryside, whether they were in the village or had gone elsewhere to work on cocoa farms or to work in those mines situated so that the miners do not live in towns. But the effect is not evenly distributed; it necessarily falls most heavily upon the rural-urban migrant groups, classified in the survey as being away in the town at the time of the survey, because by definition these classifications are composed solely of absentees.

The survey did aim at securing information about all these absentees. The important question is whether the method of data collection failed to get information on certain types of migrant. This possibility arises in three cases. The first is where the family of origin of the migrant could not be located because of the migration of the whole family; the second is where the family of origin has so changed that it no longer regards the migrant as having originated in it; the third is where the position of the migrant has altered to a position where he, or more commonly she, is no longer regarded as a member of the household.

Survey workers asked in each sampled household (and compared the answers to the questions) for details of whole families, none of the members of which would be regarded as parts of existing households, absent in the towns. The numbers proved to be small but the incidence varied. In some centres in the South and Volta an appreciable number of houses were empty at the time of the survey because of such migration, but this was much rarer in Ashanti and the North. Nevertheless, the total number of households entirely omitted in this way was probably less than 3 per cent of the number in the survey universe; definite cases of whole family migration were ascertained to amount to 2·6 per cent with another 0·1 per cent less certain. Furthermore, the relative effect of these omissions is of a lower order still, because there were also cases of whole families being absent because of migration to other rural areas. It might be noted here, so that it can be related to later findings, that only one-quarter of the rural-urban migrant families, amounting to less than 1 per cent of village families, broke their contacts with their villages of origin by disappearing into the towns and failing to make return visits or contribute to the cost of ceremonies.

There have also been reports, especially from the Volta Region, of the migration of whole villages either to another site or to join a larger settlement.* None of the survey locations included such a group, but a much larger survey would be needed to determine their national incidence. Where the site alone had changed the matter is of little concern here, for the migration of agricultural communities is a separate and important field of study; where another settlement is joined the movement may be a type of rural-urban migration or may herald such a movement getting under way.

The more serious considerations are those of changes in the family of

* Such movements were reported some years ago by medical survey teams, and more recently (in a personal communication) by Rowena Lawson from her studies of village economies in the course of the lower Volta River.

origin. The definitions used in the survey render it probable that a migrant will still be regarded as part of a village family, even if he marries and has children in the town, as long as his parents are still alive. But if they die, or in some cases if one of them dies, the resultant household or households formed from the migrant's siblings, and their spouses and descendants, will not regard the migrant as a household member. Thus some living migrants from the village will not be included in the survey. Most of them will be fairly old. Their numbers, especially amongst males, are probably not very great because rural-urban migration has increased in scale very markedly only during the last fifteen or twenty years and most of the migrants of this period are still relatively young and have surviving parents. These uncounted absentees would have been omitted only from the 'permanently absent' classifications, for by definition those away temporarily or seasonally could not be included in this group. Some confirmation for this argument appears to come from a comparison of the proportions of each age group enumerated in the 1960 census outside the region of their birth (Gil and Omaboe 1966) and the proportions of absentees in each age group found in the survey. After 55 years of age the ratio of the census to survey proportions begins to rise, but the rise is very large only in the North, being moderate in Volta, small in Ashanti, and almost negligible in the South. Furthermore, some of this rise is explicable on the grounds that the older migrants originally migrated at a time when rural-rural movements were far more important than rural-urban movements.

How serious is this omission? In terms of taking a kind of retrospective census of the rural area its effect is most marked amongst the aged, but it should be realised that persons over 55 years make up only about 6 per cent of either the survey or census population and that the permanently absent of that age made up only about 4 per cent of them or 0·2 per cent of the total. Plainly the effect is very small indeed except on the analysis of the migrant patterns of the old. The effect is smaller still in a comparison of the different migration classifications, as the other classifications have also been affected to some degree by the operation of the same process with regard to rural-rural movements.

By far the most complex consideration is, however, that of relatives who are no longer considered members of the household, or those who were never so considered. The reports of the survey workers and the findings they presented indicated certain possibilities which were subsequently confirmed by an intensive examination of these points in various survey centres. The first point is that a male who migrates permanently to the town and subsequently marries and has children is much more likely to be regarded as a member of the household absent in the town than is a female who does the same. She is more frequently assumed to be a member of another household. In terms of the social and economic structure of the rural household the viewpoint is logical, for the male is more likely to be giving continued economic assistance. In an allied research project (Caldwell 1966) it was found that sons were more likely to be giving assistance to their parents and siblings than were daughters, in both patrilineal and matrilineal societies. This is, of course, related to the fact that over one-and-a-half times as many males as females are employed, the ratio rising to almost seven times in the highly paid professional, administrative, and clerical occupations (Census 1960: Vol. IV).

The effect of this is to raise the sex ratio of the rural-urban emigrants. Thus, in the rural survey the sex ratios of all absentees in the town was 177 males per 100 females for all persons over 15 years of age and 200 for all over 25 years. The 1960 census showed that the ratio of all native-born persons enumerated outside their region of birth, whether in town or country, was 152 and 172 respectively for these two age categories (Gil and Omaboe 1966: Appendix).

In addition it was found that those children of the permanent absentees born after the initial migration are rarely considered members of the rural household even if their mothers returned to the village for their birth. That is why only 14 per cent of the long-term absentees shown by the rural survey are under 15 years of age compared with 31 per cent of those Ghanaians enumerated outside their region of birth in 1960.

The two factors just discussed act together to raise the sex ratios recorded by the rural survey for long-term absentees in the town, the figure for all such absentees being 181 males per 100 females, compared with 118 for temporary and seasonal absentees in the same survey, 120 for such absentees in the urban survey, 127 for long-term absentees in the urban survey, and 125 for all Ghanaians enumerated in 1960 in towns with more than 10,000 inhabitants, although they had been born elsewhere in the country (Census 1960: *Special Report A*). The latter figure coincides with the equivalent measure in the urban survey.

Now, what does all this signify, firstly in comparison with the 1960 census figures, and secondly in the interpretation of the rural survey findings?

The 1960 census showed that there were 3,047,000 and 3,120,000 native-born Ghanaian males and females respectively in the country, of whom 545,000 and 541,000 respectively were living in centres with over 15,000 inhabitants, thus leaving 2,502,000 and 2,579,000 living outside them. If we apply the ratios of population in the countryside to that found in the town according to the rural survey to these figures, we obtain estimates of rural population in the towns of 407,000 males and 256,000 females. But the 1960 census enumerated 306,000 males and 281,000 females as living in towns with over 10,000 inhabitants, although born elsewhere in Ghana. Thus, the estimates based on the rural survey figures are approximately 100,000 high for males and 25,000 low for females. The female deficit may easily be explained in terms of females no longer considered to be part of the household in the way discussed above.

But what of the surplus males? The explanation is rendered more complex by various side factors. For instance, the urban survey makes it clear that not all the 306,000 male and 281,000 female immigrants had come from rural localities, even as defined in this study; some certainly came from other large towns. Indeed, some are likely to have come from peripheral localities, of the outer suburban fringe type, of the very towns in which they were enumerated. In addition the census estimates of migrants into the town include babies born to long-term migrants to the town during brief visits back to the village, a category excluded in general from the rural survey. Offsetting this to some extent is the fact that the estimates were based on a fraction in which the urban migrant proportion might have been somewhat overestimated by an undercount of some rural population—namely the rural-rural migrants who have lost contact with their villages of origin and are living in places or conditions where they are unlikely to form a rural 'household' of the type on which the rural survey is based. There are also other possibilities; if the smallest localities are under-represented in the survey, and if their inhabitants are somewhat less likely to migrate to the towns, we may have slightly overestimated rural-urban migration; if many of the 'surplus' males were single migrants, a group notoriously hard to enumerate in surveys because of their mobility, we may have found fewer in our urban survey than their numbers in town warrant, and indeed disproportionately many may have returned to their home villages for enumeration in the 1960 census. In addition, the survey did not claim to be a fully balanced national survey.

However, there are probably two main reasons for the apparent surplus. Firstly, between the 1960 census and the survey, three years later, the proportion of rural-urban migrants almost certainly climbed, both because more people were migrating and because a higher proportion of migrants were making the towns their destination. It was a period when many projects requiring labour were begun in the towns, especially in Tema, and when the supply of foreign immigrants was apparently waning. The apparent increase may have been exaggerated further still by the fact that the taking of the 1960 census caused an abnormally high proportion of rural-urban migrants to return to their villages for enumeration. Every village seems to be able to cite examples of this phenomenon, especially amongst the more mobile males, an occurrence which certainly did not arise in the survey. Secondly, some of the seasonal migrants, who spend in the towns only a fraction of their total time away, appear, according to definition, as rural-urban migrants. This would raise the proportion of rural-urban migrants shown by a rural survey more than the proportion shown at any one time by an urban survey. Finally, it is likely that the estimate of female migrants in the town should be raised substantially for similar reasons, and indeed it is probably true that the number who have not been counted by the household is greater than the 25,000 surmised above to fill the gap between estimates.

Summarising, it should be said that most of the provisos listed do very little to jeopardise the validity of the rural survey. The proportions involved are small except in the case of permanent rural-urban migration. Even here, the major part of the apparent discrepancy probably arises from a real increase in rural-urban migration, and the other qualifications do not in sum have the quantitative effect in terms of migrants that their number when discussed might suggest. In the cases of babies born to long-term emigrants during visits back to the village arranged for this purpose there is more case for excluding them from the rural population than for classifying them as born there as must the census. The figures as shown in the rural survey probably come very close to measuring the effect of migration upon the rural community, because the absentees omitted, babies, women, or old men, are likely to be those who have made the most complete break and who are contributing least in the way of visits, money, or goods to their village of origin. It should be emphasised that the undercounting of migrant females is largely confined to categories absent at the time of the survey; it has hardly any effect on the returnee categories and hence only a small impact on the combined categories of those who have ever migrated.

Emigration from rural areas to the towns

In Appendix 2 the complete distributions of the migrant communities by propensity to undertake rural-urban migration, subdivided by age and migration area, are shown. Here we will try to clarify those rather complex tables by drawing out the main threads.

In Table 2:1 the distributions are presented by rural-urban migration classification and by sex. The table can be understood only if it is appreciated that household members away, either temporarily or permanently, in other rural areas are not indicated as such; they merely appear as having never left rural areas, or having permanently returned from the town, or in whatever other category fits them. Secondly, as will be seen below, the ranks of those who have never left the countryside are swollen by very great numbers of children, who may well some day migrate to the towns.

The data in Table 2:1 have been summarised in one form below the Table, but it is possible to aggregate them meaningfully in various other ways.

One-quarter of the rural population has taken part in some form of rural-urban migration, the males being markedly more mobile than the females. Nevertheless the margin is not as great as has apparently been the case in most African societies. Of those who have participated in such movements, half were away at the time of the survey.

Of those who have been away, three-quarters have participated in some

Table 2:1 Rural-urban migration classification of rural population, by sex, Ghana, 1963

(percentage distribution)

Rural-urban migration classification: Primary division	Secondary division	Tertiary division	Males	Females	Persons
(1) Has never migrated to the town	(a) does not intend to do so	(i) rarely visits town	36	48	42
		(ii) often visits town	22	21	21
	(b) intends or hopes to do so	(i) seasonally	5	4	5
		(ii) more permanently	5	4	4
(2) Has returned to rural areas after one or more migrations to the town	(a) permanent return	(i) after seasonal migration only	2	2	2
		(ii) after at least one period of more permanent migration	7	5	6
	(b) intends or hopes to go again	(i) seasonally	3	2	3
		(ii) more permanently	3	3	3
(3) Away in town	(a) temporarily	(i) visiting town	1	1	1
		(ii) seasonally	2	1	1
	(b) more permanently	(i) visits village at least once a year	8	5	7
		(ii) rarely or never visits village	3	2	2
(4) Other			3	2	3
(5) No entry			0	0	0
Totals: per cent			100	100	100
numbers surveyed			6,964	6,784	13,776[a]
Summary					
(A) Has never migrated to town [(1)]			68	77	72
(B) Seasonal migrant [2(b)(i) + 3(a)(ii)]			5	3	4
(C) Permanent returnee [2(a)]			9	7	8
(D) More permanent rural-urban migrant [2(b)(ii) + 3(b)]			14	10	12
(E) Not clear, other and no entry [3(a)(i) + 4 + 5]			4	3	4

Definitions: 'Often visits town'—at least once a year on average; 'seasonally'—for periods of less than one year, but either for more than 3 months or securing employment; 'more permanently'—indefinitely or more than a year; 'visiting'—for less than 3 months providing no employment secured, other than as a household help for relatives or selling some things produced in the village or buying some goods for consumption or sale in the village; 'other'—includes urban-rural migrants, especially teachers and other officials.

[a] Includes 28 persons of unknown sex.

Table 2:2 Rural-urban migration classification, by sex and age, Ghana, 1963
(percentage distribution)

Sex	Primary division	Secondary division	Tertiary division	0-9	10-14	15-19	20-24	25-29	30-44	45-64	65+
	Migration classification			Age group (in years)							
Males											
	(1) Has never migrated to the town	(a) does not intend to do so	(i) rarely visits town	57	50	36	23	20	23	33	45
			(ii) often visits town	15	14	22	26	25	27	28	28
		(b) intends or hopes to do so	(i) seasonally	8	8	7	4	4	3	2	0
			(ii) more permanently	5	10	11	7	5	3	1	0
	(2) Has returned to rural areas after one or more migrations to the town	(a) permanent return	(i) after seasonal migration only	1	1	1	2	3	4	2	5
			(ii) after at least one period of more permanent migration	2	2	2	4	9	9	15	14
		(b) intends or hopes to go again	(i) seasonally	2	2	2	5	7	4	3	2
			(ii) more permanently	3	2	2	4	4	3	3	2
	(3) Away in town	(a) temporarily	(i) visiting town	0	1	2	3	1	1	0	0
			(ii) seasonally	0	1	4	4	1	2	1	0
		(b) more permanently	(i) visits village at least once a year	2	3	8	13	14	13	7	0
			(ii) rarely or never visits village	2	2	2	3	2	5	3	2
	(4) Other			3	3	1	2	5	3	2	2
	(5) No entry			0	1	0	0	0	0	0	0
	Total			100	100	100	100	100	100	100	100

Females

(1) Has never migrated to the town	(a) does not intend to do so	(i) rarely visits town	62	54	39	38	39	42	53	67
		(ii) often visits town	14	14	20	24	28	25	25	20
	(b) intends or hopes to do so	(i) seasonally	6	8	5	4	3	2	1	0
		(ii) more permanently	4	6	10	4	3	2	0	0
(2) Has returned to rural areas after one or more migrations to the town	(a) permanent return	(i) after seasonal migration only	1	1	2	2	2	2	2	2
		(ii) after at least one period of more permanent migration	2	2	3	6	6	7	8	7
	(b) intends or hopes to go again	(i) seasonally	1	2	3	3	3	3	1	1
		(ii) more permanently	3	3	3	5	2	3	2	0
(3) Away in town	(a) temporarily	(i) visiting town	1	1	2	2	1	2	1	0
		(ii) seasonally	1	1	2	1	2	1	1	0
	(b) more permanently	(i) visits village at least once a year	1	4	6	6	7	6	3	1
		(ii) rarely or never visits village	1	1	2	2	1	3	1	1
(4) Other			3	3	2	3	3	2	2	1
(5) No entry			0	0	1	0	0	0	0	0
Total			100	100	100	100	100	100	100	100

form of migration involving longer term absences than seasonal migration. The latter is certainly not the typical form of migration to the towns; indeed at the time of the survey, seasonal migrants formed no more than one-tenth of those away in the towns.

Most migrants retain or re-form strong links with the village. Of those who had been or were still seasonal migrants only, one-third were at the time of the survey permanently back in the village and half temporarily back. Even of those who had participated in more permanent migration, and who were still regarded as being in some sense a member of the household, one-third were back permanently and one-sixth temporarily. Indeed the latter category made up one-quarter of all those who still regarded themselves as long-term migrants to the urban areas. Many of this group were not visiting, but had returned for a prolonged period and were tempted to go again. Of those more permanently away at the time of the survey over three-quarters visited their home village at least annually. It is statistics like these which explain the immense mammy lorry traffic on Ghana's roads.

Of those who have never participated in the movement to the towns one-eighth, mostly young people, intend to do so. For most, this means 'intend to do so in the near future', for interviewers were instructed to demand evidence of planning and not to include those with vague beliefs that they might some day go. Even of the hard core of those staying behind, one-third visited a town at least annually, and, amongst adults, the fraction approached half.

Many of these findings cannot be understood fully unless they are subdivided by age as in Table 2:2 or by migration region as is done later in this chapter.

Table 2:2 explains the operation of many of the phenomena noted in Table 2:1. For instance, the fact that 68 per cent of males have never participated in any form of rural-urban migration becomes more comprehensible when we realise that 85 per cent of 0-9-year-olds and 73 per cent of those over 65 years have never done so. The figures for the same two groups of females are 86 and 87 per cent. These proportions fall to 54 per cent for 25-29-year-old males and 70 per cent for 20-24-year-old females.

Thus it is not merely that young adults migrate. In the early 1960s young adults were going to the town on a scale that the older people had never done. This is the fundamental explanation for the rapid growth of the towns. When the survey was taken almost one-quarter of all village 20-24-year-old males and one-eighth of the females of that age were away in the towns. Furthermore the nature of long-term rural-urban migration is changing. Thus, while the household data suggest that at some time twice as many males over 60 years old had participated in such migration as females of that age, probably some exaggeration of the real position, the same is certainly not true amongst the young. In the 20-24-year-old group, the proportion of males who had undertaken such migration was only one-fifth higher than the female proportion. Indeed, it follows from the argument presented earlier that the margin might be smaller still. It is this movement towards a sex balance in migration and indeed towards family migration that explains the considerable number of children who have been away to the towns. Long-term migration does not seem to be ousting seasonal migration; amongst the young more than twice as many have participated in the former as the latter, but, interestingly, this is also the case amongst the old. However, seasonal migration remains a predominantly male undertaking, there being in the past and at present more than twice as many male seasonal migrants as females. Indeed amongst migrants from the north the ratio is three to one.

Many of these contrasts will be analysed more extensively later in this chapter.

Immigration into the towns from rural areas

The urban section of the survey was in many ways very different indeed from the rural survey. The resources expended on it were fewer. No attempt was made to secure a quantitative picture of the urban areas in which work was undertaken. This was unnecessary. The 1960 census and post-enumeration survey will be able to tell us a great deal about the movement into the surveyed centres. What was desired was a sample containing rural-urban immigrants so that their views and experiences relating to migration could be compared with the expectations of intending migrants from rural areas or the tales of the returnee migrants in those areas. We also wished to examine the internal composition of the migrant population in terms of sex and type of migration to see how it compared with the population reported in the villages as being away in the towns.

Accordingly, Accra was divided into two sections, one containing suburbs believed to house a large proportion of locally born, particularly Gas, and the other a higher proportion of in-migrants, and a selection of the latter suburbs was sampled. Survey work was also undertaken in Tema, and in immigrant suburbs of Kumasi, Sekondi-Takoradi, and Cape Coast, so that latter areas each contributed 10 per cent to the aggregate. In Table 2:3 the

Table 2:3 Comparison of total population in surveyed centres with that in predominantly immigrant suburbs surveyed by place of origin (percentage distribution)

Origin[a]	Accra-Tema	Kumasi	Sekondi-Takoradi	Cape Coast	Survey of predominantly immigrant suburbs
Same locality	47	39	31	65	28
Elsewhere in Ghana	37	49	54	30	69
Elsewhere in Africa	16	12	15	5	13

[a] Population from outside Africa excluded.
Source: Total town populations are from Census 1960: Vol. II.

composition of these immigrant suburbs is compared with that of the whole of the surveyed towns. The figures shown in Table 2:3 for the survey compared closely with an aggregate figure calculated for the surveyed suburbs from figures which have recently become available from the 1960 census (*Special Report A*).

Thus over two-thirds of the persons in the urban schedule were of the type with which the study was chiefly concerned. As many of the locally born were children, the great majority of households had some personal experience with migration.

An analysis of the origin of these persons living in predominantly immigrant suburbs reveals some interesting facts which are probably true of the urban areas as a whole. Tables 2:4 and 2:5 show that, although the population of these suburbs is predominantly rural in origin, the urban component cannot be equated merely with the locally born. A considerable proportion of immigrants claim to come not from villages but from 'towns'. For instance, one-quarter of the immigrants of Ghanaian origin come from centres with more than 10,000 inhabitants, even though such centres house only one-sixth of the population of the country and only one-eighth outside the Accra Capital District. Half the foreign immigrants claimed to have been born in towns of this size.

Considerable caution should be exercised when judging these statements. Interviewers found a strong tendency amongst respondents to exaggerate the size of their village or town of origin; this often merely arose from the fact that they had few standards of comparison and that criteria involving total numbers of inhabitants meant nothing to them. These problems were not insuperable within Ghana, for interviewers were able to take town names and check them against the 1960 census enumeration. Thus, as will be shown later from other data, it is almost certainly true that the tendency to migrate to the country's largest towns rises with the size of the centre of origin. It is greater from a medium sized town than from a large village, and in turn greater from a large village than a small one. This is not entirely unexpected. If rural-urban migration increases with social and economic change, then one would expect the larger centres to yield more emigrants. To take only one measure of social change, but one that will subsequently be shown to be an important causal agent in the migration process, the proportion of persons over 6 years of age who have been to school, but who are no longer attending and are therefore presumably potential migrants, rises steeply with the size of the centre. The proportion at the time of the 1960 census was 6 per cent in tiny villages with fewer than 200 inhabitants, 8 per cent for those with 200-499 inhabitants, 9 per cent where there were 500-999 inhabitants, 11 per cent for medium sized villages with 1,000-1,999 inhabitants, 14 per cent for large villages with

2,000-4,999 inhabitants, and 24 per cent for all centres with 5,000 or more inhabitants (Census 1960: *Advance Report*, Table 17).

The real problems arise with the foreign immigrants. In many cases the lack of recent censuses or the absence of town lists by number of inhabitants made checking impossible. Judging from the scaling down needed for the centres of origin of the Ghanaians, the same would necessarily apply to the foreign immigrants. It is most unlikely that half of them come from towns. Two of the three countries from which most foreign migrants come, Togo and Upper Volta, are not highly urbanised. However, the position is different in the third country, Nigeria, especially amongst the Yoruba, who form a considerable proportion of the total migrant stream from the country. Bascom showed that the 1952 census revealed that almost half the Yoruba lived at that time in centres with more than 10,000 inhabitants, and

Table 2:4 Distribution of population in certain immigrant suburbs of Accra-Tema, Kumasi, Sekondi-Takoradi, and Cape Coast, by birthplace, 1963 (percentages)[a]

Birthplace	Persons	Males	Females
Town of enumeration	28	24	32
Other town in Ghana:[b]			
temporary visit	1	1	(0·4)
seasonal migration	(0·2)	(0·3)	(0·1)
more permanent migration:			
visits home centre at least once a year	6	5	6
visits home centre more rarely or never	2	2	2
Village in Ghana:[b]			
temporary visit	3	3	3
seasonal migration	2	2	2
more permanent migration:			
visits home centre at least once a year	39	41	37
visits home centre more rarely or never	6	6	6
Town outside Ghana:[b]			
temporary visit	(0·1)	(0·2)	(0·0)
seasonal migration	1	1	(0·1)
more permanent migration:			
visits home centre at least once a year	4	5	3
visits home centre more rarely or never	2	3	2
Village outside Ghana:[b]			
temporary visit	(0·3)	(0·4)	(0·3)
seasonal migration	(0·4)	1	(0·0)
more permanent migration:			
visits home centre at least once a year	3	4	3
visits home centre more rarely or never	2	2	2
No entry	(0·3)	(0·0)	1
Total respondents: percentages	100	100	100
numbers[c]	3,167	1,716	1,443

[a] Percentages shown correct to nearest whole number, but decimal place shown in parentheses where this number would otherwise be zero.

[b] Towns are centres with more than 10,000 inhabitants; these have been checked for Ghana, but not outside, where the percentages are probably overstated (see text).

[c] Eight persons are of unspecified sex.

that 'If only the Yoruba of the Western Region and the Colony were considered, . . . their *index of urbanisation* [following Davis and Casis] was 42·4, exceeding that of the United States' (Bascom 1962: 699).

The slight difference between the sex ratio of 119 males per 100 females found in the survey and the figure of 116 recorded by the census for Accra-Tema is to be accounted for by the concentration on immigrant suburbs. It is this preponderance of males in the town arising from immigration that is responsible for the marked difference between the proportion of males and females born in the locality; there are in fact somewhat fewer males than females in this category because of the greater mobility of the former and hence their stronger inclination towards out-migration.

Amongst the immigrants from Ghanaian villages, more permanent immigrants outweigh seasonal and temporary migrants combined by about nine to one, or double the ratio suggested by the rural survey. This follows from the fact that seasonal migrants are entered as rural-urban migrants even if they spend only a fraction of their time away from home in the towns; but there may also be some evidence here of the relative difficulty encountered when attempting to enumerate either seasonal migrants or temporary visitors in the towns.

The findings in Table 2:4 can be aggregated in various meaningful ways, two of which are shown in Table 2:5.

Table 2:5 Major distributions of population in immigrant suburbs (percentages)

	Persons	Males	Females
(a) Rural-urban birthplace			
Urban	44	41	45
Rural	56	59	55
(b) Migration classification			
Local birth	28	25	32
Temporary visit	4	4	4
Seasonal migrant	4	5	2
More permanent migrant	64	66	61

A surprisingly high proportion of the population claims to be of urban origin. If the suspect foreign-immigrant group is eliminated the proportion drops slightly to just under 43 per cent. Admittedly many persons of urban birth are the young children of rural-urban migrants, especially where local birth is claimed, and hence the table understates the contribution of the villages to town growth.

Part (b) of Table 2:5 demonstrates the relatively much greater importance of long-term migrants than short-term migrants. It also reveals the predominance of males in seasonal migration. Temporary visits, often made either to sell or procure goods, are a more complex phenomenon. Ghanaians predominate over non-Ghanaians by more than twelve to one compared with less than five to one in the case of migration generally. Moreover, while there are more than three-quarters as many females as males amongst the Ghanaian visitors, there are only one-quarter as many amongst non-Ghanaian visitors.

Regional contrasts

The four major migration regions exhibit contrasts in the proportions of persons migrating to the towns, the type of migration, and the age and sex balance. In Table 2:6 the first two points are analysed, while sex and age differentials will be considered in the next chapter. A considerable proportion of those who have never migrated are children, but this fact does little to invalidate the comparison between areas.

Table 2:6 Migration classification by migrant areas

Migration classification	Percentage distribution of respondents by migration classification				
	South	Volta	Ashanti	North	All areas
Has never migrated[a]	66	77	86	71	73
Seasonal migrant[b]	5	2	1	8	4
Permanent returnee[c]	9	9	5	8	8
Long-term absentee[d]	17	8	7	9	12
Other, no entry[e]	3	4	1	4	3
Total: per cent	100	100	100	100	100
number	5,769	2,069	3,397	2,541	13,776

[a] Equivalent in Table 2:2 to (1) + 3(a)(i).
[b] Equivalent in Table 2:2 to 2(b)(i) + 3(a)(ii).
[c] Equivalent in Table 2:2 to 2(a).
[d] Equivalent in Table 2:2 to 2b(ii) + 3(b).
[e] Equivalent in Table 2:2 to 4 + 5.
Source: Rural survey.

Migration tends to rise with a lengthy period of economic and social change, especially as such a period is often associated with the establishment and growth of commercial centres in an area.

Thus almost one-third of the respondents in the South had, at some stage, participated in rural-urban migration.

But relative economic deprivation or a scarcity of local employment can play a role. In 1960 the Gross Value Added per Capita ranged from £80* in the South (or £61 without the Accra Capital District) to £66 in Ashanti, £43 in Volta and £30 in the North (calculated from Szereszewski 1966: 92). At some time, 25 per cent of the population of the backward and poor north had migrated to the town, compared with 19 per cent from Volta and 13 per cent from Ashanti where rapid economic expansion, especially on the Brong-Ahafo forest frontier, is occurring.

* £ Ghanaian, at par with sterling in 1960.

Distance to the towns is important. In the south, large towns are fairly common, and are always found within an easy day's journey in a mammy lorry.* Therefore, people can not only go to the town, but they can stay there without feeling cut off from their origins and often without having to consider whether to take such a major step as returning to live in the village. Thus, not only had more villagers gone to the town in the South, but five-sixths of all persons who had ever been long-term absentees were still permanently resident in the town, compared with considerably lower proportions elsewhere (Appendix 2).

Seasonal migration is especially a characteristic of the North, partly indicating its more primitive economy, but bearing witness also to the widespread existence there of agrarian subsistence farming subject to savage seasonal dry periods when food is short and the need for labour limited. At these times, the younger men of the household, as well as others, often head for the south to seek employment and earn cash. The 1960 census enumerated in the Northern Region (or appeared to do so, for undoubtedly sex differentials in age misstatement are partly responsible (Caldwell 1967a: 32-8)) one-quarter more females between 15 and 40 years of age than males, a surplus of 66,000.

Seasonal and temporary movements

As can be seen in Table 2:7, seasonal and temporary movements are particularly important amongst the young, the first but not the second being dominated by males. Relative to long-term migration, seasonal migration is most important in the 15-19-years age group, thereafter falling away comparatively steeply, especially if measured in terms of those actually away at any given time. At the time of the survey, almost one-quarter of the seasonal migrants away were 15-19 years old, while almost two-fifths were 15-24 years. Equivalent proportions for long-term absentees were one-ninth and two-ninths.

That the preponderance of young amongst the seasonal migrants is not the product of a recent upswing in such movement can be ascertained, as in Table 2:8, by confining the examination to those respondents over 15 years of age who have ever participated in seasonal migration. It can be seen that, with increasing age, the proportion of seasonal migrants who do not anticipate another migration rises rapidly, while the number away at any given time falls even more sharply, suggesting increasingly long periods between trips to the town.

Longer-term movements

The general outline of longer-term movements was shown in Table 2:2. The proportion of long-term absentees, either away in the town or temporarily in the village at the time of the survey, appeared to rise until it

* See pp. 128-9.

Table 2:7 Seasonal and temporary movements, by age and sex

Movement	Sex	Age group[a]					
		15-19	20-24	25-29	30-44	45-64	65+
(a) Percentage of all respondents in each age group participating in movements							
Seasonal[b]	Male	6	9	8	6	4	2
	Female	5	4	5	4	2	1
Temporary visit[c]	Male	2	3	1	1	0	0
	Female	2	2	1	2	1	0

(b) Ratio of seasonal migrants to long-term absentees by age group, males and females

	Age group[a]				
	15-19	20-24	25-29	30-34	45+[d]
Ratio (%):					
away and temporarily returned	47	38	42	33	30
away	33	18	13	12	7

[a] Restricted to respondents over 15 years of age because of very small numbers involved at lower ages.

[b] Either away or temporarily returned.

[c] Away only.

[d] There are insufficient respondents in the 65+ age group to justify treating it separately.

Source: Rural survey.

Table 2:8 Distribution of seasonal migrants by type and major age group (percentage distribution in each age group)

Type of migrant	Age group		
	15-24	25-44	45+
In rural area:			
will not migrate again	22	32	49
will migrate again	44	49	42
In town seasonally	34	19	9
All seasonal migrants: per cent	100	100	100
number	215	336	98

Source: Rural survey.

reached a plateau in the 20-24-year group, when one-fifth of males and one-eighth of females were away. This level was maintained in all age groups below 45 years of age, thereafter falling away. This fall arises partly from an increasing rate of permanent return with advancing age, a phenomenon outlined in Table 2:9, and partly from the fact that large-scale movement to the towns has occurred so recently that the older respondents probably had a much smaller chance of participating in very long-term movements in their youth or prime. The interviewers suspected that a proportion of the older permanent returnees from long-term absences had experienced only one or two long periods in the town, possibly by failing to return home for the wet season joining two 'drys'. For similar reasons, one should be wary of too readily accepting the 20-44 years of age plateau, for a tendency for rural-urban migrants to keep crowding into the towns even after 25 years of age may be counterbalanced by a higher rate of migration of the young as each year goes by.

A large proportion of older migrants have in fact returned to the village after periods in the town; the return rate rises steeply between 45 and 50 years of age, and is even more marked amongst females, apparently often widows, than amongst males. It is far from certain that this pattern will persist, for many of the younger migrants have secured jobs with reasonable permanence and are not casual labourers.

The high proportion of permanent return in the youngest age group is not particularly surprising; this represents the migration failure rate. If migration does fail, it is likely to do so at a fairly early stage. After what seems a long period of unemployment or of unsatisfactory employment, the young migrant, bruised by the insecurity of town life and by its incessant demands for money, will leave for the village, determined, at least at that stage, never to come to the town again.

Table 2:9 Distribution of long-term migrants by type and major age group (percentage distribution in each age group)

Type of migrant	Age group		
	15-24	25-44	45+
In rural area:			
permanently	22	22	71
temporarily	21	14	8
In town:			
visits village at least annually	45	50	14
visits village rarely or never	12	14	7
All long-term migrants: per cent	100	100	100
number	517	818	578
Percentage of all respondents in age group	18	20	29
Percentage formed by those rarely or never visiting village of all still participating in long-term migration	15	19	24

Source: Rural survey.

With longer residence in the town and with the establishment of their own town families, many migrants find their links with the village weakening. Their visits 'home' become less frequent and often briefer, as is evidenced by the falling proportion with age found in the village at the time of the survey. At the same time, the proportion who go back less frequently than once a year, a rather serious social solecism, steadily mounts, although, so strong are the connections, that it never rises above one-quarter.

The effect on rural society

The impact of rural-urban migration on village life is enormous. Let us consider for a moment the village society, as distinct from the long-term absentees, who nevertheless by their example and their visits play a very important role in rural society. Those who regard their residence as being in the village are analysed in Table 2:10.

Of those residing in the rural areas, 18 per cent of all males over 15 years old and 16 per cent of all females of that age have at some stage lived in a town as either a long-term or a seasonal migrant. A further 30 per cent of adult males and 26 per cent of adult females have frequently visited the towns. Thus almost half of the males and over two-fifths of the females could be said to be well acquainted with urban life. This is of very

Table 2:10 Percentage distribution by age group and sex of respondents permanently resident in rural areas at the time of the survey

Migration category	Sex and age							
	Males				Females			
	15-24	25-44	45+	all ages[a]	15-24	25-44	45+	all ages[a]
Has never migrated:								
hopes to do so	17	9	2	12	13	5	1	8
does not anticipate doing so								
rarely visits town	36	27	31	42	44	46	59	53
often visits town	28	33	48	26	25	30	25	23
Permanent returnees from seasonal or long-term migration	6	16	15	10	8	10	11	8
Seasonal migrants (in village or town during survey)	9	9	3	6	5	5	2	4
Visiting town during survey	3	1	0	1	2	1	0	1
Others[b]	1	5	1	3	3	3	2	3
Total respondents: per cent	100	100	100	100	100	100	100	100
number	1,125	1,601	1,284	5,967	1,271	1,819	848	6,132

[a] Includes 0-14 age group and persons not specifying age as well as age group shown in other columns.

[b] Includes persons with more varied migration histories, nearly all of whom have spent some period in a town.

Source: Rural survey.

great importance when assessing the likely speed of social and economic change, for much of the impulse towards modernisation flows from the towns, and indeed flows from outside Africa into the towns.

Amongst the village males, the incidence of past residence in the towns reaches a peak in the 25-44 age group at 30 per cent, but acquaintance with town life is greatest amongst those over 45 years, where it reaches 67 per cent. Amongst the females, the peak incidence occurs in both cases in the 25-44-year range, where it reaches 18 per cent for town residence and 49 per cent for familiarity with urban life.

Summary

One rural-urban migration stream differs from another. A major reason is the contrast between the sending areas. The mammy lorries coming into

Accra may contain refugees from a particularly harsh dry season in the North, anxious to earn cash so that their families left behind might buy food as well as transistor radios or bicycles, sitting beside youths from cocoa farms who are aware that they could earn a living in their home village but who long for the bright lights and the more sophisticated life of the capital.

The towns which beckon these travellers are more alike; the pleasures of Accra can mostly be obtained in Takoradi or Kumasi as well. The urban heterogeneity is internal; the gay life of the hotels and shops, the life which has been described so many times in each village, is one that needs money. In some suburbs of the towns most residents do live this way, but there are poorer suburbs, well known to many of the rural-urban migrants, where most residents are fighting to earn the money needed to pay the costs of merely remaining in the towns.

Nevertheless, all kinds of town life differ from that of the village. The immigrants are usually impressed by at least the outside of the cinemas, petrol filling stations, hotels, and nightclubs. There are more schools and better medical facilities. There is also a very different kind of occupational structure; jobs do not mean farming, and nearly always pay is received in cash.

Towns are different. Necessarily the way of life is at variance in many ways with that of the village. The population is surprisingly mixed and new contacts are many, even though the different ethnic groups do try to stick together. There are new ideas, some of them coming from outside the country, some being produced by the new problems being encountered in these very new segments of Ghanaian society.

The new ways of life and the new ideas do not remain insulated within the towns, for their populations are so new as to retain strong links with the countryside. The 1960 census showed that those born in the town numbered less than half in Accra, less than two-fifths in Kumasi, and less than one-third in Sekondi-Takoradi. Furthermore, many of the town-born were the young children of immigrants from the rural areas. The townspeople born outside the town of enumeration, but in Ghana, made up about one-third of the population in Accra and around half in Kumasi and Sekondi-Takoradi. Many of them certainly came from large centres, defined as towns by the census, but their move was usually to somewhere more urban than the place they left. This urban population of rural or semi-rural origin visits the villages for social reasons, for family or clan conclaves, for the ceremonies that surround births, deaths, and marriages, for celebrations and for affairs connected with the traditional or fetish shrines. In 1960 this incessant movement between village and town was catered for by 60,000 persons providing transport, almost two-thirds of them working on the lorries, and being supplemented by a further 11,500 who spent their lives maintaining these vehicles. Those returning to the village take with them industrial products bought in the town as well as ideas and behaviour patterns foreign to traditional rural life. Almost half the population of rural Ghana have some first-hand experience of the towns.

Thus, in Ghana at least, the isolation of the rural fastnesses has largely become a thing of the past. Admittedly, over two-thirds of those born in the villages have never been to the town to live, but half of these are children. Many of these children will certainly make the journey; indeed, at the time of the survey more 10-19-year-olds were planning to do so than was the case in any other age group. Nor are those who go for long periods to the town lost sight of; half were permanently or temporarily back in the village at the time of the survey.

Not all those who crowded into the towns came from rural, or even urban, Ghana. In Accra and Sekondi-Takoradi one-sixth of the population were of foreign birth and in Kumasi one-eighth. A high proportion of these people were true rural-urban migrants, for until recently national borders have not been forbidding barriers in West Africa. For many villagers in Togo and Upper Volta, Ghana's three largest towns are the nearest centres with over a hundred thousand inhabitants.

No single feature of a rural area determines the volume of migrants travelling to the towns. Socially and economically advanced areas can produce a high proportion of young people who would prefer to work in the town. In point of fact their agriculture, such as the cocoa farms of southern Ghana, may not be very labour intensive. But backward areas, such as Ghana's north, may have an agricultural system too primitive to cope fully with the harsh wet-dry cycle of the climate and expanding too slowly to provide extra employment rapidly enough. In these circumstances, a considerable proportion of the migrants may be seasonal ones, a form of existence most fitting in with the lives of young males.

Longer-term migration may produce permanent urban residence, but there are also return flows of two main types. The first arises from the failure to become established in the town or to adjust to its way of life. Many permanent returnees to the village are young and were in the towns for a comparatively short period. The second arises from the completion of what may be regarded as a town working life and the acquisition of enough capital to be able to return 'home'. This does not necessarily occur only for people of 60 or over; the return flow is quite strong at all ages after about 45 years.

3

Who is the Rural-Urban Migrant?

Some people are more likely to leave the village for the town than are others. If they can be identified, future town growth, and the impact of various social and economic changes on the volume of rural-urban movement, can be more easily predicted. Furthermore, there is a fascination in the inquiry into why such change should make some villagers forsake the way of life their ancestors have always followed while others are apparently unaffected.

The general problem

The identification of the people likely to migrate poses problems. It is undoubtedly better to ask all persons leaving the countryside why they are going, than it is to ask old town residents, who represent only the residue of the original flow, and who have long since forgotten some of their fears and some of their naïve hopes about urban life. But such subjective responses, even when honestly told, will not fully describe the most likely migrants. Few will say 'because I am young and a male'—this much is assumed or never even analysed—but those characteristics are important, as any quantitative analysis will show. Nevertheless, this does not discredit the personal approach, and in the next chapter we will examine personal responses, which can be checked against the statistical data presented here.

The other problem is the analytical approach. No one factor can fully determine an individual's propensity to migrate. Yet the application of any form of multifactorial analysis is fraught with difficulty, largely because it is impossible to define neatly the original condition of migrants. Apart from catching rural-urban migrants *en route* and during their first migration, work which is difficult but urgently needed, there are some dangers in defining migrants as those planning to depart. If the study selects those who have participated in either seasonal or long-term migration, some characteristics, such as fluency in English, may result as much from migration as from pre-migration opportunities. It is often more certain to proceed by the examination of single characteristics, or of sets of characteristics where each factor is separated out, and to discuss for each the likely effects of pre- and post-migrational experience. This approach will be followed here.

In the discussion that follows aggregates of respondents will be used to demonstrate findings, except where a marked difference between the findings for the sexes, age groups, or migration regions can be shown. Unless otherwise stated the analysis has been restricted to persons over 20 years of age, a group which is made up entirely of persons who could presumably have migrated of their own volition. Most of the analysis in this chapter has been confined to the rural survey; later we shall use the urban survey more extensively to investigate the sea-changes wrought by town life.

Size of the home centre and distance from the nearest large town

As reported in Chapter 2, the population of large towns contains amongst its immigrant residents a disproportionate number of persons from other towns (defined in the 1960 census as centres with more than 5,000 inhabitants) compared with the number from villages.

Even amongst the villages a differential exists, the larger villages producing a significantly greater proportion of rural-urban migrants than the smaller ones. The proportion of long-term absentees in the town rose with the size of the village from 8·6 per cent of the population in centres with fewer than 500 inhabitants to 14·7 per cent of those with 2,000-5,000 inhabitants. However, there was at the same time some decline in the proportion of seasonal migrants, partly because the savannah north was decreasingly represented.

However, these differentials are no greater than can be explained by differences in the incidence of schooling. The larger villages produce a greater proportion of educated persons, and education, as will be seen below, is a determinant of rural-urban migration. The 1960 census showed a continuum in the numbers over 6 years of age who had ever attended school, from 14 per cent in centres with under 200 inhabitants, to 19 per cent, 22 per cent, 26 per cent, 31 per cent, and 43 per cent as the size of the settlement increased to 200-499, 500-999, 1,000-1,999, 2,000-4,999, and finally to 5,000 persons or more.

Distance from the nearest large town (50,000 or more inhabitants) has a clear effect on migration among both males and females. Table 3:1 shows that, as distance rises, the number of long-term absentees falls steeply. Conversely, with distance the proportion who have never migrated rises except for distances over 250 miles, where the special problems of the North, and the pressure to migrate from it, at least seasonally, have left their mark.

Doubtless distance weakens the attractive message percolating out from the towns; doubtless, too, it makes it more difficult and expensive to get there. One effect is probably indirect; many of the forces working towards an increase in rural-urban migration are products of social and economic modernisation, which tend to weaken the greater distances from the towns, for, while the latter are themselves the result of such change, they are the extreme type and the centre from which change diffuses further.

But distance has a further effect. It makes the break with relatives and other villagers left behind more complete. The second part of the table shows that, for obvious reasons of expense and time, the proportion of long-term absentees who rarely or never come back rises with increasing distance between the village and the town (ignoring the first cell—for the very short distance migrants are atypical in many ways). The third part demonstrates that such problems do not lead to a high rate of permanent return to the more distant villages, partly doubtless because they are on the whole the poorest and the least likely to attract the returnee on material grounds.

Table 3:1 The effect of distance between village and town

Migration classification	Distance of village from town (in miles)				
	Under 25	25-50	50-100	100-250	over 250
Percentage distribution[a] of respondents in rural survey by migration classification and distance of village from town[b]:					
Never migrated	62	60	67	76	70
Seasonal migrants	3	6	5	2	9
Permanent returnees	6	14	10	10	13
Long-term absentees	29	17	14	8	7
Others and no entry	0	3	4	4	1
Total respondents: per cent	100	100	100	100	100
number	1,034	1,558	1,527	2,011	1,331
Percentage long-term absentees rarely or never visiting home village form of all long-term absentees	28	10	24	27	36
Percentage permanent returnees from long-term absences form of all persons who have been long-term absentees	12	66	43	61	61

[a] Distribution here is statistically significant amongst both males and females.

[b] I.e. nearest centre with more than 50,000 persons in municipality (Accra, Kumasi, or Sekondi-Takoradi).

Source: Rural survey, respondents over 20 years of age.

Sex and age

Sex and age are important determinants in most migrant streams. In Ghana, as in most developing countries, it is the young males who are most mobile. In Accra there were in 1960 over 20 per cent more males than females who were born elsewhere in Ghana. In terms of age there were disproportionately more 15-34-year-olds in the town than in the country.

The type of migration classification used in the rural survey can only indicate age at first migration by recording the age of those planning to migrate. This has two drawbacks. Firstly, although it was stressed that such planning should be for a definite move, some respondents were doubtless planning well before their departure; some may well never have left. Secondly, by definition it includes young children whose parents or others were planning their departure. Many young children were thus included, for young husbands and wives, often with young children, are more prone to move to the town than are older parents.

Even with all these provisos, Table 3:2 makes it clear that the chief planners for long-term moves to the towns are 15-19-year-olds, and that girls are almost as keen, and apparently almost as certain, to go as boys.

Table 3:2 Percentage of rural respondents in each age group planning first long-term migration to urban areas by sex and age

Sex	Age group							
	0-9	10-14	15-19	20-24	25-29	30-44	45-59	60+
Male	5	10	11	7	5	3	1	0
Female	4	6	10	4	3	2	0	0

Source: Rural survey.

Occupational contrasts

The single most important factor in the creation of a rural-urban migration stream is the occupational contrast between village and town; in the former most people are farmers while in the latter they are not, in the latter nearly all workers are paid substantially in cash while in the former great numbers are not. The 1960 census enumerated as farmers or fishermen only one-thirty-seventh of the work force of Accra, but three-quarters of all rural workers and ten-elevenths of those of the north.

It is precisely this homogeneity of village population, the fact that most men are farmers and most women are concerned both with domestic duties and farming, that makes rural occupational activity an unsatisfactory index for predicting migrational behaviour. There is, however, some evidence of the influence of occupation on migrational behaviour.

In the case of both males and females 71 per cent of those respondents reported in the rural survey as planning to migrate for the first time to the towns for a lengthy period were classified as either schoolchildren or dependent minors. The same proportions obtained for those planning a first seasonal migration. Even amongst the balance of the planners, a considerable number were young people described in the case of males as assisting with farming and in the case of females as assisting in the household, although one should not take too seriously, especially in the rural North, occupational categories which consign females to the house rather than the fields. Over one-third of older boys no longer at school, or never there, were planning long-term absences in the town.

A few other general observations can be made. Persons in specialised rural occupations, such as quarrying or mining, are unlikely to move to the town. This does not apply to farming, which in many ways is a family rather than an individual pursuit, and which is the basic, residual occupation in rural areas. Nor does it apply to craftsmanship or work in the skilled trades; young men who have obtained such employment in the village are very likely to want to try their luck in the larger towns. Thus the establishment of village crafts might well accelerate rather than retard the movement to urban areas. Rural workers described as labourers are likely to go away periodically at any time, but seasonal migrants describing themselves as farmers usually chose the dry season. Seasonal migrants are more likely to come from predominantly subsistence farms than cash farms, but this is not true of long-term movement to the towns.

Perhaps not surprisingly, those long-term absentees who most frequently revisit their home village are those who have gained employment in transport, especially on the lorries. In the towns a much larger proportion of women migrants regard their primary occupation as the one performed outside the household than is the case in the village.

The most surprising finding was that there is little statistical evidence that the returnees from the town are a particularly important source of non-agricultural skills in the village, although doubtless over a period of time such skills do flow in some fashion from the larger centres. The explanation seems to be that many of the returnees retire to their home areas with money and possessions from the town, perhaps into a house built with town money, and regard their urban skill as something which has served its purpose. Meanwhile such village crafts as blacksmithing, bicycle repairing, and weaving are performed by non-migrants who in their youth joined older village craftsmen performing these tasks and learnt from them.

Education

Possibly the most important matter to be considered is the role of education, especially formal schooling, in inducing rural-urban migration. The high proportion of schoolchildren among those planning to go to the towns is not merely a product of their youth; schooling itself turns people towards town life. Indeed, in Ghana it is often thought of as preparing people for urban occupations. Often respondents explained to the interviewers someone's migration to the town as obvious or inevitable 'because he had been to school' and another's residence in the village and occupation as a farmer 'because he had not been to school'.

Several factors are involved. One was the shortage of trained persons which lasted until after World War II. In earlier times a literate person would usually be encouraged by the mission, which was probably responsible for his literacy, to do work for the mission. Later, with the extension of the colonial administration, the government did much the same thing on a very much bigger scale (Hurd 1967: 229-30). But the content of the school courses is also important, for almost inevitably that which has been taught has hardly ever been about traditional society and has never sought to encourage a firmer establishment in that society. Rather, it has been about a foreign way of life, most closely approximated in the towns, or about aspects of society only found in the modernised sector of the economy which is identified to a considerable degree with the towns. A third factor in weakening the links of the educated with the land is probably the lack of ancestral family land with which personal identification can be made; land has traditionally been held by such larger units as the tribe or clan, and shifting cultivation has even altered the site of individual activities.

The rural survey provided strong statistical support for these arguments. The effect of education is not, of course, absolute. Some of the unschooled have strong personal drives to go to the city or to leave their home village, even though they might find their lack of qualifications a drawback in securing urban employment. Some of the educated have a cocoa farm or other inducement to stay; some of the most educated, especially in the remote areas, find themselves qualified to carry out some administrative or educational function in their home area and more suited to do so than an outsider who would otherwise have to be sent by the government.

In Table 3:3 the analysis has been confined to respondents in the rural survey over 20 years of age so that all might have had the opportunity to migrate to the towns. It can be seen that while two-thirds of the males and seven-ninths of the females without education have stayed in the village without participating in any form of migration, and without continuing to plan any migration, the proportions fall dramatically thereafter, to a point where less than two-fifths of the upper primary and middle school leavers and technically trained of either sex are content to do so. The greatest difference is between those who have gone no further than brief primary schooling, many of whom have in the past dropped out very early in the process (Hurd 1967: 226-9), and those who have had more extensive training or equivalent education. The middle school leavers have enough schooling, are sufficiently literate, and have acquired enough English to make them want a town job and to feel that they can secure it; thus it often is particularly frustrating to them to find that town employers do not always regard their proficiency in these fields as reaching the desired levels. It has been argued by Apter (1955: 165-7) and Austin (1964: 13-18) that much of the political pressure in Ghana has been caused by the problems in the town of the dissatisfied middle school leaver. The kind of primary school completion course which he has experienced leads in only a minority of cases to secondary schooling and further. In 1960 there were thirty-five times as many students in primary and middle schools as in secondary schools, this providing some measure, although perhaps an exaggerated one in view of the rapid expansion of schooling, of the scarcity of secondary school places.

Planning to migrate also rises with education, but more sharply amongst females. Seasonal migration probably reaches a peak amongst males in the brief primary schooling group, for the high proportions recorded for both males and females in the most highly educated group arises from the fact that the definition of seasonal absences could be made to cover, as some enumerators made it cover, the case of regular absence at secondary school or university. Thus some education seems to be needed to encourage even seasonal migration or to ensure its success.

What continued education does more than anything else is to promote long-term rural-urban migration. Thus almost half of those with secondary schooling or university education were reported to be in the towns, and, if the wrongly classified so-called 'seasonal migrants' are added the proportion

Table 3:3 Percentage distribution of rural respondents over 20 years of age in each educational group by migration classification and sex

Sex	Migration classification[a]	Highest level of education reached[b]			
		None	Limited primary schooling	Extended primary and middle schooling	Secondary schooling and university
Male	Never migrated:				
	no plans	65	59	38	17
	planning to do so	4	7	9	8
	Ever a seasonal migrant	8	12	9	18
	Ever a long-term absentee	19	19	40	49
	Visiting; other; no entry	4	3	4	8
	Total: per cent	100	100	100	100
	respondents	3,748			
Female	Never migrated:				
	no plans	77	65	39	26
	planning to do so	3	5	10	13
	Ever a seasonal migrant	4	8	8	18
	Ever a long-term absentee	12	20	38	43
	Visiting; other; no entry	4	2	5	0
	Total: per cent	100	100	100	100
	respondents	3,713			

[a] In this and following tables 'migrated' means migrated to urban areas, and current visitors to the town have been put in the residual category because of lack of information about their previous activities.

[b] Detailed analysis has shown groups too small for separate analysis. They have been amalgamated with the groups showing the closest migration classification pattern; thus 'Mass education' has been added to 'Limited primary schooling', 'Technical training' to 'Extended primary and middle schooling', and 'no entry' to 'none'. An examination of the individual schedules shows this to be also the closest educational correspondence.

Source: Rural survey, respondents over 20 years of age.

approaches two-thirds. It does not exceed this, because the Ministry of Education and other government bodies frequently take the opportunity to appoint to rural areas trainees who know that area and speak the language because they were raised there.

In Table 3:4 an attempt has been made to assess the contribution of each educational division to the various migration classification groups. Thus amongst males half of the long-term absentees are upper primary or middle school leavers and only one-third are the non-educated, while the respective figures amongst females are one-third and half. Nor is there evidence that this pattern is changing, for that of those planning to migrate is nearly identical with those who have already participated in long-term absences. Even a majority of male seasonal migrants have had some schooling. But the never educated dominate the group who have not lived in the town, and do not intend to do so. It is this sedentary group which must inevitably be whittled away, leading to much greater rural-urban migration and urban growth, if the pattern shown in Table 3:4 remains constant and if mass education persists or expands.

The gross migration/education distributions described in Tables 3:3 and 3:4 are obviously statistically significant. However, the analysis was carried further by subdividing each group by migration region and age, the latter being a tripartite split of population over 15 years of age into 15-29, 30-59, and 60+ age groups. The limits of the analysis set out in Table 3:5 are provided by the dwindling numbers of older persons with any education, especially amongst females and especially with movement away from the coast.

In Table 3:5, the lower limit of the youngest age group has been reduced to 15 years so as to include the younger migrants. However, this means that the 15-29 age group data must be interpreted with care, for in some cells migration has been prevented to date by continuing education. This will certainly occur to a marked extent amongst those reaching secondary school and university, to a lesser degree amongst the upper primary and middle school group, and perhaps even a little amongst the limited primary school group.

Thus, if we are to ascertain whether with time the same degree of education produces a greater tendency to move to the town, we must restrict the examination to a comparison of the 60+ age group with 30-59-year-olds. Only for Southern males, the first Ghanaians to be strongly affected by educational and other social change, do we have sufficient data. These data suggest that the likelihood of going to the town is increasing. The point, however, is not of very great importance. What is portentous is that an ever larger proportion of each oncoming group of children is subject to prolonged schooling. This is the educational factor which is helping to swell the numbers of rural-urban migrants.

The general picture presented by Table 3:5 is very clear. In every sub-

Table 3:4 Percentage distribution of rural respondents over 20 years of age in each migration classification by education and sex

Sex	Migration classification	Highest level of education reached				Total respondents	
		None	Limited primary schooling	Extended primary and middle schooling	Secondary schooling and university	Per cent	Number
Male	Never migrated:						
	no plans	63	10	25	2	100	1,972
	planning to do so	34	9	50	7	100	243
	Ever a seasonal migrant	44	11	34	11	100	345
	Ever a long-term absentee	34	6	50	10	100	1,036
	Visiting; other; no entry	46	7	36	11	100	152
	Total respondents 3,748						
Female	Never migrated:						
	no plans	83	8	9	0	100	2,574
	planning to do so	50	11	36	3	100	163
	Ever a seasonal migrant	60	14	23	3	100	201
	Ever a long-term absentee	52	10	35	3	100	639
	Visiting; other; no entry	71	6	23	0	100	136
	Total respondents 3,713						

Source: Rural survey, respondents over 20 years of age.

Table 3:5 Percentage of rural respondents over 15 years of age who had never migrated to town, by sex, migration region, age, and education

			Percentage of respondents who had never migrated to the town by highest type of education reached					
Sex	Migration region	Age group	None	Limited primary schooling	Extended middle schooling	Secondary schooling and university	Statistical significance[a] per cent	Total respondents
Male	South	15-29	55	66	54	47	5	757
		30-59	64	59	37	15[b]	0·1	291
		60+	70	62	53	—[c]	5	161
	Volta	15-29	68	83	64	28	5	273
		30-59	70	80	63	0[b]	5	291
		60+	NC	NC	NC	NC	NC	61
	Ashanti	15-29	87	85	79	65	1	516
		30-59	50	73	61	12[b]	NS	462
		60+	NC	NC	NC	NC	NC	78
	North	15-29	71	80	59	50	5	438
		30-59	66	56	26	25[b]	0·1	472
		60+	NC	NC	NC	NC	NC	92
Female	South	15-29	70	66	63	32	0·1	854
		30-59	75	72	44	44[b]	0·1	823
		60+	NC	NC	NC	NC	NC	177
	Volta	15-29	80	70	66	43[b]	5	339
		30-59	74	62	33	—[c]	5	280
		60+	NC	NC	NC	NC	NC	29
	Ashanti	15-29	88	80	78	73+	5	637
		30-59	90	90	78	—[c]	—[d]	392
		60+	NC	NC	NC	NC	NC	62
	North	15-29	79	43	36	100[b]	0·1	434
		30-59	85	67	—[c]	—[c]	—[d]	350
		60+	NC	NC	NC	NC	NC	30
						Total respondents		8,299

[a] Level of statistical significance of distribution by education (chi-square test).
[b] Fewer than 10 respondents in cell, so aggregated with adjoining cell for significance test.
[c] No respondents in cell.
[d] Insufficient respondents with any education to warrant significance test.
NC Not calculated because of insufficient respondents with any education to warrant calculation.
NS Not statistically significant at 5 per cent level.

Source: Rural survey, respondents over 15 years of age.

division where calculation is possible except one, there is a statistically significant association between the incidence and extent of education and migration to urban areas. Even the exception yields a significant association if the examination is confined to those who have received some schooling. What is noteworthy is that brief attendance at primary school is not of great importance in inducing rural-urban migration. Many of those who had a little primary schooling are not literate, cannot make themselves understood in English, and have learnt comparatively little about the outside world. In fact in about one-third of the cells those with limited primary schooling have shown a lesser tendency to migrate than those with no education.

Of the thirty-two cells where male and female migration tendencies can be compared, in only three have more females than males from the same region and in the same age group migrated. Two of the discrepancies are

Table 3:6 Propensity for rural-urban migration by region subdivided by sex and age groups and standardised for education
(in each line propensity inversely related to point score)

	Region			
	South	Volta	Ashanti	North
Whole sample	21	32	43	24
Sex:				
male	11	21	23	15
female	10	11	20	9
Age:				
15-29	10	18	28	14
30-59	11	14	15	10
Sex and age:				
male				
15-29	5	9	16	10
30-59	6	12	7	5
female				
15-29	5	9	12	4
30-59	5	2	8	5

Note: The data in Table 3:5 showing the proportion of persons who 'Never migrated' were reassembled into twenty-four divisions by sex, age, and education. Each division contains four percentages, one for each migration region. Twelve divisions were discarded for scaling because they were not calculated owing to insufficient data or because one or more individual cells contained fewer than ten respondents (in all but one case these divisions were ones where the respondents were 60+ years old or were 30-59 and had reached secondary schooling or university). The remaining twelve divisions, containing the great majority of respondents, were then scaled by regions from 1 to 4, from the lowest percentage of 'Never migrated' to the highest, and these scalings were then awarded one to four points respectively. These points were then aggregated in various ways; the lowest aggregation in each set of four regional comparisons indicated the lowest propensity to remain in the village and hence the highest propensity to participate in rural-urban migration.

Source: Table 3:5 presenting data of rural survey respondents over 15 years of age.

found in the Volta Region. This is evidence of a sex differential in migration even after age, education, and region have been standardised.

It is possible to scale the migrational tendencies of the various regions, subdivided where desired by sex or age divisions. This has been done in Table 3:6 where in each case the lower the point score the lower the proportion who had never migrated to the town and hence the higher the propensity for rural-urban migration.

The point score in Table 3:6 confirms that even when education and age have been standardised, propensity for rural-urban migration has been greatest in the South, which has experienced the most socio-economic change, and in the North, which has experienced the least change, but where the pressures to migrate are very great for three reasons: an agrarian structure which cannot adequately cope with a savage dry season, a largely subsistence economy which cannot produce cash incomes on a sufficient scale to allow the purchase of various tempting industrial products, and the magnitude of the contrast in living conditions between itself and the more economically developed areas further south. Migration has been least in Ashanti, where, although income per head is no higher than in the South (Szereszewski 1966: 92), it has probably been increasing more rapidly, and where 'boom' conditions in the cocoa farming frontier areas have provided plenty of jobs.

The analysis by sex shows that the differentials in migration propensity between the South, North, and Volta are much more marked amongst males than females. Only in Ashanti is there a markedly greater tendency than elsewhere for educated women to stay in the village. No such tendency exists in the North. The relative lack of Northern women in the southern cities, the lack which in 1960 produced a sex ratio in the Accra Capital District for those born in the North of 180 males per 100 females, compared with 114, 117, and 141 for those born in the rest of the South, Volta, and Ashanti respectively (calculated from Census 1960: *Advance Report*, 13), is simply the product of very low female educational levels in the North. In 1960 almost five times as many males as females in the North claimed past school attendance and the proportion climbed to over forty times amongst those over 55 years of age (calculated from *Advance Report*, 30-1). Nowhere in the other three migration regions does the first educational sex ratio rise above three and one-third or the second above six (see also Caldwell 1967a: 48-54).

The analysis by age indicates that it is only in recent years, perhaps since 1950, that the South has definitely outdistanced the North in proportional production of rural-urban migrants, although it should be noted that it has probably always led the North in terms of long-term absentees and hence in the number of migrants in the towns at any given time. Probably only since World War II, with at first conditions of high prosperity in the cocoa industry and then the continued pushing out of cocoa-growing areas,

Table 3:7 Migration patterns and literacy amongst rural respondents over 20 years of age

Sex	Migration classification[a]	Literacy category[b]					Total respondents	
		Illiterate	African only	English and African	English only	Other	Per cent	Number
(a) Percentage distribution in each literacy category of respondents by migration classification and sex								
Male	Never migrated	69	67	50	38	48		
	Seasonal migrant	5	5	9	3	26		
	Permanent returnee	14	13	13	9	13		
	Long-term absentee	9	14	24	48	13		
	Other; no entry	3	1	4	2	0		
	Total respondents: per cent	100	100	100	100	100		
	number	2,025	219	1,077	396	31		
Female	Never migrated	81	72	53	47	100		
	Seasonal migrant	3	6	7	4	0		
	Permanent returnee	8	12	12	10	0		
	Long-term absentee	6	8	25	38	0		
	Other; no entry	2	2	3	1	0		
	Total respondents: per cent	100	100	100	100	100		
	number	2,884	215	393	220	1		
(b) Percentage distribution in each migration classification of respondents by literacy category and sex								
Male	Never migrated	62	6	24	7	1	100	2,257
	Seasonal migrant	44	5	42	6	3	100	235
	Permanent returnee	56	6	30	7	1	100	486
	Long-term absentee	27	4	39	29	1	100	660
	Other; no entry	55	7	3	35	0	100	110
Female	Never migrated	83	4	6	7	0	100	2,784
	Seasonal migrant	60	7	9	24	0	100	128
	Permanent returnee	72	7	14	7	0	100	335
	Long-term absentee	47	4	27	22	0	100	377
	Other; no entry	80	5	12	3	0	100	89

[a] 'Never migrated' includes visitors to the town at the time of the survey; 'Seasonal migrant' and 'Long-term absentee' include those temporarily in the village at the time of the survey; 'Permanent returnee' includes those who have been either seasonal or long-term absentees.

[b] The 'Illiterate' are the completely illiterate—those who cannot make out a simple sentence or notice board; 'Illiterate' includes 'No entry'; 'Other' is made up of those literate in Arabic, except for two persons literate in French.

Source: Rural survey respondents over 20 years of age.

especially in Brong-Ahafo, has Ashanti fallen so far behind in its tendency to produce rural-urban migrants. Nevertheless, even here their actual numbers have doubtless increased very considerably.

The more detailed breakdown by age and sex only slightly modifies the picture already drawn. Perhaps its most interesting suggestion is that during the earlier migration period, perhaps until the late 1940s, Volta Region women, probably Ewe migrants to Accra, were the most likely females to participate in rural-urban migration.

Literacy

If education makes rural-urban relocation easier, then it is possible that this is mainly a function of some of its individual strands, the production of literacy or the improvement in spoken English. Both are much harder to analyse meaningfully than is education. Schooling is usually finished before the decision to move to the town, or the decision to stay there if the schooling itself necessitated a move, is made. But literacy or spoken English may be as much or more a product of migration as its cause. When acquired before migration, they might often be little more than a reflection of educational levels attained.

Amongst both males and females in the rural survey there was a positive association between literacy and rural-urban migration, an association that was stronger when literacy in English was involved. Thus Table 3:7 shows that, while 69 per cent of adult male and 81 per cent of adult female illiterate respondents had never migrated to the town even seasonally, this was true of only 47 per cent of males and 51 per cent of females who were literate at all in English. The test applied tried to differentiate between those completely illiterate and the balance, and so simple sentences of basic English were administered and judged liberally. Originally records were also separated according to ability to read only, to write only, or to read and write, but the first two categories were found to be very small indeed.

Most respondents who were literate in any language were literate at least in both English and their native language, the proportion rising to almost two-thirds amongst males and falling to just below half amongst females. One reason is the pattern of schooling—although, when judged as liberally as here, literacy rates exceed schooling rates—for primary schools begin to teach in the local language and subsequently switch to English. Those who are literate in an African language only tend to be the very early school drop-outs who have remained in the village or those who have learnt from others in the village. Thus, especially amongst males, this group is little more likely to have migrated from village to town than is the illiterate group. Conversely, those literate in English only contain a very high proportion of long-term absentees, especially those who have been in the town since they were very young, who find English suffices and who might have little use for reading a language used only in a distant area where notices or records are few and even then usually not in the vernacular. But, if one has a use for both forms of literacy, one can fairly readily be acquired once the other has been mastered; hence the high rate of literacy in both languages of seasonal migrants.

There is certainly a relationship between literacy and rural-urban migration. Over two-thirds of the male long-term absentees and almost half the male seasonal migrants are literate in English compared with less than one-third of those who had never migrated. Doubtless many migrants have acquired this skill as a result of their migration; but the high proportion of long-term and seasonal migrants who are literate in both English and their native language may well be partly a product of the work of the village primary schools which in this way help to provide the expertise so useful

Table 3:8 Migration patterns and spoken English amongst rural respondents over 20 years of age

Sex	Migration classification	Spoken English category[a]			Total respondents	
		No English	Poor English	Fair or good English	Per cent	Number
(a) Percentage distribution in each spoken English category by migration classification and sex						
Male	Never migrated	69	62	44		
	Seasonal migrant	5	6	8		
	Permanent returnee	13	16	13		
	Long-term absentee	10	14	32		
	Other; no entry	3	2	3		
Total: per cent		100	100	100		
number		2,109	393	1,246		
Female	Never migrated	80	67	48		
	Seasonal migrant	3	7	7		
	Permanent returnee	8	14	11		
	Long-term absentee	7	10	31		
	Other; no entry	2	2	3		
Total: per cent		100	100	100		
number		3,061	196	456		
(b) Percentage distribution in each migration classification by spoken English category and sex						
Male	Never migrated	65	11	24	100	2,257
	Seasonal migrant	45	11	44	100	235
	Permanent returnee	55	13	32	100	486
	Long-term absentee	31	8	61	100	660
	Other; no entry	60	8	32	100	110
Female	Never migrated	87	5	8	100	2,784
	Seasonal migrant	63	11	26	100	128
	Permanent returnee	76	8	16	100	335
	Long-term absentee	57	5	38	100	377
	Other; no entry	82	4	14	100	89

[a] Those classified as 'Poor English' had real difficulty in making their meaning understood to the interviewers when speaking English.

Source: Rural survey respondents over 20 years of age.

for survival in the town. Evidence that this is so, and of the role of the school in producing literate would-be migrants, is provided by an examination of all the respondents planning long-term migration to the towns. Half were literate in both English and their native language, products of schooling to at least the mid-primary level, one-quarter were literate in only one, many of them lower primary drop-outs, and one-quarter were illiterate. Amongst these respondents, the great majority of them between 10 and 25 years of age, there was no sex differential in the planning of urban migration by degree of literacy; the fact that 60 per cent more males than females were planning such a move was entirely the product of a sex differential in literacy, evidence of the sex imbalance in rural schooling.

Spoken English

Even more difficult, because of its interrelation with schooling, and because of its being both cause and effect, is the analysis of spoken English. The mastery of English is certainly related to rural-urban migration, as the pattern shown in Table 3:8 reveals (significant for each sex). It will be noted that nearly all respondents classified as having 'fair or good English' had been classified as to some degree literate in the language as well as about half those with 'poor English'. It is in fact usually easier to read a notice in a foreign language than to keep up even a simple conversation.

Seven-tenths of the males and four-fifths of the females with no English have never lived in the town at all, while in neither case is this true for even half of those with fair or good English. Acquisition of some English certainly plays a role in the original decision to migrate. Fewer than two-fifths of the young people planning to migrate have no spoken English while over two-fifths have fair English or better. Here again there is no sex differential amongst planners with the same degree of spoken English, but more boys than girls make plans because more than one-and-a-half times as many at this age do have some command of the language.

The benefit gained by having some English for successful settlement in the town is not confined to the securing of office jobs or other positions demanding it as an employment qualification. The population of Ghana is fractionated into many language groups and the rural-urban migrant often finds that his own language cannot be used to communicate with many people in the town; in these circumstances he needs some form of lingua franca. The most extreme case is Accra, for Ga is the language of those who are native to the area, but it is spoken as a first language by insignificant numbers of persons outside the city. The rural-urban migrant settling in for long-term residence will probably find that he has to acquire some Ga for his everyday needs; he will probably also use at least the basic vocabulary of some Akan language, for such languages are spoken by the Ashanti, Fante, and related groups and are used widely, even amongst northerners, as a lingua franca.

But English also plays an important role, especially for formal purposes and when coming into contact with officialdom, and is essential for office positions, many forms of retailing, and in any other task where it is necessary to come into contact with a wide range of people. This is truer for men than women, for the latter may be mainly engaged in looking after children or in petty trading, where English may at times be a help but is not really essential. Thus over three-fifths of the male long-term absentees have fair English compared with less than two-fifths of the females. However, it is possible, especially if one is a dependent wife, to live in the immigrant suburbs without any English at all. The table shows that almost one-third of the men and over half the women do so, figures which were confirmed by the urban survey, which showed that in the predominantly immigrant suburbs one-third of the entire population spoke no English at all.

An examination of all rural survey respondents by separate migration regions, major age groups, and sex showed that there has long been a positive association (significant in all cases) between participation in rural-urban migration and command of spoken English in the North, from which migration was a major undertaking, and in Ashanti, where it was the most unusual to migrate. The association is weaker in the South, where towns abound, and weakest of all in Volta, partly because Ewes moving to Accra have long tended to live amongst their fellows there. There is some evidence that with the coming of mass migration to the town and mass education to the villages, the distinction between the person with fair spoken English migrating and the one without it staying in the village, is less marked than it used to be.

Position in the family

There is an association, as is seen in Table 3:9, between the number of living siblings in a family and the propensity of each to migrate to the towns. This relationship persists when the examination is confined to members of the same sex. There are probably at least three different forces at work. Members of larger families are slightly older in average age, but this should affect the picture very little, as the examination has been confined to persons over 20 years of age, and migration patterns do not vary suddenly with age—in fact they tend to vary in a direction which would produce the opposite association to the one noted here. The first important influence is probably related to chain migration, a phenomenon which does exist and which will be analysed later. Members of large families are more likely by random chance to have at least one sibling in the town, and, as will be seen, persons with a close relative already in town are the most likely to migrate. The other important influence is that when there are few children, as we learnt from village discussions, there is greater pressure, especially on an only surviving son, not to go to the town, or if once gone to return. This pressure becomes very strong indeed if the elder male household heads (fathers, grandfathers, or uncles) die. This pattern of higher incidence of permanent return where the family is smaller is clearly visible in the table. In all sections of the table there is a statistically significant difference between the migration patterns of 1-2 siblings and 3+ siblings.

The ascertainment that children in relatively small families were more encouraged to stay at home or to return home if they did migrate suggested that such pressures might be exerted on the elder children irrespective of family size; perhaps in smaller families such children merely formed a larger fraction of all children. This inquiry was pursued, as is shown in Table 3:10,

Table 3:9 Percentage distribution of rural respondents over 20 years of age by migration classification, number of siblings, and sex

Sex	Migration classification	Number of siblings (including respondents)[a] 1	2	3	4	5+
(a) By total number of siblings						
Male	Never migrated	62	68	63	62	50
	Seasonal migrant	6	6	9	5	7
	Permanent returnee	15	14	8	11	11
	Long-term absentee	13	10	19	21	30
	Other; no entry	4	2	1	1	2
Total:	per cent	100	100	100	100	100
	respondents 3,748					
Female	Never migrated	77	85	77	77	65
	Seasonal migrant	3	3	1	4	5
	Permanent returnee	10	4	8	3	8
	Long-term absentee	7	7	13	13	20
	Other; no entry	3	1	1	3	2
Total:	per cent	100	100	100	100	100
	respondents 3,713					
(b) By number of siblings of the same sex						
Male	Never migrated	63	63	59	58	49
	Seasonal migrant	6	6	8	6	8
	Permanent returnee	14	12	8	9	14
	Long-term absentee	13	17	24	26	28
	Other; no entry	4	2	1	1	1
Total:	per cent	100	100	100	100	100
	respondents 3,748					
Female	Never migrated	77	76	72	61	68
	Seasonal migrant	3	3	4	3	5
	Permanent returnee	10	5	6	10	8
	Long-term absentee	8	13	16	22	18
	Other; no entry	2	3	2	4	1
Total:	per cent	100	100	100	100	100
	respondents 3,713					

[a] There is evidence that in some cases the respondent was shown as having no siblings when the fact could not be properly ascertained.

Source: Rural survey respondents over 20 years of age.

with some difficulty. Siblings were defined as full or half siblings reared together; but often only some of the rearing was in the same household. Position was amongst siblings ever born, not merely the survivors. Respondents were frequently confused by questions about the exact number and order of siblings. Ultimately data were only completely sure for half the males and one-third of the females and it was on this residue that the analysis was carried out.

The distribution patterns are statistically significant only in the case of males, on whom more pressures about responsibilities to the village family are put. Nevertheless, in all sections of the table there is for both sexes a greater propensity for long-term absence amongst the younger siblings. There certainly appears to be a more pronounced tendency for the first two sons and the first daughter to remain behind and for the eldest of each

Table 3:10 Percentage distribution of rural respondents over 20 years of age by migration classification, position by age amongst siblings, and sex

Sex	Migration classification	Position amongst siblings 1st	2nd	3rd	4th	5th+	Insufficient data
(a) By siblings of both sexes							
Male	Never migrated	62	60	54	49	54	
	Seasonal migrant	7	7	4	6	8	
	Permanent returnee	13	9	10	12	7	
	Long-term absentee	16	22	31	29	29	
	Other; no entry	2	2	1	4	2	
Total:	per cent	100	100	100	100	100	
	number	742	539	272	159	188	1,848
Female	Never migrated	74	71	74	70	64	
	Seasonal migrant	2	4	4	6	6	
	Permanent returnee	8	8	5	4	8	
	Long-term absentee	14	14	16	19	22	
	Other; no entry	2	3	1	1	0	
Total:	per cent	100	100	100	100	100	
	number	345	340	211	125	175	2,517
(b) By siblings of the same sex							
Male	Never migrated	60	60	53	53		
	Seasonal migrant	6	7	6	8		
	Permanent returnee	12	9	10	10		
	Long-term absentee	20	22	29	27		
	Other; no entry	2	2	2	2		
Total:	per cent	100	100	100	100		
	number	922	555	241	190		1,840
Female	Never migrated	74	70	69	65		
	Seasonal migrant	3	4	6	5		
	Permanent returnee	8	5	7	6		
	Long-term absentee	13	19	17	22		
	Other; no entry	2	2	1	2		
Total:	per cent	100	100	100	100		
	number	623	341	146	100		2,503

Source: Rural survey respondents over 20 years of age.

sex to return permanently. Presumably the pressure for permanent return is exerted on both long-term absentees and seasonal migrants, so in Table 3:11 the examination of permanent return amongst all who have been away in the town is pursued further.

Table 3:11 confirms that all forms of rural-urban migration are less likely in the case of the two eldest sons and the eldest daughter. It also shows clearly that the eldest son and daughter are much more likely to return permanently even when they have participated in movements to the towns. This, especially when the parents die, is probably partly the result of family pressure, and partly the result of new opportunities in the village, especially farming or other occupational opportunities, caused by the death of the parents.

Because these pressures to stay or to return are felt more strongly by males, and because the need for sudden return is experienced more by those 30-59 years of age than younger or older migrants, a special examination by migrant region was made of males of this age. This study suggested that the pressure not to migrate at all is strongest on the eldest in the South and Ashanti, where there may well be cash-cropping farms to help administer, and that the pressure on the eldest to return permanently is a feature of all Ghanaian rural society.

Table 3:11 An examination of permanent return amongst rural-urban migrants over 20 years of age by position, by age amongst siblings, and sex

Sex		Position amongst siblings[a] 1st	2nd	3rd	4th	5th+
(a) By siblings of both sexes						
Males	Percentage ever migrated form of all respondents	36	38	45	47	44
	Percentage permanent returnees form of all ever migrated	36	24	22	26	16
Females	Percentage ever migrated form of all respondents	24	26	25	29	36
	Percentage permanent returnees form of all ever migrated	33	31	20	14	22
(b) By siblings of the same sex						
Males	Percentage ever migrated form of all respondents	38	38	45	45	
	Percentage permanent returnees form of all ever migrated	32	24	22	22	
Females	Percentage ever migrated form of all respondents	24	28	30	33	
	Percentage permanent returnees form of all ever migrated	33	18	23	18	

[a] The respondents noted in Table 3:10 with insufficient data have been omitted here.

Source: Rural survey respondents over 20 years of age.

These patterns are not merely historical; they still persist. Amongst young males the proportion planning their first long-term migration to the towns is one-and-a-half times as great for fifth or more sons as it is for first or second sons. The disproportion is smaller but still recognisable amongst daughters.

Conjugal condition

Rural-urban migration patterns and conjugal condition certainly affect each other. However, the interrelation is complex. Most intending migrants are single, but then most young males, the group with the greatest motivation towards urban migration, are single. Amongst males of the 15-29 age group, 20 per cent of those planning to migrate for a long period are married compared with 26 per cent of those expecting to remain at home. Table 3:12 shows that, whilst only 6 per cent of the married are planning long-term migration, 9 per cent of the single are doing so. These findings are statistically significant (at 5 per cent level) but may be affected by age variations even within the 15-29 range. The planning of seasonal migration is apparently little inconvenienced by marriage.

If the examination is confined to maturer males, the 30-59 age range for instance, it is found that the single are one-and-a-half times as likely and the widowed twice as likely to be planning a first rural-urban migration as are the currently married. The margin is much greater in terms of planning seasonal than long-term migration, for almost as large a proportion of the married envisage eventually transferring the whole family for a long or indefinite period as do the unattached envisage moving themselves.

An analysis of the interrelation has been carried out in Table 3:13. There is some evidence, even when age standardisation is in effect carried

Table 3:12 The planning of migration by conjugal condition, males, 15-29 years of age

Migration classification	Percentage distribution of respondents by migration classification in each conjugal condition[a]				
	Married	Single	Widowed	No entry	All conditions
Never migrated:					
no plans	49	51			51
planning seasonal migration	5	5			5
planning long-term migration	6	9			8
All migrated and visiting[b]	40	35			36
All migration classifications: per cent	100	100			100
number	524	1,404	6	50	1,984

[a] 'Married' includes all persons with some kind of continuing relations with and obligations to a member of the opposite sex.

[b] Includes all migration classifications, except those listed above.

Source: Rural survey male respondents, 15-29 years of age.

out by confining the examination to specific age groups, that the single are more likely to be seasonal migrants. Many of these single older males work

Table 3:13 Migration classification and conjugal condition of rural males over 20 years of age

Migration classification	Conjugal condition					Total respondents	
	Married	Single	Widowed	No entry	All married conditions	Per cent	Number
(a) Percentage distribution of respondents in each conjugal category							
Never migrated	61	59	69		60		
Seasonal migrant	6	8	4		6		
Permanent returnee	14	8	15		13		
Long-term absentee	16	22	9		18		
Other; no entry	3	3	3		3		
Total: per cent	100	100	100		100		
number	1,597	978	79	94	3,748		
(b) Percentage distribution of respondents in each migration classification							
Never migrated	70	26	2	2	—	100	2,257
Seasonal migrant	63	34	1	2	—	100	235
Permanent returnee	78	17	2	3	—	100	486
Long-term absentee	64	32	1	3	—	100	660
Other; no entry							110
Distribution of all respondents	69	26	2	3	—	100	3,748

Source: Rural survey respondents over 20 years of age.

Table 3:14 Migration classification and number of wives of rural males over 20 years of age

Migration classification	Number of wives							Total respondents	
	0	1	2	3	4+	No entry	All married respondents	Per cent	Number
(a) Percentage distribution of respondents in groups by number of wives									
Never migrated	59	60	65	65	60		60		
Seasonal migrant	8	6	5	8	4		6		
Permanent returnee	9	13	22	16	22		15		
Long-term absentee	20	18	7	11	14		16		
Other; no entry	4	3	1	0	0		3		
Total: per cent	100	100	100	100	100		100		
number	993	1,921	419	110	48	257	3,748		
(b) Percentage distribution of respondents in each migration classification									
Never migrated	26	50	12	3	2	7		100	2,257
Seasonal migrant	34	48	9	4	1	4		100	235
Permanent returnee	18	51	19	4	3	5		100	486
Long-term absentee	31	53	4	2	1	9		100	660
Other; no entry	31	57	3	0	0	9		100	110
Distribution of all respondents	26	52	11	3	1	7		100	3,748

Source: Rural survey respondents over 20 years of age.

on the farms of relatives such as parents or brothers and are in many ways analogous to similarly placed persons in the pre-modern farming of Europe. The fact that the migration behaviour pattern of widowers differs from that of non-widowers is simply a product of age; this is the migration pattern of earlier times and is exhibited by the aged. Most other apparent differentials in the table disappear with standardisation for age. No distinctive regional patterns emerged from separate analyses of the relationship between conjugal condition and migration.

The striking point to which Table 3:14 seems to bear witness is that long-term absentees are unlikely to have more than one wife. The fact that permanent returnees are most likely to be polygynous suggests that urban monogamy arises from the financial and other difficulties of practising polygyny in the town rather than from any change in outlook that might be caused by the urban environment. The fact of a greater incidence of rural polygyny and of the problems of such marriages in the town has been attested elsewhere (Caldwell 1967a: 71-3; Caldwell 1968b: 54-6).

In Table 3:15 the analysis of the marriage patterns of long-term absentees and of permanent returnees from long-term absence is carried further. It is striking that, whilst less than one-seventh of the 30-59-year-old married males away for long periods in the towns are polygynists, almost one-third of the permanent returnees of the same type are polygynists. Permanent returnees are in fact somewhat more likely to have more than one wife than those who have never migrated, a condition which may arise from their greater affluence. Some of the same points are borne out by the examination of those over 60 years of age, but the total number of respondents was so small that too much reliance should not be placed on the findings.

Table 3:15 Number of wives currently possessed by long-term absentees, permanent returnees from long-term absence, and total population, males, 30-59 and 60+ years of age

Age group	Migration classification	Percentage distribution of respondents by number of wives						Total respondents	
		0	1	2	3	4+	No entry	Per cent	Number
30-59	Long-term absentees	11	67	7	3	1	11	100	384
	Permanent returnees from long-term absence	13	56	20	4	2	5	100	225
	All males in age group	13	60	15	4	1	7	100	2,101
60+	Long-term absentees	14	47	0	10	5	24	100	21
	Permanent returnees from long-term absence	30	32	17	6	8	7	100	66
	All males in age group	11	50	17	7	7	8	100	392

Source: Rural survey male respondents, 30-59 and 60+ years of age.

An examination of these age groups by migration region showed that the patterns noted persisted in each of them. The only modifications are that Ashanti males are somewhat more likely than those from other regions to be polygynous in the town, especially in Kumasi, and it is permanent returnees to the North who are most likely to acquire more wives than their fellows who have never migrated.

Children being supported

As with conjugal condition, any analysis of the restraining effect exerted on migration by the necessity for supporting children is rendered difficult by the fact that most Ghanaian males do not have children at the age when the incidence of first rural-urban migration is highest. Three-quarters of all rural male respondents in the 15-29 age group had no children, and the fraction was similar amongst those with no immediate plans to move from the village.

However, the kind of analysis carried out in Table 3:16 does suggest that the supporting of two or more children may do something to reduce mobility, a suggestion that is further borne out, in so far as the number of respondents is great enough to provide any kind of evidence, by the migration pattern of the relatively few respondents of this age with three and higher numbers of children. The same general pattern is observed in each migration region. There is no evidence from the residual category, 'all migrated and visiting', whether the children were born before or after migration.

Table 3:16 The planning of migration by number of children being supported, males, 15-29 years of age

Migration classification	Percentage distribution of respondents in each migration classification by number of children being supported[a]				
	0	1	2+	No entry	All numbers
Never migrated:					
no plans	52	45	47		51
planning seasonal migration	5	6	5		5
planning long-term migration	8	8	6		8
All migrated and visiting[b]	35	41	42		36
All migration classifications: per cent	100	100	100		100
numbers	1,473	131	242	138	1,984

[a] Children where the majority of support is by the respondents.
[b] Includes all migration classifications except those listed above.
Source: Rural survey male respondents, 15-29 years of age.

Amongst males 30-59 the patterns become clearer, although by this age only a small proportion, 5 per cent, of males are still planning a first migration. Of those who were planning a long-term absence one-quarter were supporting no children and half less than three; this compares with less than one-sixth and less than two-fifths respectively amongst those who had not migrated and were not planning to do so. Children were fewer still amongst those planning a first seasonal migration; over two-thirds were supporting no children at all.

When all adult male population is examined certain relationships between migration classification and number of children being supported appear, and most persist even after age standardisation. For instance, in Table 3:17, the relation between seasonal migration and the support of few or no children is a real one. Amongst those males who marry particularly late, usually single males working on relatives' farms, there is a high incidence of seasonal migration. Long-term absentees do have smaller families, at least while they remain in the towns, partly because of lesser polygyny and partly because of a pattern of lower female fertility in urban areas (Caldwell 1967c). It is more difficult to establish with certainty a higher level of child support amongst the permanent returnees, but, even when age is controlled, there appears to be a tendency this way, perhaps associated with higher marital and polygyny levels. The high level of non-response was caused by the very real difficulties in the Ghanaian situation of deciding whether the respondent was the major support of a particular child.

Table 3:17 Percentage distribution of rural male respondents over 20 years of age by number of children being supported in each migration classification

Migration classification	Number of children being supported								Total respondents	
	0	1	2	3	4	5-9	10+	No entry	Per cent	Number
Never migrated	31	9	11	8	7	16	7	11	100	2,257
Seasonal migrant	42	12	11	9	7	12	2	5	100	235
Permanent returnee	21	8	9	11	10	24	8	9	100	486
Long-term absentee	35	7	9	10	7	13	3	16	100	660
Other; no entry	27	17	13	8	8	13	0	14	100	110

Source: Rural survey male respondents over 20 years of age.

Relatives in urban areas and chain migration

As will be seen later, Ghanaian migrants to the town usually go first to join a relative or fellow villager. Thus, there is no doubt that such movements are often of the chain migration type, whereby once migration from a certain family or village begins it tends to gain momentum. Some families and some villages have proportionately much higher representation in the towns than have others. The sample was large enough to allow an examination of this phenomenon on a personal basis; detailed analysis of the 1960 census could establish its existence on a village basis.

Table 3:18 examines first the position of those currently visiting the towns at the time of the survey, for such visits often precede more permanent migration. It can be seen that visits to the towns from families without relatives already living there are practically unknown. Only 39 per cent of the respondents who had not migrated at the time of the survey came from households where any member was living in the towns at that time, but they provided 98 per cent of the current visitors to the towns.

The same holds true, although to a less marked extent, in the planning of first migration to the towns. Of those male villagers who had never lived in the town and who were in the rural areas at the time of the survey, 36 per cent had close relatives in the town. But 47 per cent of those planning seasonal migration and 48 per cent of those planning long-term migration had relatives there. Females, perhaps less inclined to set off for an unknown and friendless destination, showed more evidence than males of chain migration. Thus, while only 41 per cent had close relatives in the town, 48 per cent of those planning seasonal migration and 62 per cent of those planning long-term migration had such relatives there.

The evidence for chain migration exists in the data not only for visitors and planners, but for those who have actually lived in the towns. Of those in

Table 3:18 Aspects of chain migration to the towns, males and females over 20 years of age

Sex	Respondents	Numbers of members of household living in town[a]				
		0	1	2	3-4	5+
	(a) Percentage of non-migrant and visiting respondents visiting towns at the time of the survey by number of members of household living in the town at that time					
Male	Never migrated plus visitors (number)	1,441	373	204	155	84
	% current visitors	0·1	4·0	2·5	9·7	6·4
Female	Never migrated plus visitors (number)	1,617	473	302	258	144
	% current visitors	0·1	1·7	3·3	10·7	7·6
	(b) Percentage of non-migrant respondents planning to migrate to towns at the time of the survey by number of members of household living in town at that time					
Male	Never migrated (number)	1,440	358	199	140	111
	% planning first seasonal migration	4·0	3·6	8·5	8·6	7·2
	% planning first long-term migration	4·9	5·9	7·5	10·7	12·6
Female	Never migrated (number)	1,616	465	292	240	134
	% planning first seasonal migration	3·0	1·7	5·1	4·2	8·2
	% planning first long-term migration	1·7	3·2	3·1	5·0	6·0
	(c) Percentage of total respondents in rural areas at time of survey who had never lived in a town by number of members of household living in town at that time					
Male	All in rural areas[b] (number)	1,965	491	279	222	137
	% who had never lived in a town	73	73	71	63	57
Female	All in rural areas[b] (number)	1,964	556	457	311	178
	% who had never lived in a town	82	84	86	77	75

[a] Respondents providing insufficient data omitted.

[b] I.e. excluding respondents in the town at the time of the survey.

Source: Rural survey respondents over 20 years of age.

the rural areas at the time of the survey, nearly three-quarters of the males with no relatives in the town had never themselves lived there, but the proportion fell steadily to about three-fifths for those with four or more relatives in the town. The comparative fall for females was from about five-sixths to about three-quarters.

Each of the three phenomena described above can be seen in the table to be not merely true of the dichotomy between those with relatives in the town and those without. Visiting and migration increase in volume as the number of close relatives in the town increases; the irregularities in this progression can be ascribed solely to the small number of respondents in each category. Even so, the patterns discerned are all statistically significant.

Economic condition

The survey workers were asked to classify the households in each centre according to whether the living standards of the members appeared to be markedly above, markedly below, or much the same as those of the villagers in general. As shown in Table 3:19, two-thirds of all households were listed as average, somewhat more than one-sixth as above average, and somewhat less than one-sixth below.

These economic levels are associated with migration, the division between the economic levels of respondents who had never migrated and the rest being statistically significant in the case of both sexes. The pattern was the same for each sex, so both sexes are analysed together in the table in order to increase cell size.

Table 3:19 Apparent economic level of rural respondents over 20 years of age and migration classification

Migration classification	Percentage distribution of respondents by apparent economic level				
	Above average	Average	Below average	Total respondents[a] Per cent	Number
Never migrated:					
total	17	67	16	100	4,830
not planning migration	16	67	17	100	4,500
planning seasonal migration	22	66	12	100	199
planning long-term migration	31	53	16	100	131
Visiting town at the time of the survey	21	68	11	100	88
Seasonal migrant	24	68	8	100	359
Permanent returnee	27	62	11	100	792
Long-term absentee	24	66	10	100	1,013
All respondents[b]	19	67	14	100	7,237

[a] Excludes, except for 'All respondents', 379 respondents who were either in 'Other; no entry' migration classification or for whom there were insufficient data on economic level.

[b] Excludes only 224 respondents for whom there were insufficient data on economic level.

Source: Rural survey respondents over 20 years of age.

It is clear that households above the average economic level tend to produce a disproportionate number of persons planning rural-urban migration and almost certainly a disproportionate number of actual migrants to the town. Amongst all respondents who had never migrated and who lived in economically above average households 10·3 per cent were planning either seasonal or long-term migration to the towns, compared with 6·3 per cent and 5·6 per cent in economically average and economically below average households respectively. A similar pattern is observed amongst those visiting the town.

There are probably two explanations for these relationships. Firstly, economically above average households are more likely to have been able to keep children at school, and, as we have already seen, length of schooling is positively associated with propensity to migrate to the towns. Secondly, as will be discussed below, economically above average households probably owe their condition partly to the absence of some of their members in the towns; and the presence of some members in the town is likely, as noted before, to encourage chain migration there.

There is little doubt not only that households of above average economic level produce more rural-urban migrants, but also that such migration raises the economic level of the household that produces them. In households of below average level only one-fifth of the members were long-term absentees, seasonal migrants, or permanent returnees; but in the better-off households two-fifths belonged to these categories. The explanation is simple enough. In many villages those who have worked or are working in the town are the main source of cash to buy those goods which raise apparent, and real, living standards. The process may be self-reinforcing in that some of the money may be used to keep more children at school, who may in turn be thus encouraged to go to the towns and may be so qualified to earn higher urban incomes. Not all the wealth derived from the town is money remitted back; as will be seen later, much is in the form of goods, often brought back temporarily or permanently by the rural-urban migrant. The role of the permanent returnee, who may even have built and furnished his house with money earned in the town, is important. One-sixth of the members of economically above average households were permanent returnees, compared with one-tenth of the members of average households, and one-twelfth of below average households.

Summary

The characteristics of the rural-urban migration movement examined in this chapter may be divided into five types; factors related to geographical, economic, agricultural, and social conditions which are subject to relatively slow change; the biological factors of sex and age, which cannot in themselves change but which may not continue to bear the same relationship to the likelihood of migrating; factors especially in matters of education, where government policy decisions are important; factors of family structure; and such factors as chain migration and economic condition which are themselves part of the mechanics of rural-urban migration.

In the first group, it can be shown that the volume of rural-urban migration is likely to be greater from larger centres, probably because of higher educational levels and possibly because of greater general affluence there. Distance is also important, the volume of movement to the towns tending to be least from the furthest villages, at least if the north, with its special problems, is excluded from the examination. These measures may merely reflect the degree of social and economic change, which is greatest in larger centres and nearest the bigger towns. There is little doubt that such change produces an accelerating, and non-reversible, rural-urban flow of migrants.

In the same group we may place the nature of the rural and urban society. The town is the major supplier of many types of desirable occupation and of cash incomes; fundamentally this is the explanation for rural-urban migration. To what extent the saturation of the supply of migrants for certain occupations, or the slower change in urban occupational structure, determines the size of the migration stream or selects the type of migrant is a complex matter only indirectly approached in the following study. Rural society itself is heterogeneous; seasonal migrants, but not long-term migrants, are more likely to come from subsistence than cash farming areas. In fact a degree of modernisation, such as cash farming, may well serve to swell rather than reduce the long-term rural-urban migrant stream. There is evidence that young persons who have been employed by craftsmen in the village are particularly likely to seek their fortune in the town. However, the true heterogeneity of the rural areas lies in the contrast between its major regional divisions. Rural-urban migration is often very great in areas such as Ghana's South where forces alien to the traditional economy and culture have been longest operating; but it can be almost as great from such backward areas as Ghana's North, if living conditions are sufficiently bad and if they are starkly contrasted with adjacent richer areas where towns are to be found.

In the second group are found the characteristics of age and sex. It is predominantly the young people who move to the town, particularly those between 15 and 29 years of age. It is an acceleration of the migration which has resulted in town populations having a disproportionate number of young adults; although the effect is accentuated by a tendency for at least some of the older migrants to return to the village. Increasingly, the time when the decision must be made whether to go to the town or not has become that age in a young person's life when he has finished his schooling and must decide on an adult occupation. There have also been more males than females in the migrant stream, a fact which in the past at least has been largely but not entirely a product of a sex differential in rural education. Amongst today's youngsters the educational differences are growing smaller, and girls of the same educational standing as boys are almost as likely to want to go to the town. This will provide a very interesting test of the flexibility of the urban occupational structure. Has the greater number of urban male jobs in the past merely been a reflection of the greater supply of boys from the country? If girls come in increasing numbers can adequate places be found for them? Alternatively, has the marked reluctance in the villages to send girls to school or to keep them there been a realistic appraisal of their earning power and chance of employment in the non-agricultural sector of the economy?

Of the factors determining the volume of rural-urban migration, the one which can be most easily varied by governmental decision is education. In Ghana, perhaps in all tropical Africa, the fact of education, and its degree, are powerful determinants of rural-urban migration. The decision taken in Ghana to increase vastly over a small number of years the amount of schooling being offered may well be necessary in order to attain desired targets of social and economic modernisation; but the corollary has inevitably been a very considerable boosting of the population flow into the towns, which itself has helped to increase urban unemployment. Whether the rise in educational levels can help in the creation of a modern economy fast enough to absorb the migrants into urban occupations, or whether increasing urban unemployment will tend to stem the flow in spite of rising levels of schooling, has yet to be seen. Certainly a reduction in the sex differential in rural education, especially in the North, seems likely to reduce in time the male surpluses in the immigrant suburbs of the towns. Associated with the educational effect in inducing rural-urban migration, partly explaining it and partly adding to it, is the greater tendency for the literate, especially those literate in English, and the English-speakers to go to the towns.

Family conditions also play a part. Probably the most important is the nature of the family from which the migrant came. The eldest children, especially the two eldest sons and the eldest daughter, are less likely to migrate, and more likely to return if they do migrate. They are more likely to acquire responsibilities to the family in the village and they are more likely to find occupational openings there when a father or an uncle dies.

Another aspect of the family is much less important than we had hypothesised before the investigation began. Few potential migrants are hindered from moving to the town by the possession of wives and children. The main reason is that the decision whether to go or not is usually taken between 15 and 25 years of age, when few Ghanaian males are married. Even when marriage has occurred, Ghanaian wives and children are usually, as we shall see in a later chapter, surprisingly mobile, and prepared either to accompany a migrating husband or to follow him later. Few persons are inconvenienced by wives or children. But where wives, especially polygynous wives, and children, especially large numbers of them, may prove to be inconvenient is in the town itself. Accommodation is often insufficient, sustenance must be paid for with cash, and families cannot be put into the fields to grow food. Children may not even be of much value for carrying water or fuel; and conversely the pressure to send them to school, thus incurring expense, is usually much stronger than in the village. The migrant in the town is likely to marry later, restrict himself more frequently to a single wife, and have fewer children at a comparable age than a non-migrant in the village. But this may be more the result of circumstances than conviction; he may easily reverse this position after his permanent return to the village, especially as those who decide on permanent return may be the very ones whose convictions were not altered by urban life.

An even more important role played by the family in the migration process is the encouragement of successive members to go to the town. Sometimes wives follow husbands and children follow fathers. But there is also no doubt that a young man or woman is much more likely to move to the town if he or she already has a brother or sister there, or perhaps an uncle or aunt. Furthermore, two or three siblings in the town apparently prove to be a greater attractive force than one. Thus some families and some villages are much more strongly represented in the towns than others. This is a classical example of chain migration.

Migration and return migration bind town and village together in a complex relationship. One aspect of this relationship is economic. The wealthier village households more often keep the children at school, and this, and possibly other aspects of life amongst the rural better-off, produces a higher incidence of rural-urban migration. In its turn this migration raises the living standard, by the flow of wealth from the town, of the residual members of the household, a fact which is certainly noticed by non-migrant households.

Two general points might finally be made. The first is that the phenomena described are only tendencies, although often pronounced ones. Many unschooled boys, many members of poorer households, even some polygynists, do migrate, even though fewer proportionately do so than persons with the opposite characteristics. The second is that the pattern described implies that rural-urban migration, and consequently urban population, are likely to increase very much in the years ahead. The reasons are the continued spread of schooling, literacy, and spoken English, the rise in rural living standards, and the certainty with each year of continued rural-urban migration that more villagers have relatives in the town. More generally, all kinds of social and economic change work towards increasing the flow to the towns, and such change is visibly penetrating ever further into traditional Ghanaian society.

4

Rural Push and Urban Pull

The use of household surveys

Early in the preliminary testing stage of the survey, it was found that in a substantial proportion of rural households, especially in remoter areas, it was impossible to interview selected respondents alone or indeed to prevent older members of the household intervening during the questioning. In the event it was decided to make a virtue of the problem, and to fit in with the nature of rural society by structuring full household interviews. These were held with 585 urban households and 1,782 rural ones, the present and absent members respectively making up the 3,167 and 13,776 individual respondents discussed earlier. In the rural survey 794 households were in the South, 143 in Volta, 513 in Ashanti, and 332 in the North.

The interviews thus became quite ceremonial occasions. All members of the household currently resident in the village were usually present. Providing certain politenesses were observed and many of the general remarks were made to the head of the household, no difficulty was usually encountered in directing questions, either personally by the interviewer or through the head of the household as the circumstances seemed to dictate, to the members of the household concerned in each question. Thus those planning to leave for the town usually explained the attractions of the town, although elders frequently added remarks about what other recent emigrants had felt. Most interviewers felt that these discussions usually added to the quality of the analysis and led to a more introspective concern with real motives for action. Where the method was in danger of breaking down, such as when rural respondents were loth to explain that one motive for emigration was to get away from the family for a while, the interviewers turned the discussion to the reasons for young people from other households leaving.

Household interviews did not permit the cross-tabulation of replies with individual characteristics. However, such characteristics as age, marital status, migration classification, and so on were easily obtained for individuals. The accuracy of such data, when collected by this method, appeared to be greater than that obtained in individual interviews because of conscientious group discussion, which often called the attention of various members of the family to flaws in the information they produced from memory. These characteristics did permit the kind of cross-tabulation employed in Chapter 3. The household interviews permitted a valuable comparison of the patterns of motivation and experience between the major migration regions, and in the ensuing chapters all significant regional differences are noted.

One point should be kept in mind during all the analysis that follows. The data gathered are often a record of family reporting on past events or of present opinions. This is, of course, true for much of the data of the social sciences, even those published by the census. Nevertheless, the degree to which distortion is likely or the probability that emotional responses will bias the answers varies from question to question; the possibility of its existence should at no time be ignored. Where the questions seek to ascertain attitudes, then it is of significance to report the distribution of those viewpoints even where it is felt that many of them are not grounded in logic.

More important is the fact that the distribution of responses is a distribution of respondents giving certain responses. Thus the relative frequency of responses does not show the relative strength of different views in households; indeed, if nearly all respondents held a certain response to be somewhat more important than another, and all confined themselves to a single response, the former would appear to be by far the most important in the tabulation of results. In reality this position is never reached. One reason is that multiple responses are taken into account in all questions where simple dichotomies are not involved. The other is that the simple distribution of responses by respondents often seems to come close to the intensity with which various views are held in the community. In subsequent testing, households voicing the dominant views were acquainted with the other views and in a surprising number of cases it was argued that these were also more weakly held family views.

The urban pull

The households were first questioned on the reasons for contemporary migration to the towns. Emphasis was placed on the fact that we were discussing why people were now going, rather than on why past migrations had taken place, and that we were most interested in movements to the biggest towns, Accra and Kumasi being quoted as the kind of place we had in mind.

Respondents were encouraged to choose only the major reason for migration, but when they insisted that a second reason was also important this too was recorded. The fact that this occurred more frequently amongst the more voluble town dwellers helps to explain their higher rate of response for some of the replies which were essentially supplementary to the economic ones.

The outstanding fact about Table 4:1 is the emphasis on economic motives; the vast majority of the respondents explained rural-urban migration in terms of more money and a better standard of living in the town rather than insufferable economic conditions in the village. If those who saw the increase in the flow as largely occurring in the two-way trading movement between country and town are added to the major economic category, then nineteen out of twenty village households described the movement in terms of jobs, money, and increased ability to purchase consump-

Table 4:1 Responses to the question, 'More people are going to the big towns (e.g. Accra, Kumasi) now. Why do you think this is so?'

Responses	Rural survey Number	Per cent[a]	Urban survey Number	Per cent[a]
To obtain jobs, money, consumer goods	1,567	88	479	82
Preference for town life, preference for town husbands	166	9	48	8
To become 'civilised', sophisticated, for prestige	79	4	45	8
Desire to travel and enjoy new experiences	61	3	44	7
To gain education or training	60	3	44	7
To join immediate relatives	31	2	31	5
Problems of the village:				
land shortage	13	1	2	0
poor rural facilities	36	2	13	2
village or family difficulties	40	2	6	1
Trading purposes	124	7	71	12
Other	6	0	8	1
Total: responses	2,183[b]	121[b]	791[b]	133[b]
respondent households	1,782		585	

[a] Percentage of households giving response.
[b] Adds to over 100 per cent because of multiple responses.

tion goods. These latter categories cannot be separated, for most households spoke of them together, taking it for granted that one flowed from the other.

In the southern part of Ghana it was often assumed that the prospect of migrating was tempting but rarely that it was occasioned by grim necessity. One old man in the cocoa-farming area said that the young men left, 'Because they dislike farm work and they go into the towns in search of quick money', while another said of the girls, 'Some go after money; some go with the mind to practise prostitution'. But a 35-year-old woman in Somanya, less than an hour's mammy lorry drive from Accra, explained her own moves to and from the city as 'in search of jobs; it is in the big towns where one gets many customers if one is a trader or food-seller'. Often education was mentioned, as when a migrant, temporarily back in a Brong-Ahafo village, argued, 'The educated people do not get jobs to do in the village'. In the North the decision to leave home was often a result of much stronger pressure. A middle-aged man, who had never left the Bolgatanga area, pointed out that, in the southern towns, 'There are many jobs to be done there for money; money cannot be had in the villages and nobody would like to leave his grandparents if the desire to earn money were not great'. Another, in the Kongo area, as remote from Ghana's large towns as it is possible to be, complained, 'Less and less foodstuff is got from the farms these days; people go to the towns to get money to buy more food to feed their families'. The long-term migrant interviewed in the town was often very certain that he had taken the right course. In a wealthy suburb, one would hear statements like the following from the household head in Accra's wealthy Ridge Area, 'For work; there are more prospects of employment in Accra, especially for the educated, and new development and works offer opportunities even for manual labour'. Much the same sentiment was echoed in a poorer suburb of Cape Coast: 'To work as labourers for cash; to buy either fish or European foods to go and sell'.

But though employment provides the major lure to the town, in few migrants' minds is it the only one. In the course of many of the interviews, attitudes were expressed such as the following from the Akwapim Ridge, an area of almost continuous interconnecting small towns in the original cocoa area near Accra: 'The life in the village is rather boring and they want to be in the towns where life is more lively'. Further afield, in the new cocoa country of Brong-Ahafo near the Ivory Coast border, an old man said, without contradiction by the younger members of his family, 'They do not want village life, and as parents are not having any control over them as it used to be in the olden days, they go when they wish'. In Wa, in the far north-west, a 33-year-old man, temporarily returned from working in a southern town, described one of the reasons for going away as 'To get in touch with modern amenities—football matches, prominent persons from foreign countries'.

Often prestige was mentioned and surprisingly frequently the term 'civilised' was used, as if in its classical sense. 'It depends on the mind of the individual. People want to be in big towns only to be thought of as being big or important.' 'They want to be civilised—to see what is going on in the town.' It was felt in an Ashanti village, 'They want to change where they live; people in the town look down upon the villagers—therefore, they want to go and be town people'.

A minority expressed the antithesis between village and town more in terms of the failings of the former than the attractions of the latter. Even in Aburi, immediately to the north of Accra, one household explained, 'Everybody is struggling for existence, and, since there are no jobs in the village, they should go into the big towns for jobs', and another thought, 'It is because there are no jobs here for many of them, and also that many jobs available are mainly for the unskilled'. In Kpandu in the Volta Region, a household head who was a permanent returnee from the towns argued, 'It is because of the amenities lacking in the village, for instance, lack of good roads, football, dances and other social entertainments, and lack of good water supply'. Further north, village difficulties often provided concrete reasons for departure: 'Some misbehaved in the village and they knew that if they remained they would suffer disgrace', and 'Some elope with their wives because their wife's parents would not consent to the marriage'.

There were statistically significant differences in the replies from the various migration regions. In Ashanti fewer households, less than three-quarters in fact, mentioned economic reasons for migration, a fair commentary on booming conditions in the new cocoa and timber areas. In the distant and traditional North proportionately almost three times as many households as elsewhere talked of preference for town life, the need to become civilised, and the advantages of having travelled, and six times as many quoted strife or difficulties within the village or family as reasons for leaving. The accusation of the practice of witchcraft against a relative sometimes provided an urgent reason for sudden departure. Land shortage was most often mentioned in Volta, particularly in the southern part.

The rural pull

Yet the fact remains that, for all the temptations of town life, most Ghanaians still choose to remain in the village. The reason for this was rarely given adequately while discussing reasons for migration, so, as shown in Table 4:2, a specific question was asked about the forces binding people to the village.

Table 4:2 Responses to the question, 'Some people stay in the villages all their lives. Why do you think this is so?'

Response	Rural survey		Urban survey	
	Number	Per cent[a]	Number	Per cent[a]
Have a village job:				
farm specifically mentioned	741	42	218	37
farming not mentioned	417	23	104	18
Prefer village life	484	27	221	38
Family or village ties	320	18	69	12
Difficulty in migrating:				
lack of education or literacy	153	9	72	12
lack of money	129	7	30	5
Life in town more expensive than in village	41	2	27	5
Other reasons	140	8	46	8
Total: responses	2,425[b]	136[b]	787[b]	135[b]
respondent households	1,782		585	

[a] Percentage of households giving response.
[b] Adds to over 100 per cent, because of multiple responses.

Almost two-thirds of all village households give as a reason—and nearly always the first reason—for remaining the adequacy of rural employment. By implication this suggests that inadequacy of employment is a ground for migration, and thus that there is more 'rural push' than might have been thought from Table 4:1. Checks on some of the interviews showed that the rural job meant was usually farming, even when it was not specifically described as such. There is no doubt that amongst those who have already migrated to the town there is a little more scepticism than there is in the village about either jobs or family ties keeping people in the village; there is a greater readiness to ascribe it to personal lack of motivation to move or lack of education.

In rural areas where cash farming was practised the most common explanations for staying in the village were, 'Because they have jobs there and farms from which they get substantial income which is able to maintain them', or 'Those who take to farming are satisfied with their calling and stay; again it is necessary that some should stay in the house to care for the old and infirm'. The possession of farms in the area was not always considered entirely satisfying, for, in the words of a Western Region household, people stay in the countryside 'because they have some immovable property here, but they are looking forward to the day when jobs will come to the village'. In Accra a rural-urban migrant would often reply with understanding, 'They think when they come they won't find work and since they are already established in farming, fishing and other village activities, they don't want to leave their village'. But a townsman, born in the city, was much more scathing: 'Conservatives are not moved—they have not heard of town attractions; family ties are too strong; no stimulus to make them move; they think a small town life better; their jobs, like farming, tie them to the villages'.

Rural households often argued that many preferred village life but the case was surprisingly often qualified. 'They are the old who cannot start life afresh; most of them have houses and some rely on remittances from children and relatives in the towns.' 'Such people are mainly those whose relatives value them so much that they cannot afford to let them go to the town; others are so lazy that they would not like to go to the towns.' The successful migrant in the town is much more likely to put emphasis on fears of the town or difficulties in adjustment. In Accra's New Town a young technician from the Volta Region explained, 'The majority of people in my village spend all their life on farming; this therefore causes them to stay in the village all their lives; others also think that they may be looked upon as uncivilised, especially where traffic is concerned'. Another in the migrant slum of Nima said, 'They feel life here is so difficult that they cannot cope with it if they come to big towns'.

In the North, family, village, and traditional ties were often particularly strong. Farmers near Bolgatanga explained, 'They are the heads of their families who must be present in the village always to offer sacrifices to the Gods of the household for the welfare of its members', and 'they want to keep to their own place so that when they die their spirits will easily join those of their ancestors'.

Education was frequently mentioned. In the cocoa-growing area of the Eastern Region, a young female schoolteacher maintained that the young adults who remained behind were 'Not educated and can't move because they may not be able to have any job', while a middle-aged farmer said, 'Such people are illiterates who work on their own cocoa farms; some are wealthy landowners who have their own shops which they keep'.

Statistically significant differences between the replies from the various migrant regions occurred. In the South the view that those with satisfactory local jobs stayed and those without did not was particularly widespread, being expressed by three-quarters of all households compared with half elsewhere. This may be a sign of marked and prolonged socio-economic change. In the North proportionately five times as many households as elsewhere spoke of family ties and seven times as many of the importance of such village positions as chieftancy and being an elder. The inability to change the way of life or to cope with town life or its accompanying traffic was mentioned two-and-a-half times as frequently in the North as elsewhere. The ascribing of failure to migrate to lack of education was far more frequent in the South and Volta, the most highly educated areas, as was the explanation of the absence of a certain job. The lack of money weighed most heavily in the South and Ashanti; as these are the wealthiest migrant regions, it was obvious that money as a factor in migration decision-making

Table 4:3 Responses to the question, 'Tell me three or four things which sometimes make town life (in Accra, Kumasi, or Sekondi-Takoradi) pleasant'

Responses	Rural survey Number	Rural survey Per cent[a]	Urban survey Number	Urban survey Per cent[a]
Entertainment:				
in general (including residual category describing holidays, radios, etc.)	816	46	280	48
cinemas	417	23	143	24
bars, clubs, dances, women	251	14	154	26
life exciting and faster; greater visual beauty	363	20	114	20
Facilities:				
better shopping and marketing facilities	725	41	128	22
better transport (and cultural) facilities	540	30	206	35
water supply	515	29	111	19
electricity supply	442	25	88	15
medical and health facilities	341	19	96	16
educational facilities	104	6	41	7
Economic:				
better chances of employment, higher wages	720	40	208	36
less communal labour and lower taxation	25	1	32	6
Personal:				
higher prestige	185	10	55	9
freedom from village, family, and traditional ties	52	3	41	7
Total: responses	5,496[b]	307[b]	1,697[b]	290[b]
respondent households	1,782		585	

[a] Percentage of all respondent households.
[b] Adds to over 100 per cent because of multiple responses.

is more important where money has been of major importance in everyday life. In contrast to these differences, the preference for village life was described with much the same frequency, one-quarter to one-third of the households, everywhere.

The pleasures of the town

The pleasures of town life certainly attract the migrant. But the pleasures are not necessarily identical with the reasons for the migration; indeed migrants can usually list aspects of life in town which are pleasant and others which are unpleasant. Doubtless such things do war in the potential migrant's mind when he is trying to decide whether to embark on a journey to town or not. Accordingly the respondent households were asked two questions, shown in Tables 4:3 and 4:4, first on the pleasant side and then on the unpleasant side of town life. The questions also provided a valuable check on whether these pleasures and perils appear in the same light after a period of town residence.

Most respondent households listed three of the pleasures of the town, a majority regarding economic opportunity as a feature rather than a pleasure of the large centre. The replies left no doubt that the non-economic attractions of the town are very considerable and are of two major types, the importance of each group being roughly comparable.

Entertainment is important to the Ghanaian rural-urban migrant. Furthermore, with prolonged town residence it becomes if anything even more important, especially in the category of bars, clubs, dances, and women. This category is hardly divisible, as its components are often all participated in at the same time. The general category 'entertainment' probably covers exactly the same things as are named in the two categories below it, although such residual answers were also included here as those drawing attention to the fact that one could listen to a radio almost anywhere in a big town and that there were definite 'holidays' when work was not expected. What never ceases to surprise an outsider is that rural-urban migrants from green, forest-covered mountains find the city with its shanty-town periphery not merely more lively than the village but visually more beautiful. They refer to buildings, neon signs, and even to roads and advertisements.

The urban way of life and its pace is important; the reputation of Accra and Kumasi in this respect stretches far beyond the borders of Ghana—north to the Niger and further.

Women repeatedly spoke of the fashions and the opportunities for 'dressing properly' in the towns, and others of 'the opportunity to witness all important ceremonies'. Migrants in Accra referred to 'the general busy atmosphere' and to 'moving abreast with the changing times, the fashions and the haircuts'.

The praise for the town's facilities was largely a complaint about all that makes village life most onerous. A Volta Region family spoke of 'the availability of your needs when you want them'. The fact that one could buy most things in the town, and buy them on any day of the week, was mentioned hundreds of times. Some, like an old rural-urban migrant in Accra, added the rider, 'It is easy to buy one's requirements once there is the means'.

Transport is important, as anyone will realise who has watched the long queues of walking humans slowly trudge along the remoter roads of Ghana. In the poorer areas the number of lorries is small and few can afford them. In the towns transport can often be afforded for both people and goods. It is commonly not appreciated by the foreigner, or even the town-born, just how much rural labour goes not directly into farming but into the carrying of water and fuel. In the North one can watch women and children trudging far across the countryside on a hot, dusty path to a distant waterhole, and each person may do the journey several times a day. In the town the carrying of water, except perhaps the last few yards from a community tap, is done by pipes. In the town petty traders bring the market to the house so that much of the buying does not mean carrying goods back.

One aspect of village life always noticed by those returning from the towns is its darkness; often one sees at night only dimly lit patches in the house doorways. But in the town one can talk outside during hot, stifling nights lit perhaps by street light or shop sign. A young man who had come to Accra from the Volta Region felt that, 'Electric light, especially at night, makes Accra pleasant'.

Finally the town has medical and educational facilities, the contrast between town and country being more marked in the case of the former than the latter. Accra-Tema, Kumasi, Sekondi-Takoradi, and Cape Coast had in 1960 far more medical and health personnel than the Upper, Northern, Brong-Ahafo, and Volta Regions combined, though possessing less than one-third of the population. The Accra Capital District alone, with its relatively short distances and 7 per cent of the country's population, contained 35 per cent of the nation's doctors, far more than the Upper, Northern, Brong-Ahafo, Volta, and Eastern Regions together, a combined area with a substantial majority of all Ghana's population (Census 1960: Vol. IV).

The town is also a place of escape, sometimes from communal labour and local official or unofficial exactions, and sometimes from the closeness of village and family ties. In Brong-Ahafo a permanent returnee, who had married and was rearing six children, explained somewhat nostalgically that in Kumasi 'there is no envy from anyone and one can meet his few neighbours and enjoy himself'. Envy of the successful is often very potent in the village and can be focused on the relatively wealthy returnee or even on the relatives of the successful absentee. In Accra's New Town an immigrant observed, 'Nobody cares about what others do'.

It was in the comparatively sophisticated villages of the South that the entertainment facet of town life was most mentioned, while in the needier hamlets of the North such things are overshadowed by the desire for employment. Comparatively few Northern households demand of the town the joys of street lighting or of household electricity, but proportionately twice as many mentioned health facilities, whose rarity still scars their home region. It has been argued that northern males outlive northern females because so many spend parts of their lives in the south where they can obtain medical treatment (Hilton 1968). Over half of all respondents who spoke of overstrong village and family ties were in Ashanti, perhaps a reflection of the tight embrace of the traditional Ashanti family.

The perils of the town

However, whatever the attractions of town may be, there are also drawbacks which tend to repel both the villager gazing from afar and the town resident himself. Nevertheless, it is significant that, when a question was asked about the drawbacks of urban life, the replies, shown in Table 4:4, averaged only 2⅓ drawbacks per household in the rural survey and slightly under 2 in the urban one.

The attraction of villagers to the towns is not a simple process. Urban areas do have a forbidding side to their nature, and this is not mere rural

Table 4:4 Responses to the question, 'Tell me three or four things which sometimes make town life (in Accra, Kumasi, or Sekondi-Takoradi) unpleasant'

Responses	Rural survey Number	Rural survey Per cent[a]	Urban survey Number	Urban survey Per cent[a]
Economic:				
shortage of money and employment	496	28	178	30
cost of living	783	44	218	37
cost of housing	782	44	200	34
cost of food	385	22	84	14
Social:				
thieves, burglars, criminals	465	26	32	6
bad housing, slums, poor sanitation	212	12	160	27
general social evils	167	9	34	6
shortage of women	27	2	1	0
Way of life:				
traffic and accidents	352	20	57	10
excessive noise	275	15	24	4
life too fast, impersonal or unfriendly	207	12	60	10
Residual:				
all other complaints (many very specific)	84	5	88	15
Total: responses	4,235[b]	239[b]	1,136[b]	193[b]
respondent households	1,782		585	

[a] Percentage of all respondent households.
[b] Adds to over 100 per cent because of multiple responses.

apprehension, for migrants with years of town life behind them still reiterate many of the charges. In many ways Table 4:4 provides the complementary picture to Table 4:3. We first saw that the virtues of the town were the entertainments and the facilities the villages lack; conversely, the vices of the town are the heightened need for money at every turn and the breakdown of the social controls of traditional life.

The major protest against town life is that against the wholly exchange economy in contrast to the partially subsistence economy even of the wealthy villages in the cocoa country. Everything must be paid for. It is an overwhelming experience for the less tutored new arrival from the countryside to find that the common Ghanaian foodstuffs are exclusively an item of commerce in the way that only foreign imports, such as kerosene or sardines, are in the village. He finds that in the long run one must acquire housing, which is neither built nor acquired from relatives as easily as in the rural areas. Furthermore, shortage of money, or of cash-paying jobs with which to earn it, means real personal crisis in the town and not the mere inconvenience it may cause at home. In both rural and urban surveys three-fifths of the unpleasant aspects of town described were economic; indeed if bad housing is included in this category the proportion rises towards two-thirds in the former and three-quarters in the latter.

Urban-rural communication, and degree of agreement about problems, is much better in terms of factual problems, such as the financial ones, than it is when judging the way of life of the towns. In rural households considerable bitterness was often expressed about the economic problems of the towns, partly because the most vocal members were in many cases permanent returnees who had found town life unsatisfactory. In the far northwest of the country interviewers were told in one household that in the town there were 'too many taxes; every need must be paid for with money; unemployment brings too many problems; accommodation is difficult'; and in the far northeast they were told that in Kumasi there was a 'lack of land for farming, and everything has to be bought with money'. In Accra a man from a southern village complained, 'The cost of living is too high, and rent and means to get it mean heavy advance payments', while in Cape Coast a migrant from a relatively near village said, 'When there is a scarcity of foodstuffs, the cost of living is high'. Often the money was needed for things which would not have seemed necessities back home. A returnee to Tutu, north of Accra, said that in Accra there were 'too many temptations to spend money', while a migrant in that city from Mampong, not far from Tutu, reported, 'People overestimate and overspend because of attraction to lots of novelties, and therefore incur debts at the month's end'.

The most startling shock to many newly arrived immigrants is the failure of the town to exert collective control over crime. This shock comes in spite of the fact that tales about urban crime percolate so readily back into the countryside that villagers relate far more stories about it than do town residents. In Enyinasi in the far west interviewers were told that in town 'Thieves make life unpleasant and there are unnecessary fights', while northerners spoke of 'Stealing, robbery and burglary'. In Tema, a migrant from the Navrongo area of the North talked of rural-urban migrants being a particular target for criminals and described 'the presence of gangsters who exploit the ignorance of villagers'. Often there is great concern about children becoming involved with the shadier elements of the town; a migrant in Cape Coast pointed out that 'When children go out, parents get worried'. In fairness to the towns it should be explained that the urban-born usually blame crime upon poor, unplaced, rural-urban migrants and regard its seat as being in the squatter, shanty suburbs.

There are other social problems. In the words of one immigrant, 'Drinking alcohol in Accra is becoming too much', while another in Takoradi protested about the 'prostitution in the towns'. This was seen by some as evidence of, and by others as a solution for, the shortage of women in the towns, especially in immigrant suburbs. The 1960 census had shown that there were almost twice as many men over 20 years of age as women in Accra's Nima, almost the prototype of the immigrant shanty town. However, as a migrant from a village near Bawku in the north pointed out, prostitution did lead to 'contagious diseases'.

One of the things that do not unduly worry new immigrants but become an increasing source of grievance with length of urban residence is the condition of the poorer housing. A migrant to Accra from the Akim Oda area complained of the 'unhealthy rooms leased for hire—sanitation is too poor, there is a lack of public stand-pipes'.

Not all migrants become adjusted to town life. A 65-year-old widow, who had given up seasonal migration, argued, 'If illiterate, life in town is unpleasant, and there is too much noise'. A temporary returnee to Salaga in the north felt, in spite of his decision to return to Kumasi, that 'town life is noisy and fast; accidents often occur'. A migrant in Takoradi complained of 'the fast life [using 'fast' in a different sense] which compels people to follow fashion blindly'. Another worry was the degree to which the migrant had to rely on himself; there was no one to catch him when he fell. This was felt most by migrants from the more traditional north, especially if they belonged to small tribes whose numbers were few in the southern towns. A household head in the Kongo area warned, 'You get no family help when in trouble'.

Some migrants echoed the insecurity commonly felt in the shanty suburbs. 'The police are always checking your activities', and there are 'too many rules to observe'.

What was remarkable about the answers was the almost total lack of significant differences between the responses from the four major migration regions in the rural survey. In this sense there is a greater homogeneity in urban-rural difference than had been expected. Almost the same proportion and the same type of economic complaints about the town were voiced by returnees in southern villages 30 miles from Accra as in northern villages 400 miles away. However, proportionately twice as many northerners as others complained that the towns were full of strangers, lacked courtesy, and broke with traditional ways, but this may merely reflect the fact that the towns are socially and in terms of distance further from the North than from anywhere else. Kumasi is an Ashanti creation, the Volta Region comes within 50 miles of Accra, and the South contains that city as well as Sekondi-Takoradi; there is no equivalence to this position in the north—a move to a really large town means going one, two, or three hundred miles to places where the climate, the food, the languages, and the traditions are very different. Northerners were also more prone to complain of the lack of women or the break with wivcs. With 216 males per 100 females for all North migrant region immigrant population in the Accra Capital District in 1960, this was understandable when compared with the South or Volta, each with ratios of 140, but less explicable in terms of the Ashanti ratio of 239; perhaps the Ashanti felt less frustrated because their womenfolk were relatively near and hence more easily visited.

The pleasures of the village

In the process of deciding whether to migrate or not, not only does the town repel as well as attract, but the village itself both attracts and repels. On average both urban and rural respondents can think of more good features of the town and bad ones of thc villagc than thcy can thc oppositc, but the margin is not very great. The disadvantages of the village, shown in Table 4:5, could be surmised from the previous questions, but some points are made with greater emphasis.

Table 4:5 Responses to the question, 'Tell me three or four things which sometimes make village life pleasant'

Responses	Rural survey Number	Rural survey Per cent[a]	Urban survey Number	Urban survey Per cent[a]
Economic:				
low cost of living	798	45	221	38
cheap (and fresh) food	1,065	60	301	52
accommodation free or cheap	619	35	104	18
Social and way of life:				
enjoyment of farming	417	23	49	8
enjoyment of keeping livestock or hunting	228	13	16	3
quiet life	742	42	152	26
mutual help by family and friends	236	13	128	22
traditional and family culture	86	5	88	15
Total: responses	4,191[b]	236[b]	1,059[b]	182[b]
respondent households	1,782		585	

[a] Percentage of all respondent households.
[b] Adds to over 100 per cent because of multiple responses.

Both villagers and townsmen agree, the former with a little more emphasis, on the economic advantage of the village in terms of consumer spending, at least in terms of the goods that are available in the countryside. Townsmen put smaller store on the rural way of life, on farming, hunting, and living quietly, partly because rural-urban migration has been a selective process removing to the city precisely those people who least desired these aspects of rural life. But townsmen do miss the security of the village family and do feel cut off from their own specific traditions; often these strains are not fully appreciated until residence in the town is fully established.

No one questions the lower cost of living in the village. A household in Dormaa-Ahenkro in western Brong-Ahafo described the position there: 'Rent rates are lower; meat can be obtained by the villagers themselves; not a large sum of money from one's income is used in personal necessities and one can save more'. An 80-year-old permanent returnee in the south cited 'cheap food, low and sometimes free rent'.

West Africans do not seem to exhibit the fierce love of farming found in some other agrarian societies, but many of the rural people of Ghana are fond of the agricultural way of life for not wholly economic reasons. In the frontier forest land of the Western Region we were told of 'free land and plots for farming', but it was only the town-born who said of the village, 'Nature is seen at its best—the growing crops'.

Townsman and villager alike appreciated the countryside for its quietness and lack of urban strains. Village returnees spoke in the south of the 'quiet nature of the place' and described 'no traffic—no danger in movement'. Others appreciated the lack of the giddy life and of the opportunities for consumption spending. In the south a woman in Mampong praised the fact that there were 'not many attractions' and another near Swedru Angona the 'few attractions and temptations'. Many praised the freedom from those restrictions and official interference, which apparently worry migrants so much in the towns. There are 'only a few regulations to obey', there is 'freedom of movement', and 'You can keep work without police interference'. Town also means the disciplined workforce of the modern economy; a migrant from a small coastal village said in Takoradi of his home-place, 'You work under nobody's control'.

The returnees and the absent migrants agree that in the village, unlike the town, there are 'advantages from family and relations—help is easily obtainable'. 'Family life is compact; there is a sense of belonging together.' Social control is stronger; a household resident only 60 miles from Accra indicated that there are 'few ruffians', and another that 'children are not corrupted by town life'.

Many appreciate the traditional culture. A household in the south pointed out that 'Herbs for traditional medicines are available', while a migrant family in Cape Coast spoke nostalgically of the festivals, especially the yam festival. But it was a young man of town birth, educated in the modern Ghanaian schooling system, who longed to hear the village 'folk stories'.

Often rural life was praised for some. A family living near Bolgatanga in the far north argued that 'You are very happy in the village if you are not often sick' and 'Village life is easy for married life'. A literate migrant from the Volta Region said in Accra, 'The illiterate, who cannot read or write, find the village more pleasant'.

Some regional differences were significant in the rural survey. The cheapness of village food was felt most strongly in lush Ashanti and least strongly in the dry North. The pleasure of farming as such was referred to most frequently by households in the traditional North and least in the South, which has experienced much change. The joys of hunting were rarely mentioned in the South, which has least unused land, but more often elsewhere. Almost one-quarter of Northerners spoke of the advantages of living with family and relatives but the proportion was much lower elsewhere. Where government authority is still weakest, in the far-flung reaches of the North, proportionately four times as many households pointed out the advantages of living at a distance from the police, soldiers, and political upheavals of the city than occurred elsewhere.

The unpleasant side of the village

But the village also has its unpleasant side. In fact both rural and urban residents can enumerate on average more unpleasant than pleasant features. Table 4:6 shows that respondent households in the rural survey averaged almost one-fifth more replies than did those in the urban survey.

Many of the economic complaints are of lack of employment, such as that voiced by the household in Fete along the coast to the west of Accra: 'School leavers cannot get jobs here'. But other sources of grievance lie in the nature of rural work itself. Near Kpandu in the Volta Region, a permanent male returnee to the village complained, 'The work you can do to live on is too laborious; the profit you make from the laborious work is too little'. A migrant in Accra protested that in his native village of Tekinta in the Western Region there was 'too much work done by all—men and women'.

Most respondent households just grimly listed the facilities which existed in the town but not in the village, much as is shown in Table 4:6. More generally a household head in the Old Tafo district of the Eastern Region complained of 'the lack of certain amenities, the unhealthy conditions, and the difficulties in obtaining your needs—you are almost always in a fix'.

Similarly, complaints about entertainment were almost always along the lines of pointing out what could be enjoyed in the town but not the village. Many of the general statements about dullness probably referred at least partly to the lack of institutionalised entertainment. In the south a

Table 4:6 Responses to the question, 'Tell me three or four things which sometimes make village life unpleasant'

Responses	Rural survey Number	Per cent[a]	Urban survey Number	Per cent[a]
Economic:				
no work or no suitable work, especially for the educated	577	32	131	22
crop failures	117	7	51	9
Facilities:				
lack of facilities or amenities	312	18	119	20
inadequate water supply	662	37	216	37
shortage of consumer goods	584	33	93	16
bad roads, poor transport, poor communications	549	31	114	20
poor preventive medical and health facilities	382	21	118	20
much disease and sickness	324	18	107	18
lack of electricity	338	19	134	23
poor educational facilities	94	5	28	5
Entertainment:				
no nightclubs, bars, dances, etc.	552	31	129	22
no cinema	128	7	14	2
Way of life:				
life is dull or uncivilised	289	16	108	19
laziness, disobedience, lack of respect	118	7	28	5
Social:				
family pressures or troubles (conflicts about traditional religion, practice of witchcraft)	91	5	28	5
Total: respondents	5,117[b]	287[b]	1,418[b]	243[b]
respondent households	1,782		585	

[a] Percentage of all respondent households.
[b] Adds to over 100 per cent because of multiple responses.

35-year-old married man with four children who had always lived in the village said that 'life is almost always monotonous—very dull and uninteresting'. In the Volta Region a permanent returnee complained of 'the feeling of being in the bush away from civilisation', while a migrant from that region said in Accra that, back home, 'life seems dull and there is no change'. In Kumasi an Ashanti rural-urban migrant described his village as 'showing no sign of social advance'.

The embrace of village life often proved suffocating. Respondents referred to the 'strict observance of many old-fashioned customs', to family 'quarrels', and to 'a lot of restrictions' within the family and village.

In terms of significant regional differences, the absence of work, particularly for the educated, was felt most strongly in the South, where educational levels are higher and competition for jobs demanding educational qualifications strongest. The lack of electricity is felt most strongly in the South and Ashanti, perhaps because these are the areas where it already exists most widely. The absence of health facilities is most felt in the North and Volta, least in the South, which is a direct reflection of where they are most lacking and most prevalent. The lack of nightclubs, bars, and dances is felt to a much smaller degree in the more abstemious North, where Moslem culture, although only claiming a minority as adherents, has had a marked effect. Really dangerous family troubles, often involving accusations of the practice of witchcraft against relatives and necessitating sudden migration for reasons of safety, is by far the most common in the North and least common in the South, the frequency in the latter being less than one-eighth of that noted in the former. Similarly crop failure is much more a peril in the North, where it was commented upon four times as frequently as in the rest of the country.

The case for male migration to the towns

Males have been more likely to migrate to the towns than females, although this situation may be passing, for the 1960 census recorded larger surpluses of immigrant males in the Accra Capital District amongst older adult age groups than amongst the younger ones. The male predominance was greater in migrant streams from more distant and more traditional areas. Nevertheless, as shown in Chapter 3, this predominance may be related more to sex differentials in education in the sending areas than to differentials in available employment in the towns.

To what extent do rural household attitudes support and even condition the sex differential amongst the rural-urban migrants? Some of the answers are given in Tables 4:7 and 4:8. A comparison of the two tables shows that, while five-sixths of rural households favour young men going to the towns for at least a while, barely half feel the same way about young women. As one might anticipate, the margin is considerably smaller in urban households. Similarly, while rural households listed between three and four times as many benefits as harmful experiences accruing to young male migrants to the town, the balance sheet for females was almost equal, and, in the field of moral danger, four times as many believed the women to be in danger as felt that way about the men. There is very definitely stronger emotional pressure exerted on girls to stay in the villages than there is on boys. The exception is when the former are joining husbands or going to form a marriage with a specific person, or when older women are extending their trading activities.

Two points are fundamental to a proper understanding of the table. The first is that, although urban dwellers are often self-selected and are significantly less suspicious of the town than are the villagers, the pattern of response is surprisingly similar, suggesting good urban-rural communications and an approximation of beliefs to realities. The second is that the question placed the emphasis on the 'goodness' of the move and hence on human values. For many of the respondents the economic motivation was

Table 4:7 Responses to the questions, (a) 'Is it a good thing for boys or men to go to the town (i.e. a big town like Accra, Kumasi, or Takoradi) for a while?' (b) 'Why do you think this?'

Responses	Rural survey Number	Rural survey Per cent[a]	Urban survey Number	Urban survey Per cent[a]
(a) 'Is it a good thing for boys or men to go to the town?'				
Yes	1,474	83	499	85
No	255	14	47	8
Residual (most highly qualified responses)	53	3	39	7
Total respondent households	1,782	100	585	100
(b) 'Why do you think this?'				
Migration is a good thing:				
to obtain knowledge and ideas, to become sophisticated	935	53	448	77
to obtain better jobs and raise their standard of living	590	33	86	15
to further their education or to learn a trade	130	7	57	10
to supply the village with goods	30	2	9	2
Sub-sectional total responses	1,685	95[b]	600	104[b]
Migration is not a good thing:				
they may become criminals if unsupervised	194	11	50	9
the parents or family suffer from the loss	124	7	27	5
they may forget their traditions and culture	90	5	36	6
the farms will suffer; others will have to work harder	84	5	11	2
Sub-sectional total responses	492	28	124	22
Total responses	2,177[b]	123[b]	724[b]	126[b]

[a] Percentage of households giving response.
[b] Adds to almost or over 100 per cent because of multiple responses.

assumed; what they were concerned with then was the effect on the migrant and his family.

Over three-quarters of urban households, and more than half the rural households, argue that sophisticated, 'civilised', 'modern' ways of life can be learnt only in the town, although many make the point that having learnt such behaviour one can then return to the countryside. The view was expressed in a household near Kpandu in the Volta Region that 'by going to the town they broaden their outlook. One feels very bush when one has never been to the town. Such visits can even bring new ideas which will help in improving life in the village'. In Brong-Ahafo it was said, 'Yes, they get change of mind and become capable of discriminating between good and bad things', while in Wa in the far north it was felt, 'They get to the town and try to change their old-fashioned way of life; they get some improvements both mentally and physically'. Most rural-urban migrants living in the town were even more definite. In Accra a 31-year-old man from the Volta Region said, 'Yes, in order to come and see things in Accra for yourself and not depend on what you hear, to buy things not got in the village, and to watch games', while a younger immigrant in Tema replied earnestly, 'To learn to know how one can live profitably even in his own village, to learn something and then apply it in the village'. This is certainly a conscious example of the role of rural-urban and urban-rural migration in diffusing economic change.

The discussion of employment was often qualified by reference to 'rural push' or 'urban pull' factors. It was stated in a household in Aburi, where the educational output far exceeds the supply of suitable positions, 'If there are no jobs for them in the villages it is good for them to go', while a household in Dwinyama, Ashanti Region, cautiously put the supplementary view, 'It is good if they have some work to do there'. In some replies two specific values of migration were argued. One was that often schooling, further education, or trade training could be obtained or made use of only by going to the towns. The other is the value or even the necessity of remittances of money or goods from the town. In the far north a frequent response was that of a Chiana family, 'Yes, it is good; they return with plenty of money to help their relatives'.

There were also fears about the effect of the town on the migrant, the chief being that he might get into trouble with the law because of lack of supervision, bad company, or the strains of unemployment. The following are representative viewpoints, all presented as evidence against migration: 'There is suffering if boys have no close relations in Accra'; 'They are likely to be corrupted by bad company'; 'Their going always lands them in miserable conditions; they are removed from their loving parents'; 'They may get corrupt morals and become thieves when they have no work to do'; 'They will be influenced by ideas which may be bad'. Sometimes there were qualifications according to either age or aim: 'It is good for men but not for boys, because, since there are no jobs for the men to do [in the village], it is better they go and find work elsewhere; on the other hand boys become corrupted if they have no proper care in towns'; 'Only if they go with the mind to work and get some money and come back and marry at home; but it is bad for those who go aimlessly'.

Almost as important, at least in the view of rural households, was the harm done by migration to the village. A man who had migrated but who subsequently returned permanently explained, 'It leaves the aged in a helpless condition; it also depopulates the villages'. In Brong-Ahafo it was said, 'They must stay and look after their families', while in the North it was explained, 'People who go to sell their things in the town and return shortly after do not make town-going bad, but to desert the village for the town permanently is bad'. Sometimes these sentiments arose from a feeling that traditional ties should not be broken: 'It is not a good thing if they stay there permanently because they forget all about their culture; it is preferable to remain in the village'. More often it was economic: 'They must stay in the village and farm before they travel to anywhere'.

In the rural survey regional differences were not particularly marked. In the more developed South the largest proportions felt that a move to the town was a good thing, but of course such movements in this area involve shorter distances than elsewhere and much less likelihood of lengthy breaks with village and family. Social reasons for going predominated in the South, while grimmer economic reasons were more common in northern households. The most marked difference in reasons why migration was a good thing was on the acquisition of skills; replies favouring the learning of town skills were much more commonly given in the traditional agrarian North, where few of the trades of the South are practised. Only in the case of the temptation to crime in the towns, a feeling most frequently expressed in Ashanti, were there any significant regional differences amongst the negative answers.

The case for female migration to the towns

The support for female migration to the towns is considerably weaker, especially in rural households. In fact the division of these questions by sex was decided upon only after preliminary field trials had shown that replies on the subject were frequently qualified according to sex.

Table 4:8 Responses to the questions, (a) 'Is it a good thing for girls or young women to go to the town (i.e. a big town like Accra, Kumasi, or Takoradi) for a while?' (b) 'Why do you think this?'

Responses	Rural survey Number	Rural survey Per cent[a]	Urban survey Number	Urban survey Per cent[a]
(a) 'Is it a good thing for girls or young women to go to the town?'				
Yes	923	52	395	68
No	785	44	129	22
Residual (mostly highly qualified responses)	74	4	61	10
Total respondent households	1,782	100	585	100
(b) 'Why do you think this?'				
Migration is a good thing:				
to obtain knowledge and ideas, to become sophisticated	674	38	362	62
to obtain better jobs, raise standard of living, supply village with goods	317	18	65	11
to find a husband or make a marriage	194	11	49	8
Sub-sectional total responses	1,185	67	476	81
Migration is a bad thing:				
they may become prostitutes if unsupervised	711	40	159	27
the parents or family suffer from the loss	76	4	23	4
they may forget their traditions and culture	96	5	14	2
the farms will suffer; others will have to work harder	34	2	10	2
Sub-sectional total responses	917	51	206	35
Total responses	2,102[b]	118[b]	682[b]	116[b]

[a] Percentage of households giving response.
[b] Adds to over 100 per cent because of multiple responses.

Table 4:8 shows that only half the rural households believed in female migration; even in the towns almost three times as many households were against it as were hostile to male migration. The reasons given for favouring female migration were broadly similar to those described for males, except that one-seventh of all answers described the advantages of securing a town husband and few mentioned the acquisition of skilled training. Further probes on this point, set out in Table 4:9, show that there was widespread understanding for the former aim, and that its object was rather similar to that of much other rural-urban migration, namely to effect a transition from traditional agrarian life to that in the more modernised sector of the economy and society.

The contrast between Tables 4:7 and 4:8 lies in the rather extraordinary concentration on a single theme in the opposition to female migration. It is not destitution, crime, or the loss of family ties which are feared; it is the temptations of prostitution.

The need for sophistication, by which non-traditional manners are meant, is felt strongly. Often this need was expressed by the womenfolk of the household and assented to by the menfolk. In Enyinasi in the Western Region if was felt that 'Girls should go; they want to get cultured like the boys'. The two wives of a polygynist in the Volta Region agreed, 'It is a good thing; they improve upon their life there, they learn to dress, to speak and even to walk properly; they become very smart'. Similar views were widely expressed; 'They must be given a chance to go and see new women's clothes in order to make their choice before they get married'; 'Manners [i.e. urban and imported ways of behaviour] are not taught in the rural areas, and both girls and boys can learn manners only by visiting the town for a while'; 'It is a good thing sometimes, for village girls can learn a lot of things such as the proper way of cooking and dressing and in general can learn personal cleanliness'. Sometimes the emphasis was more on broadening the outlook: 'Yes, for a change of outlook and to keep abreast with the times, to buy new things, see new places and keep in touch with civilisation'; 'It improves their status in life; they see more modern things in Accra'. An Ewe immigrant in the Nima squatter area of Accra said with conviction, 'Yes, they must see the big developments in the big towns'. Sometimes importance was placed on the effect on the rural areas: 'Yes, women are better at imparting what they learn to others; the village, therefore, gains from the visits of its girls to the big towns'.

Employment, both as a way of earning money, and as a change in way of life, was frequently discussed. An Eastern Region household replied, 'Yes, to have a break in monotonous life and for employment'. In the Western Region it was said, 'Women should go; girls have no work there to do, but women might like to start commercial businesses which can be greatly helped in the town'. Full-time or part-time petty trading was often mentioned, as by the Accra household which pointed out, 'They can come and work for jobs and also do some trading'. Other occupations were also mentioned; in Kumasi it was said, 'Yes, so that they can learn jobs such as seamstresses'. Educational qualifications were commonly made, as for instance the observation of a household near Bawku in the far northeast, 'Young women and girls who have gone to school and want to seek employment in the town can go, but others who are illiterates must first have responsible relatives to care for them'.

From over one-third of all households, both rural and urban, the question evoked warnings about prostitution. The following comments are typical of 751 statements: 'Girls can easily be tempted into leading bad lives'; 'No, except they go with their husbands, they will be corrupted'; 'It is not polite [i.e. proper] for women to travel without going with their husbands or to them'. From the north, 'It is not good for young women or girls to visit; there are many temptations that can easily turn a young girl from her actual self to a rogue or harlot'. From Accra, 'Unless they have protection and work and also a proper place to stay, they fall victims to unscrupulous men and often become worse off than before'. From Cape Coast, 'Girls tend to become involved in immoral practices when they visit big towns'. From Kumasi, 'Girls become prostitutes when they are jobless in the towns'.

Often the major emphasis was placed on the effect on the village or the family. In the Western Region it was said, 'Girls can easily fall into the trap of prostitution, and this brings diseases to their home village'. In the Volta Region, 'They become spoilt and bring a bad reputation on their homes'. A young male rural-urban migrant to Tema reported, 'City life is likely to corrupt the village girl and she may corrupt other village girls when she goes back'. A household in the Upper Region reported, 'They return to be very unruly to their parents—they come back as prostitutes'.

The villages also have other problems. Female migration can 'reduce the woman population in the village'. Furthermore, it was said in Akuse that 'Those who stay rather longer [in the towns] tend to think they know better than their mothers and are a little difficult to handle'.

Regional differences, as measured by the major migration regions, were marked. In the South 67 per cent of households favoured some degree of female migration to the towns; this dropped to 63 per cent in Volta, tumbled to 39 per cent in Ashanti with its strong rural family tradition, and finally reached 29 per cent in the more traditional North. There was no equivalent contrast in the type of reason given for favouring or disfavouring migration, except that a significantly greater number of northern households emphasised the difficulty of fitting the returned female migrant back into the local society. This may be less a difference in viewpoint than a reflection of the fact that the traditional, agrarian North retains a way of life that is much further from that of the southern towns than is found any longer in any large areas of the rural South.

The different pattern of response shown by the regions on the question of male and female migration meant that within each region very great differentials by sex of potential migrant occurred in the replies. Thus, whilst of every nine households in the South and Volta, eight favoured male migration at some time, only six were prepared to countenance female migration. The picture in Ashanti and the North was very different. In each area seven in every nine households favoured male migration, but in the former fewer than four and in the latter fewer than three saw any merit at all in female migration.

Although a large minority of respondents saw no merit in female rural-urban migration, and although only one-tenth justified such migration in terms of making a suitable marriage, nearly all respondents understood why village girls might wish to make a town marriage. Table 4:9 shows that when the question was asked directly, even the proportion of households that gave disparaging reasons fell as low as one-fifth. There is little division of opinion on the fact that a wife's lot can be very different indeed in the town from on the farm.

Table 4:9 Responses to the question, 'It is said that some girls prefer to find husbands who live in town. Why do you think this is so?'

Responses	Rural survey		Urban survey	
	Number	Per cent[a]	Number	Per cent[a]
Living conditions are better in the town	1,111	62	343	59
The town way of life is better, more interesting, more civilised	649	36	235	40
They are lazy, wish to avoid farm work or village life	390	22	102	17
Total: responses	2,150[b]	120[b]	680[b]	116[b]
respondent households	1,782		585	

[a] Percentage of households giving response.
[b] Adds to over 100 per cent because of multiple responses.

Both men and women supplied answers that strongly suggested that the gulf between rural and urban life is greater for women than men. Furthermore, there was surprisingly little difference in the pattern of replies between the rural and urban surveys; the only significant contrasts were a greater tendency in the village to refer to laziness and more frequent mention in the town of drawbacks in village social life.

Townsmen had few doubts. A wealthy man, born in Accra, said girls aimed at such marriages 'for prestige and to be introduced to high society; a husband in town with a good job and probably a car is the dream of all girls'. Near Chiana, in the Upper Region, it was reported, 'Women have many needs and only husbands in town can provide them'. Sometimes the same needs were listed with a good deal more disapproval: 'they like high life in town and quick money and a sure source of income'.

Most respondent households assumed that the town wife would have many more possessions. Near Bolga in the north it was pointed out, 'They get enough food in town to eat and they also get many clothes to wear'. A migrant couple from the Volta Region, living in Accra when interviewed, knew well why girls wanted to be town wives, 'To be better looked after in town, to enjoy town life—after seeing how girls married to husbands in town are kept up they prefer to find husbands in town to those in villages—to run away from tribal restrictions'. One of three wives in a northern polygynous union explained, 'They get nice clothes to wear; they learn better ways of caring for their babies'.

The way of life itself is important to many. Near Swedru in the south it was pointed out, 'They make such marriages an opportunity to experience the town life', while a rural politician, living amongst his own people in an urban immigrant suburb, maintained, 'They enjoy modern life in the towns by doing that'.

The style of life, the whole question of urban and urbane manners, is a central issue. Near Agona Swedru, a town with about 20,000 inhabitants, a 24-year-old wife asserted, 'They hope to be married to more civilised and richer people—men in better businesses'. Another wife, a rural-urban migrant in Accra, reported, 'It is because men in the town are more lively and more polite'. A male, born on the outskirts of Accra, maintained, perhaps with insufficient knowledge of the rural hinterland, 'They'll have the opportunity of living in the towns and will set certain standards so that when they go back to their villages they will be on top of the world'. A Kumasi husband, born and bred in the city, explained the girls' preference, 'Because they want educated men—men who can look after them and who are cultured'. There was some dissent; a town-born wife replied, 'I don't agree with this point because a girl who is not used to town life finds it very difficult to understand a man who lives in the town'.

Status counts. In Cape Coast a household of local origin explained the desire for such marriages: 'because of the education town people have had; they [the wives] also rise in status'. In the same centre a young male rural-urban migrant from the Western Region was somewhat more sceptical: 'This is a fashion; the girl is proud to say, "my husband works in town and lives in town"; they feel elevated in position'.

There is near consensus on life being more easeful for women in the town. In Odumase in Brong-Ahafo the desire for town husbands was explained, 'because most men in the towns are well employed and so can afford to care for their wives'. These facts can have another construction put on them. In Mampong in the Eastern Region a household insisted, 'Some are too lazy to work on the farm and they want to go to the town'. Somewhat more judiciously a family near Kpandu in the Volta Region weighed the position: 'You see there is nothing like farming and hard manual labour in the town; when married to a husband who lives in the town, one is assured of some comfort, nice clothing, neat dressing and enjoyment of all the facilities of the town'. Sometimes the contrasts were a little surprising; a widow in Asuoboa, Ashanti Region, concluded, 'they are too lazy to go to farm; there [in the town] they are able to find jobs to help their husbands'.

The problems of marriage within the village were usually, but not always, put by rural-urban migrants in the town. They were the universal problems of small communities where people live in very close contact with one another. A wife in the Volta Region sympathised with the desire for a town marriage: 'They feel they will have a more peaceful married life with a husband in the town, for at home rumour-mongering breaks a lot of unions'. Sometimes the anonymity of the town was its greatest attraction. A couple who had migrated from the Volta Region to Takoradi felt that many girls prefer the town 'because they feel townsmen make better husbands; moreover, all their [the girls'] failings are known to the men of the village, and when they are known to be bad they seek husbands in the towns'.

The pattern of response was similar in the major migration regions. The only statistically significant deviation was a markedly smaller agreement in Ashanti, where the rural economy has been expanding rapidly, than elsewhere that town life did mean higher living standards, and much more agreement that it was the lazy who left the farms.

Urban-rural contrasts

In the course of preliminary trials before the main survey interviewers noted how frequently two assertions were made about the differences between town and village life. The first was that village life compared with town life was more 'manageable' or less complex. It was a life to which a person of rural origin was adjusted by upbringing and tradition. On the contrary, town life constantly presented unexpected and unfamiliar difficulties to the newcomer, and even after a residence of years was capable of springing surprises and raising almost insoluble problems. The second was that town life corrupts. Corruption in this sense is a difficult concept because different respondent households emphasised aspects of it to varying extents. Everyone meant that to some degree there is a temptation in the towns to commit offences recognised by the law as crimes; in the villages the temptation and the opportunity is smaller and the social controls are stronger. But some respondents meant that people behaved improperly in their occupations or immodestly in their daily lives without actually transgressing any laws. Others meant that the rural-urban migrant in the town failed to observe many of the traditions or show the kind of respect for them that they would have in their home villages.

Therefore, it was decided that in the main survey direct questions would be asked on both points to see how widespread agreement on them was. The results are summarised in Table 4:10.

Table 4:10 Responses to the questions, 'These statements have sometimes been made; do you agree with them? (a) Village life is more "manageable" than town life'; (b) 'Town life corrupts'.

Responses	Rural survey Number	Rural survey Per cent	Urban survey Number	Urban survey Per cent
(a) 'Village life is more "manageable" than town life.'				
Yes	1,506	85	470	80
No	222	12	74	13
Residual or qualified	54	3	41	7
Total	1,782	100	585	100
(b) 'Town life corrupts'				
Yes	1,162	65	376	64
No	459	26	97	17
Residual or qualified	161	9	112	19
Total	1,782	100	585	100

The large numbers of respondent households agreeing with the statements, especially the first, is very remarkable. Urban life is in Ghana still new and seemingly impermanent. Most town residents are not yet soaked with the kind of urban traditions which make the countryside, rather than the town, appear to be hostile and strange. There are at present few Ghanaians who believe that they could not easily cope with village life, but only small numbers feel the same about existence in the towns.

There was remarkable agreement between the rural and urban surveys. The only discrepancy of any size occurred in the residual category. This is explained almost entirely by the town-born in the urban survey who qualified their response by saying that town life was not easily managed by the newcomers or the village-born and who held that it was the poor immigrants into the town who were easily corrupted. Nevertheless, the closeness of the urban response to that of rural households demonstrates further that town life has not yet had time to embed itself deeply into Ghanaian society.

In the more advanced South one-sixth of rural households denied that town life was any less 'manageable' than village life, but in the North fewer than one in twenty-five did so (statistically significant). No such division occurred, however, on the question of corruption. Northerners may find it more difficult to understand and follow the ways of the town than do people further south, but they are not for this or any other reason more likely to attribute sin to the city.

The urge to move to the town

In 56 per cent of the respondent rural households some member of the household had been to the town to work, while in 68 per cent of the urban households one or more members had been born in rural areas. These households were questioned on the motives for migration, the feelings of the migrants, and the restraints placed on them as set out in Table 4:11.

Table 4:11 Responses to the questions, (a) [rural survey] 'Why did they [the rural-urban migrant members of the household] go to the big town?' [urban survey] 'Why did they [the rural-born members of the household] come to the town?' (b) 'Did they themselves favour going (coming)?' (c) 'Did anyone say anything against their going (coming)?' (d) [if 'yes' for (c)] 'What did they say?'

Responses	Rural survey Number	Rural survey Per cent[a]	Urban survey Number	Urban survey Per cent[a]
(a) 'Why did they go (come) to the town?'				
To find jobs or to earn money	763	77	304	77
Because they were educated	184	19	58	15
To seek further education or to learn a trade	52	5	61	15
To join other members of a migrant family	63	6	156	39
Total: responses	1,062[b]	107[b]	579[b]	146[b]
respondent households	990		396	
(b) 'Did they themselves favour going (coming)?'				
Yes	861	87	364	92
No	112	11	27	7
Residual and very qualified responses	17	2	5	1
Total	990	100	396	100
(c) 'Did anyone say anything against their going (coming)?'				
Yes	105	11	39	10
No	866	87	343	87
Residual and very qualified responses	19	2	14	3
Total	990	100	396	100
(d) [if 'yes' for (c)] 'What did they say?'				
Responses suggesting town bad for the migrants	35	33	24	62
Responses suggesting migrants' departure bad for village	50	48	26	67
Total: responses	85[b]	81[b]	50[b]	129[b]
respondent households	105		39	

[a] In (a), (b), and (c) percentages of 990 rural households where members had gone to the town at some time to work and 396 urban households where one or more members had been born in rural areas; in (d) percentages of 105 rural households and 39 urban households replying 'yes' to (c).

[b] Adds to less or more than 100 per cent because of failures to answer and multiple responses.

In Table 4:11 the rural and urban questions in Part (a) were asked in slightly different ways. The effect of this was to obtain answers in the former explaining family movement in general, while in the latter, where individuals were specifically mentioned by asking about their births, the subsequent movements of wives joining husbands and children joining parents were also recorded. In some cases the children join their parents in order to begin or continue their schooling, and this too was picked up to a greater extent by the urban survey approach. The other responses show clearly how dominating is the economic motive in rural-urban migration. They also support earlier findings by showing how inevitable many feel the migration of the educated to be.

Few migrants are pushed unwillingly to the town by family pressures based on the need for extra income or for cash income. Probably no more than one-tenth of migrants are in this category, and a substantial number of these are the wives of husbands or the children of parents determined to move to the town.

On the other hand another tenth of migrants go to the town in spite of the attempts of at least some of their relatives to dissuade them, and almost certainly many more potential migrants are actually deterred. As might be expected, migrant households in the town are more voluble about explaining the arguments put forth against migration than are the residual rural households. But both surveys make it clear that the dangers and unsuitability of the town are stressed somewhat less than is the loss to the village or village family. The resistance to migration often varies with the circumstances; a household in the Chiana area of the far north explained, 'At the time of the dry season there was no work for them, so there was no need to object to their decision'.

The major migration regions showed some significant differences in response. In the North five-sixths of all movement was ascribed simply to job-seeking, while the proportion fell almost as low as one-half in Ashanti. It was in the latter, where incomes have been climbing quite steeply while educational levels have lagged behind the South, that most emphasis was placed on movement for schooling and on the inevitability of the migration of the educated. It was in the Volta Region, where a tradition has grown up amongst the Ewes of partially supporting the rural population by remittances from the town, that the greatest pressure on reluctant young men to migrate was reported. Perhaps this is why Volta, together with the North, also recorded higher rates of attempted dissuasion from migration. Temporary and long-term movements to the town are important from the Volta Region, but there is evidence that they occasion a good deal of emotion and argument. It is here too, more than elsewhere, that the arguments predominantly centre on the harm of departure on the village than on the harm of the town on the migrant.

The urge to stay in the village

In four-fifths of the rural households there are adults who have never worked for any period in a town. Half the urban interviews were conducted in households which regarded themselves as parts of families, some adult members of which were still in the rural areas and had never worked in the town. The series of questions set out in Table 4:12 were designed to ascertain what reasons were generally held to explain this pattern of behaviour.

Once again a considerable number of respondents, one-ninth in the rural survey and one-sixth in the urban survey, explained the phenomenon in terms of education or mental inability to secure urban jobs or cope

Table 4:12 Responses to the questions, (a) 'Why did they [the adult members of the family who had never worked in the town] stay in the village?' (b) 'Did they themselves favour staying in the village?' (c) 'Has anyone said they should go to town?' (d) [if 'yes' for (c)] 'What reason did they give?'

Responses	Rural survey Number	Rural survey Per cent[a]	Urban survey Number	Urban survey Per cent[a]
(a) 'Why did they stay in the village?'				
Family responsibilities	507	36	141	48
Possession of a farm or land	435	31	98	33
They have enough money or possessions or a good job	440	31	31	11
They are uneducated or too simple	150	11	49	17
Total: responses	1,532[b]	109[b]	319[b]	109[b]
respondent households	1,398		294	
(b) 'Did they themselves favour staying in the village?'				
Yes	1,218	87	241	82
No	114	8	24	8
No response or very qualified	66	5	29	10
Total	1,398	100	294	100
(c) 'Has anyone said they should go to town?'				
Yes	111	8	51	17
No	1,205	86	216	74
No response or very qualified	82	6	27	9
Total	1,398	100	294	100
(d) [if 'yes' for (c)] 'What reason did they give?'				
To find jobs or earn money	60	54	22	43
To buy and send, or bring back, goods	49	44	16	31
No response or residual responses	2	2	13	26
Total	111	100	51	100

[a] In (a), (b), and (c) percentages of 1,398 rural households where some adult members had never worked in the town and 294 urban households claiming some adult family members in rural areas who had never worked in the town; in (d) percentages of 111 rural households and 51 urban households replying 'Yes' to (c).

[b] Adds to more than 100 per cent because of multiple responses.

with town life. Of the remainder, those who claimed some kind of 'rural pull' factor, almost two-thirds of the rural households saw it primarily as having an adequate job or income in the countryside. Half spoke specifically of access to land. This does imply a belief also in rural push; such large numbers of respondents would hardly point to the importance of the availability of farm land in keeping people in the village if the absence of such land were not known to be a factor in promoting migration. Nevertheless, the rural pull factor is by no means exclusively economic. A sizeable minority of households placed primary responsibility for the inability or lack of desire to move on family responsibilities. Sometimes these were seen as fundamentally ties of emotion and tradition; on other occasions as largely practical problems such as removing the only adult male who could assume various kinds of occupational responsibilities. Urban respondents placed significantly greater emphasis on these ties. They frequently held that older relatives pointed to available land as a means of discouraging younger members of rural households from migrating or even from expressing the desire to do so. If this is indeed the case, which seems probable, then at least some of the younger members of village households kept their peace during the rural survey interviewing. In the survey regional differences in the pattern of response were not significant, except that the Ewe households of the Volta Region placed greater emphasis on family responsibilities.

On the whole it was those who wanted to remain in the village who saw compelling reasons for doing so. There is little evidence that the rural Ghanaian family dominates its younger members to the point of determining whether they migrate or not regardless of individual wishes. Perhaps one-tenth stayed behind against their own desires; roughly the same fraction as Table 4:11 suggested had migrated reluctantly. The regional analysis did show a statistically significant division between the North and Ashanti on one hand and the South and Volta on the other. In the former there was a much closer correlation between staying and wanting to stay, while the latter areas obviously contained a good number of dissatisfied potential migrants staying on to work the farms or look after the family. On the whole they are, of course, closer to the towns and perhaps penetrated more by the temptations of town life.

Most adults who choose to remain in the village are not frequently urged to do otherwise. The most persistent urging comes from relatives who have already migrated to the towns, a fact which helps explain the phenomenon of chain migration noted earlier. It also explains the higher 'yes' response in part (c) of Table 4:12 in the urban survey, for necessarily all the urban households analysed here, but not all the rural households, had members in both town and village. Regional patterns did not exhibit great differences; potential migrants in the Volta Region receive somewhat more encouragement to go, while in the Ashanti Region, where rural work is usually available, they receive markedly less encouragement.

There is no dispute or regional variation in the reasons given for encouraging such migration. While potential migrants might feel within them the twin temptations to earn more and to enjoy the fast way of life in the city, relatives, especially those in the village, rarely see the latter as an argument for moving. The case put forward is nearly always that for transferring some of the wealth of the town to the countryside or at least to specified families within it.

The dependence of the village on the town

Such viewpoints do raise the question of the dependence of the village on the town for goods or money to buy goods, especially manufactured and imported products. Thus, as shown in Table 4:13, the respondent households were asked, perhaps in a rather extreme way by reference to being 'very poor', about this dependence.

Table 4:13 Responses to the question, 'If everyone in your village [or your village of origin] stayed in the village and no one wanted to go to the town, do you think that the village people would be very poor?'

Responses	Rural survey Number	Per cent[a]	Urban survey Number	Per cent[a]
Yes	820	46	228	39
No	851	48	294	50
No response or question does not apply	111	6	63	11
Total	1,782	100	585	100

The question was directed in urban households at those persons of rural origin, although it was answered readily enough in terms of either village of personal origin or of parents' origin. Half of all rural households believe the system of rural-urban migration, coupled with the reverse flow of remittances and goods, to be essential to the rural areas; and it was plain that a large fraction of even those replying 'no' thought that it made an appreciable difference to rural living standards. The slightly lower affirmative proportion in the urban survey seems to be largely attributable to rationalisation by those who have ceased sending remittances, or who have never sent them, to the villages.

The regional analysis was particularly interesting, and demonstrated quite convincingly that poverty is a relative concept. The need for remittances was felt most strongly in the coastal part of the country which has been subject to the forces of change for a very long time. Thus 49 per cent of households in the South, and 62 per cent of those in Volta, an area with a long migration tradition, felt that without migration the villages would be poor. But the proportion feeling this way fell to 38 per cent in Ashanti, and, somewhat surprisingly, to 28 per cent in the poor but traditional North.

Summary

Those responses which appear to be of major importance, largely because of the extent of agreement found, are summarised in Table 4:14.

It is quite clear that there are urban pushes as well as pulls and rural pulls as well as pushes. It is also apparent that the overriding forces are economic and that the net flow of migrants is from the village to the town only because of a differential in favour of the latter in the number of job opportunities or in the income earned by labour. The family evidence supports the views of the households about the general position. There is widespread belief that rural-urban migration plays, through the urban-rural flow of money and goods, an important role in the rural economy.

Nevertheless, there are supplementary non-economic forces, of which by far the strongest rural pull is a reluctance to break close ties with the family and the village. This is reinforced by an urban push. For most Ghanaians

Table 4:14 Summary of certain responses to questions on rural push and urban pull

Response	Percentage of households giving specified response	
	Rural survey	Urban survey
Motives for migrating:		
migrants are going for economic reasons	88	82
family members went for economic reasons	77	77
Motives for not migrating:		
non-migrants remain for		
economic reasons	65	55
non-economic reasons[a]	45	50
family members remain for		
economic reasons[a]	62	44
non-economic reasons[a]	36	48
Villagers would be very poor if there were no migration	46	39
Village life is more 'manageable' than town life	84	80
Town life corrupts	65	64
Male migration is a good thing	83	85
Female migration:		
is a good thing	52	68
may lead to prostitution	40	27
Attractions of:		
town life		
facilities[a]	150	114
entertainment[a]	103	118
village life		
simple economic conditions[a]	140	108
family and village way of life[a]	96	74
Disadvantages of:		
town life		
complex economic conditions[a]	138	115
social problems[a]	49	39
way of life[a]	47	24
village life		
lack of facilities[a]	182	159
lack of entertainment[a]	38	24

[a] More than one response in a multiple response question has been added, resulting in some households being represented more than once.

town life is still something alien and somewhat frightening; and it is certainly true that there are aspects of existence, especially for immigrants, in the raw, new cities of tropical Africa that are turbulent.

Nevertheless, the greatest urban push factor, like the pull factor, is economic, but is concerned mostly with expenditure rather than income. The rural-urban migrant is usually appalled, on entering the fully cash economy, to find that everything has to be paid for, often at high cost. His precious wages are rapidly eroded by what appear to be unfair exactions. The returnee in the village often praises the low or negligible cost of basic housing and food and indeed the simplicity and small number of economic decisions he has to make. The rural-urban migrant usually goes from an economy that is still partly subsistence to one that is fully cash and acquisitive. Furthermore he enters the new economy in a very disadvantageous position; he is unfamiliar with much of its working and he is poor and hence often in a difficult bargaining position. It is true that he may in time help exploit the new rural-urban migrants, often from his own area, but, when migration decisions are made, that day is still far off and does not affect decisions. When the city is described as less 'manageable' than the village, problems of this type are usually meant.

The contrast between the village and town style of life is also important, but complex, for both push and pull factors are involved. In truth rather similar features of city life repel some and attract others. The swirl of life, the entertainment facilities, and the lack of traditional village restraints add to the lure of the city but many are apprehensive of such things. Indeed the majority of respondents in the town as well as in the bush agree that town life corrupts, and very great numbers of respondents discussed, at some point in the interviewing, theft and prostitution, most of them identifying both with the corrupting influence of towns.

Yet, to many migrants and non-migrants, the contrast between the dearth of entertainment and facilities in the village and their presence in the town is very clear. It is interesting that greatest emphasis was placed on the difference in the provision of facilities—lighting, water, hospitals, and so on. Thus the attraction of 'city lights' runs not only to jobs and cash, but to such mundane things as the provision of facilities.

Finally the regional analyses revealed that there are many types of rural-urban migration, depending on where the movement starts and where it finishes. Short-distance migration from such socially and economically advanced areas as the Akwapim Ridge into Accra is very different from the movement from the near-subsistence villages of the savannah north down hundreds of miles to Kumasi. The latter involves not only greater adjustment problems for the migrants on arrival at the town but sometimes insuperable problems of adjustment for both the migrant and the home village should he (or, more seriously, she) return from the town permanently.

5

The Migration

Questions on the planning of migration and of the process itself were directed in the rural survey at those members of the household who were intending to go to the town for the first time and in the urban survey to those household members who had come from villages and small towns. The greatest number of responses to any of the questions immediately following were from 1,224 rural households or 69 per cent of all those in the rural survey and 532 urban households or 91 per cent of all those in the urban survey. The remainder contained no eligible respondents. In fact for specific questions the number of eligible households usually fell below 1,224 and 532 respectively and so percentages were calculated from the various eligible totals. The numbers of rural households, as would be anticipated, fell somewhat short of the 1,252 individuals reported in Chapter 3 as planning migration.

Rural knowledge of the town

In many developing countries a controversial question is whether migrants go to the town as a result of factual knowledge about town life and rural-urban differences or whether, on the contrary, they are lured on by essentially false pictures arising partly from faulty communications and partly from the inability of persons unfamiliar with the town to interpret correctly the information that is received.

A series of four questions, set out in Table 5:1, attempted to probe the position in Ghana.

Part (a) of Table 5:1 shows that seven out of every nine intending migrants in the rural areas believe that they know what town life is like. For the remaining two-ninths the migration must be very much a gamble. The lower 'yes' response in the urban survey is partly a product of poorer communications and fewer town visits in earlier times and partly a reflection of the fact that, with the wisdom of hindsight, fewer actual migrants believe that they really did have any idea of the nature of the towns, Interestingly enough, there is little regional variation in claimed knowledge about the towns.

In the years immediately before the survey the mammy lorries had multiplied and the proportion of the population with relatives in town to

Table 5:1 Responses to the questions (a) [rural survey] 'Have you any idea what life in the town is like?' [urban survey] 'Did you have any idea what life in the town was like before you came here?' (b) [if 'yes' for (a)] 'How did you learn about life in the town?' (c) [urban survey only] 'Is life in the town just like you thought it would be?' (d) [if 'no' for (c)] 'In what ways is it different?'

Response	Rural survey Number	Rural survey Per cent[a]	Urban survey Number	Urban survey Per cent[a]
(a) [rural survey] 'Have you any idea what life in the town is like?' [urban survey] 'Did you have any idea?'				
Yes	956	78	283	63
No	268	22	170	37
Total	1,224	100	453	100
(b) [if 'yes' for (a)] 'How did you learn about life in the town?'				
From a visit	624	65	101	36
From returned migrants or hearsay	336	35	181	64
From radio, newspapers, books, films	20	2	24	8
Total: responses	980[b]	102[b]	306[b]	108[b]
respondent households	956		283	
(c) [urban survey only] 'Is life in the town just like you thought it would be?'				
Yes			200	63
No			115	37
Total			315[c]	100
(d) [urban survey only—if 'no' for (c)] 'In what ways is it different?'				
Town worse than imagined:				
overcrowded, insanitary, unattractive, various social evils			45	39
fewer jobs, money harder to earn			27	23
cost of living higher			27	23
Town better than imagined:				
fewer adjustment problems, more 'manageable'			53	46
Total: responses			152[b]	131[b]
respondent households			115	

[a] Percentages calculated in (a) from 1,224 rural survey households and 453 urban survey households feeling eligible to respond, in (b) from 956 rural survey households and 283 urban survey households responding 'yes' to (a), in (c) from 315 urban survey households feeling eligible to respond, and in (d) from 115 urban survey households responding 'no' to (c).

[b] Adds to over 100 per cent because of multiple responses.

[c] Respondent households are greater in (c) than (d) because some who replied 'no' to (c) did not feel earlier that they would claim having any idea of the town.

visit had also climbed steeply. There is no doubt that the mobility of the population, especially in terms of short-term town visits, increased rapidly. Hence intending migrants at the time of the survey were much more likely than their predecessors to have visited the town at least once before deciding to migrate. Doubtless this increase in visiting is affecting to some degree the whole country, but the incidence of visits is very different in the various migration regions. In the two areas containing large towns, the South and Ashanti, visits explained over two-thirds of all knowledge, but the fraction was nearer half in Volta and the North.

The information received from the mass media is surprisingly small. The explanation is not merely illiteracy or poverty. Part of it lies in the fact that films were almost always, and books usually, foreign imports which said nothing about Ghana's towns. Part lies in the fact that the press was at the time of the survey, as it had been for years before, a political one, granting little space for anecdotal description of everyday life in the towns. This was also true of the radio, which, in addition, does not easily convey impressions of ways of life. Since the survey television has arrived in Ghana, and it is quite possible that this medium, with increasing numbers of out-of-doors telecasts in Accra, Kumasi, and Takoradi, will play a significant role in promoting rural-urban migration. The original code of possible responses also envisaged that respondents would have learnt about the towns in schools from urban-born or urban-trained teachers. However, only a handful claim to have derived information in this way, and they have been included in the 'hearsay' category. It is possible that those who merely say that people told them about the towns do contain large numbers who learnt, perhaps informally, from the village teacher what he had experienced in the towns.

Nevertheless, most Ghanaians do not pursue a mirage to the towns. Communication between town and country is surprisingly good. Although only about one-third of the migrants already in the town had derived their pre-migration impressions from visits, almost two-thirds found these impressions approximated reality.

Even amongst those who found their impressions markedly astray, almost half had been too apprehensive of the town. Those who had been disappointed numbered only about one-sixth of all rural-urban migrants questioned in the town, but the tendency to remain in the town is obviously a selective process. The great majority of disappointed migrants might well have departed for the village long ago. In Lagos it was found that many persons of this type remained in the city for only a very short period (Ejiogu 1968). The unexpected deficiencies of the town divided almost evenly into lesser economic opportunity than expected and greater social problems or insufficient facilities to cope with problems of urban living.

Planning for the journey

The anticipated uses of town money. The chief motive for migration is the desire to earn town cash so that it can be put to a variety of uses. It seems reasonable to suppose that some of these uses, beyond those of basic keep, must be envisaged at the planning stage; indeed that they form an integral part of the decision to migrate. Hence, as shown in Table 5:2, eligible rural households were questioned on the matter, and eligible urban households were asked about actual expenditure patterns for comparison.

The great majority of intending migrants plan to save some of their urban earnings, and the experience of the migrants already in urban areas shows that this is possible. Even in apparently poverty-stricken squatter areas, such as Accra's Nima, four-fifths or more of the households manage to make some savings; after all, for many this is the chief purpose of migration. The flow of wealth to the villages is by no means restricted to those who specifically mentioned remittances; wherever migrants make savings some of it is likely to find its way back to the home villages as money, remitted or taken, or as goods, often in the form of presents.

Many villagers planning migration assume the town to be similar to the village and overestimate the need or the possibility of owning housing there. Subsequently they realise that most townspeople rent accommodation, even temporary shacks.

But the earnest potential migrant very much underestimates the demands of consumption expenditure on fashionable clothes, and on the city

Table 5:2 Responses to the question [rural survey] 'If you earn more money in town than you need to pay for food and housing there, what do you intend to do with the money?' [urban survey] '. . . , what do you do with the money?'

Responses	Rural survey		Urban survey	
	Number	Per cent[a]	Number	Per cent[a]
Expenditure in town:				
save it				
means unspecified	357	29	249	47
at post office or bank	464	38	63	12
send home remittances	208	17	114	21
spend it				
on a house	306	25	49	9
furniture	89	7	44	8
use it to marry and establish a family	75	6	26	5
buy clothes (usually 'nice clothes')	226	19	173	33
spend it				
enjoyment (unspecified or general)	57	5	119	22
beer, drinks, etc.	3	0	55	10
Sectional total	1,785[b]	146[b]	892[b]	167[b]
Expenditure in village:				
save it				
means unspecified	145	12	92	17
at bank or post office	89	7	7	1
spend it				
on a house, land, or farm	845	69	167	31
furniture	9	1	3	1
use it to marry and establish a family	64	5	22	4
buy clothes	29	2	6	1
spend it				
enjoyment (unspecified or general)	3	0	3	1
beer, drinks etc.	1	0	3	1
Sectional total	1,185[b]	97[b]	303[b]	57[b]
Total: responses	2,970[b]	243[b]	1,195[b]	224[b]
respondent households	1,224		532	

[a] Percentages of 1,224 eligible rural survey households and 532 eligible urban survey households.

[b] Adds to nearly or over 100 per cent because of multiple responses.

bars and dancing places. These are part of the way of life of the town and certainly reduce the potential for saving.

For some migrants the town plays an important role in traditional society. It provides the money to meet the necessary bride wealth payments to make a desired marriage and establish a family. This is particularly true for people from the North, where the existence of southern towns has certainly had the effect of raising the value of bride wealth.

Two qualifications should be made about the expenditure envisaged or practised back in the home village. The first is that some respondents classified urban-rural remittances as town expenditure and others as rural savings, and no meaningful distinction can be made between them. The other is that some forms of rural expenditure, such as giving money or goods to relatives for consumption or schooling, or to fellow villagers for ceremonies associated with marriages, deaths, and births or other festivities, are so much assumed to be the reason for saving that they are not listed as specific planned or current expenditure.

The great majority of intending migrants award the highest expenditure priority to the establishment of a firm base back in the village to which they might well later return permanently. Thus in over two-thirds of the rural households the need for building or buying a village house or a farm was discussed. As the years pass in the town the hope of being able to do this, or even the desire to do so, sometimes dwindles, but one-third of respondent urban households reported having already made such expenditures.

There were some statistically significant differences by migration region. Migrants from the Volta Region were particularly concerned with building a village house back home, while those from the North predominated in the discussion of setting up a farm. It was northerners, too, who most frequently discussed the possibility of using town-earned money as capital for trading purposes back in their home areas.

The desire for a town job. An integral part of the decision to migrate and the making of plans to do so is usually some concept of a desirable town job. This is frequently something as far away from farming as possible, for instance an office job, and, in the case of those who have been to school, something that uses the skills acquired during education. Such aims tend to tax the employment possibilities of the town, but, as Table 5:3 shows, large Ghanaian towns, especially the capital, do provide a good deal of office employment, or at least employment around offices. Such towns are primarily commercial and administrative centres rather than manufacturing ones.

The rural-urban migrants are probably somewhat optimistic but not wildly unrealistic. The 1963 rural-urban migrant stream contained a high proportion of young, educated persons with qualifications certainly exceeding on average those of the general Accra population. However, some, even of the educated, will probably have to accept positions in the skilled

Table 5:3 Responses to the question [rural survey only], 'What job would you like to get in the town?' and occupational data for Accra in 1960

Response	Number	Per cent[a]	All employed, Accra Municipality, 1960 (percentage distribution)		
			Both sexes	Males	Females
Professional, administrative, clerical[b]	372	30	17	22	9
Sales workers[c]	181	15	30	9	72
Farmers, fishermen, etc.	55	5	4	6	1
Skilled and services[d]	274	22	39	49	17
Labourers	188	15	10	14	1
No response	154	13	—	—	—
Total	1,224	100	100	100	100

[a] Percentage of 1,224 eligible rural survey households.

[b] In rural survey includes seven desiring to further their education or training.

[c] Includes petty traders.

[d] Includes drivers.

Source: Rural survey and Census 1960: *Special Report A,* Table 10.

trades rather than around offices; they may indeed earn higher incomes by doing so. Similarly, many of the wives will probably eventually take up petty trading in order to help out the family budget. The apparently higher rate in the survey for labouring jobs is probably more a statistical artifact than the migrants under-selling themselves, for the census skilled category includes the assistants and mates of skilled workers.

When questioned further, approximately half the intending migrants claimed to have already experienced some employment in the urban work they desired. This, of course, included nearly all the farmers and labourers. Nevertheless, it was clear that the obtaining of rural employment in non-farming occupations, even part-time employment, provided a strong temptation to a young adult to try his fortune in the same field in the town. This applies particularly to male skilled and semi-skilled workers, and to a lesser extent to female petty traders. In a rather similar sense schools give young people the feeling that they have already experienced 'white collar' employment. However, a smaller proportion of intending migrants with specific occupations in mind claimed experience in clerical work than in any other desired occupation. Pre-migrational work experienced in desired occupations is certainly on the increase, presumably as a result of economic change in rural areas, as significantly fewer migrants in the urban survey claimed prior experience in the jobs they sought.

Those who had no previous experience in the desired job were questioned further. Nearly half were seeking employment in occupations which they pointed out needed no experience or were quite easily picked up on the job. But over half were hoping either for further training or apprenticeships, or at least the kind of acquired, specific experience which would subsequently count as a definite qualification. There is no doubt that in this way the large towns serve, and are seen, as great training areas for the modern economy. However, significantly fewer migrants in the urban survey claimed that in fact they had managed to acquire specific training and qualifications; about four-ninths claimed to have done so.

The urban workforce appears to be surprisingly stable, if not in terms of specific employment, at least in terms of specific occupation. Only 36 per cent of migrants questioned in the urban survey claimed to have worked since reaching the town in any occupational field other than the one they had entered on arrival.

The migrants' views on the employment situation were of particular interest. The towns of tropical Africa, and of Ghana in particular, have grown rapidly in recent years. But this has not necessarily meant that employment is more abundant, for the pressure of rural-urban migration has grown and the number of rural-urban migrants with some kind of qualification for urban employment has increased enormously. By 1963 there was probably a slackening in at least the foreign investment in tropical African cities, and in many unemployment rates were rising (van de Walle 1968). The migrants in the urban survey were asked, 'Is it easier to get work in Accra [or Kumasi, Sekondi-Takoradi, or Cape Coast] now than when you first came here?' Only 22 per cent of the respondents said 'yes', 10 per cent were undecided or said the position was much the same, while most of the 68 per cent who replied 'no' went on to observe that it was probably harder. Thus, as measured in Ghana in 1963, urban opportunities for individuals had not grown, although urban employment had over the previous twenty years increased enormously.

The family and migration

Preliminary surveys had established that migration in Ghana can be a drawn-out affair, with husbands, wives, and children making the journey at different times as a beach-head in the city is made and consolidated. Accordingly, questions were asked on the point both about anticipated movements from the rural areas and about the past movements of migrants already in urban areas. Unfortunately, as was established by subsequent checks, the tight control kept during the immediately preceding questions on those planning imminent first-time migration was relaxed. Part of the problem was a defect in the organisation of the questionnaire, a flaw which had not been detected in preliminary testing. The result was that the question was also answered in rural areas by considerable numbers of respondents either planning migrations other than their first, or only generally considering migration and with no definite plans.

The findings, nevertheless, remain of value in the rural areas even if describing in many cases migration that was not imminent and that might not even take place. In urban areas the data present no problems.

Of male migrants in urban areas interviewed in the urban survey 43 per cent were married prior to migration. Almost exactly half of this number, making up just over one-fifth of the total male migration stream, were accompanied by their wives at the time of migration. Interviewers reported, however, their suspicion that this proportion was probably higher than the facts warranted; they had the impression that some of the older migrants were not clearly distinguishing between migrating with their wives and being joined by them soon afterwards. Of the married migrants who were not accompanied by their wives, two-thirds later sent for them. Only about one-sixth of married migrants and one-fourteenth of the total left their wives permanently in the village. Thus long-term rural-urban migration may lead to temporary splitting of spouses but rarely to near-permanent separation. There was no evidence from the rural survey that in contemporary migrations wives are more likely to accompany their husbands than in the past; indeed, the opposite may well be the case. However, it is anticipated that nine-tenths of the wives at first left behind will be subsequently sent for, so there may be a continuing decline in the proportion of permanently split marriages.

Only two-fifths of migrants in urban areas had children at the time of first migration, but over half brought them. Usually when children came the wife had also done so. In contemporary rural-urban migration fewer children may at first come, but it is anticipated that all but about one-eighth will eventually join their parents in the town. During the transition period to the town, most children left by fathers back in the village are looked after by immediate relatives—mothers, if present, or otherwise grandparents, siblings, or uncles; some may later stay with more distant relatives. Non-relations, friends, chiefs, elders, play an almost negligible role in caring for family members during the period of transition, although during the planning stage of the survey some had suggested otherwise.

Significantly fewer migrants from the North arrive in town accompanied by either wives or children and significantly fewer send for them later. In fact, well over two-fifths of the children of long-term migrants from the North may never be brought to the southern towns.

In spite of the emphasis placed here on stages of movement from the village to the town, many relatives, such as parents or nephews and nieces, for whom the migrant feels wholly or partially financially responsible, must stay in the village. 'Dependants' of this kind were reported to be in rural areas by about half the urban households containing any migrants.

The journey

Intending migrants in the rural survey and all migrants in the urban survey were asked, as shown in Table 5:4, about the means of transport used.

The major difference between the two surveys is caused by the high 'no response' rate, partly the result of persons being too young to remember the trip. The other noteworthy difference arises from the decline in foot migra-

Table 5:4 Responses to the question [rural survey], 'How will you travel to the town?' [urban survey] 'When you first went to a big town, by what means did you travel?'

Response	Rural survey Number	Rural survey Per cent[a]	Urban survey Number	Urban survey Per cent[a]
Lorry	1,084	89	394	74
Bus	29	2	2	0
Train	140	11	35	7
Other transport (car, boat, plane)	38	3	14	3
Foot	20	2	32	6
No response	0	0	55	10
Total: responses	1,311[b]	107[b]	532	100
respondent households	1,224		532	

[a] Percentage of 1,224 eligible rural survey households and 532 eligible urban survey households.

[b] Adds to over 100 per cent because of multiple responses.

tion. Until the mid-1930s walking was an important means of migration, but in recent times it has been of little significance. Road transport, and above all mammy lorry transport, completely dominates the picture, although by 1963 competing bus routes were beginning to spread.

Regional differences (all significant) did occur. Only in the South and Ashanti were any migrations by train planned, for the simple reason that these were the only two major migration regions in which railways were found. However, they also accounted for five-sixths of all journeys planned by car, although they were not, of course, the only areas with roads; this difference was a reflection of relative income levels in the regions. Finally, and significantly, three-quarters of the planned foot journeys were by northerners. Usually they formed merely the first part of a journey, for the days have gone when men walked the whole way from the savanna to the coast. Nevertheless, most of the northern journeys on foot were expected to be quite long ones, in contrast to the few relatively short movements listed elsewhere.

The system of migration in Ghana was in 1963 largely sustained by the mammy lorry. These are trucks on which wooden sides have been built, with wooden posts extending further upwards to support the beams and canvas of the roof. Within them low benches are placed from side to side so that up to 40 persons can share a somewhat jolting ride. The most distinctive part of the lorries is usually their painted exteriors, on which statements, in either English or Ghanaian languages, are boldly written. These take the form of sayings, proverbs, or advice from the owners, and to foreigners are often very cryptic indeed. An assistant to the driver collects fares. On competitive routes these were in 1963 about one penny per mile, but could often be lowered by negotiation; on the other hand, on lonely roads where sometimes only a single lorry plied, fares could be considerably dearer, with scant hope of negotiation. In the North some of the walking took place to major roads where a number of lorries were to be found. The seemingly most important and exciting place in many towns and villages is the lorry park, a dusty open space usually located near a market. It is here that the lorries call, terminate, or start. The journey is not usually accurately timetabled, and the bus may start hours later than the driver forecasts, often because he is awaiting a full load or some passenger who has been capriciously delayed. In the migrant's memory of his first trip, the initial assembly at a village lorry park, the long, bumpy journey with its many halts, the change of lorries at another park where one vehicle finishes its run, and the final exciting arrival in the busy lorry park of a great town, all remain clearly etched.

Arrival in the town

Nevertheless, the migrant faces a whole range of urgent problems the minute he disembarks in the city. The first is where he will stay. The matter is important because most migrants have no job, nor even a very clear idea about the labour market. They need a period, while looking for a job, in accommodation that is cheap, or preferably free. It is better still if they can get it with someone who is sympathetic to their need for a job and whose knowledge of jobs, or even personal intervention, can help secure employment. In addition, adjustment to town life takes time and there are new modes of behaviour to be learnt; in the circumstances there is much to be said for staying with someone who initially will not expect too much and who can be used as a model or even as a teacher.

More often than not the migrant already knows, when he dismounts from the mammy lorry in the lorry park, with whom he will be staying. Often he does not know how to get there. He will seek advice from bystanders, often from people from his own area. He is not helped by the fact that city addresses are often inexact and hence have to be descriptive. To whom does he go? To determine this eligible respondents were asked the question in Table 5:5.

Over half the potential migrants in the rural areas expected to stay at first with relatives or fellow villagers. If to these are added those joining their nuclear families, mostly wives going to husbands and children going to parents, the proportion exceeds two-thirds. The combined proportions in the urban survey were somewhat lower, but this was expected as partly reflecting the pattern of an earlier time. With the rapid growth of town population, far more rural Ghanaians have relatives or friends from the village in the towns. Thus chain migration is becoming ever more important as a mechanism for moving population from countryside to town; indeed, it helps to explain the acceleration in urbanisation. At the same time older mechanisms for ensuring labour of adequate volume and type have become of smaller importance. A smaller proportion of employers, apart from the government, offer accommodation.

Table 5:5 Responses to the question [rural survey], 'Whom will you stay with when you get to the town?' [urban survey] 'Whom did you stay with when you first came to Accra (or Kumasi, Sekondi-Takoradi, or Cape Coast)?'

Responses	Rural survey Number	Per cent[a]	Urban survey Number	Per cent[a]
Relatives (other than spouse, parents, or children)	405	27	48	21
Friends (usually fellow villagers)	401	27	25	11
Rented accommodation or board	289	20	56	24
Nuclear family (spouse, parents, children)	204	14	54	23
Chief (elective chief of rural group in town or equivalent person)	125	8	11	5
Employer or apprentice master	53	4	36	16
Total	1,477	100	230	100

[a] There are a few multiple responses in the rural survey but the large number of respondents is mostly explained by the inclusion of more than one eligible individual from some households. In the urban survey the large non-response rate has been caused by failure to remember, especially amongst migrants who were young at the time of arrival. In the circumstances the responses have been percentaged as a proportion of total responses.

With the growth of training in schools and technical institutions, the system whereby masters took young apprentices into their own houses and boarded them so that they were often almost indistinguishable from their own children has become of much less significance. If migrants do not know any specific person in the town, they often seek out the most important persons among their own ethnic group, frequently a kind of elective chief of the specific immigrant community. It is usually one of his tasks to provide personally the necessary initial accommodation or to suggest someone who can do so. The system is made easier by the tendency for the various ethnic groups to settle in clusters. It might be noted that this system of securing accommodation was not used as frequently as we had been led to believe, and that it usually requires the payment of some board, although this might not be exacted at the outset. It is the northerners who still adhere most to the older patterns (statistically significant), being four times as likely as the others to seek accommodation from a 'chief' and three times as likely to secure it by apprenticeship. In fact the system of elective chiefs is far stronger and far more important in the southern towns amongst the northerners than amongst others; it is one of their shields against the very great cultural stresses produced by their transition between markedly contrasting societies. A common response was, 'I will go to the Zongo [i.e. strangers' or immigrant quarter] Chief'.

Table 5:5 does a great deal to explain just how poor rural-urban migrants are able to cling on in the town until they are in a position to earn money. The relatives or fellow villagers with whom they stay are under rather strong pressure to help with the search for a job, if only out of self-protection. By the time the migrant is in a position to find his own housing, he has learnt a good deal about town life; he has also learnt how to find adequate housing without paying too much. Those who pay rent from the outset have above average earning capacity, and are much more likely to be able to secure housing, especially government accommodation, through their job.

Seeking help from town relatives or fellow villagers

The assistance given to migrants on their arrival in town is so important a part of the whole rural-urban migration process that several questions were framed to probe it further. In the rural survey a series of questions, set out in Table 5:6, was put as part of the section of the survey directed to the 1,508 rural households where some members were either back from permanent or seasonal migration to the town, or currently in the town and their position known to the village household. Similarly, questions were put to 500 urban households,* eligible because they contained rural-urban migrants.

Table 5:6 Responses to the question [rural survey only], 'Are people who have gone to the town always happy to help their relatives who want to go to the town?'

Response	Number	Per cent[a] Respondents	Responses
Yes	1,108	73	77
No	332	22	23
No response	68	5	—
Total	1,508	100	100

[a] In this and the succeeding question responses are shown as a percentage of 1,508 rural survey respondents and 500 urban survey respondents. However, as there are reasons why eligibility to answer some questions is different from that in other questions, percentages of total responses are also shown.

Most rural households agreed that town relatives are happy to help the new arrivals from the village, although a substantial number of 'yes' responses were qualified, as in the words of a response from Aburi in the Eastern Region: 'Some are happy to help but others are not'. In terms of major migration regions there was a significant difference between the South and Volta on one hand, where the 'yes' response averaged over 80 per cent, and Ashanti and the North on the other, where it was under 70 per cent. The explanation amongst the Ashanti may well be that, having fewer relatives in the town than do most families in the South and Volta, there is less choice amongst town relatives and a greater chance of not find-

* This number is somewhat below the 532 urban households replying to questions in the survey section dealing with migration; there is a slight variation in eligibility for the two sections depending on whether links with the village have been retained.

ing one willing to take in a migrant. The explanation amongst the northerners is that the move from the north is such a considerable undertaking that many migrants, a great number of them illiterate, become cut off from families and do not always view the arrival of a little-known relative with pleasure. This position is aggravated by the fact that most northerners in the towns are poorer than the average urban population and in a more difficult financial condition for supporting relatives.

It became obvious in the preliminary trials that few urban residents would state that they were not prepared to help their rural relatives, so the question was approached indirectly, as shown in Table 5:7.

Table 5:7 Responses to the questions [urban survey only], (a) 'In what way do you help relatives from your village who want to come to live in Accra (or Kumasi, Sekondi-Takoradi, or Cape Coast)?' (b) 'Do you help other people from your village when they come to Accra?' (c) [if 'yes' to (b)] 'In what way do you help them?'

Response	Number	Per cent[a]	
		Respondents	Responses
(a) 'In what way do you help relatives from your village who want to come to live in Accra?'			
Provide temporary accommodation and food, and help find jobs	224	45	51
Help find jobs	52	10	29
Help out with money if needed	126	25	12
Help find accommodation	33	7	8
No response	65	13	—
Total	500	100	100
(b) 'Do you help other people [i.e. non-relatives] from your village when they come to Accra (or Kumasi, Sekondi-Takoradi, or Cape Coast)?'			
Yes	270	54	83
No	56	11	17
No response	174	35	—
Total	500	100	100
(c) [respondents answering 'yes' to (b)], 'In what way do you help them?'			
Provide temporary accommodation and food, and help find jobs	126	47	55
Help find jobs	59	22	26
Help out with money if needed	23	8	10
Help find accommodation	20	7	9
No response	42	16	—
Total	270	100	100

[a] In (a) and (b) percentages of 500 eligible respondent households and in (c) percentages of 270 respondent households replying 'yes' to (b).

The numbers failing to respond in part (a) of Table 5:7 are not very meaningful, as some migrants in the town are almost entirely cut off from relatives, or have never been asked for accommodation, or, because they themselves are boarding, are in no position to provide it. However, the relatively greater 'no response' rate in (b) and its cumulative climb to (c) are very significant indeed, and prove clearly that many households do not feel the same responsibility towards fellow villagers as towards relatives.

The most one can do is to provide transitional board and help locate jobs. Perhaps over half of rural-urban migrant households in the towns are prepared to do all this for relatives, and a somewhat smaller fraction, drawn almost entirely from this group, for fellow villagers as well. A 30-year-old man from one of the Bolga villages in the Upper Region, now living in Kumasi with his wife and three children, said in a matter-of-fact way, 'They get free boarding and lodging until they get work'. A wealthier and more influential migrant in Takoradi reported, 'I help them financially, find accommodation and arrange jobs for them'.

Far more frequently than with relatives, townsmen feel that their only obligation towards fellow villagers is to devote some time and use their superior knowledge of the town in searching for jobs, contacting others (often of the same ethnic group) and generally advising. It is far less common to give or lend money to fellow villagers than to relatives.

It is probably fairly close to the truth to say that up to four-fifths of urban migrant households give at least minimal help, and usually far more, to relatives from the village, but that a majority give no assistance at all to non-relatives. Nevertheless, sufficient help is forthcoming to illuminate clearly the process of chain migration.

Table 5:8 Responses to the question [rural survey only], 'If people from the village go to the town to live, do the relatives treat them fairly ("unfairness" might consist of working them too hard or giving them too little food or money for their work)?'

Response	Number	Per cent[a]	
		Respondents	Responses
Yes	934	62	65
No	250	17	17
Some do and some do not	256	17	18
No response	68	4	—
Total	1,508	100	100

Table 5:9 Responses to the question [urban survey only], Are you always pleased to help relatives, and others, from your village when they come to live in Accra (or Kumasi, Sekondi-Takoradi, or Cape Coast); or are there sometimes difficulties?'

Response	Number	Per cent[a]	
		Respondents	Responses
Yes	240	48	64
No, or 'there are often difficulties'	135	27	36
No response	125	25	—
Total	500	100	100

Nevertheless, the system does not always work smoothly or without rancour. In the villages one frequently hears stories of town relatives exploiting migrants, especially young females, by working them hard as unpaid domestic labour. In the town one quickly realises that some people who do give assistance do so grudgingly or with heavy heart. The questions in Tables 5:8 and 5:9 were designed to test the extent of these feelings.

A striking testimony to the efficiency with which the system has worked to date in Ghana is that almost two-thirds of eligible rural households feel that the migrants are fairly treated. Only one-sixth are unqualified in their complaints.

Some rural families regard lodging and assistance as their right. In Bolga, in the far north, a 35-year-old family head, planning his first seasonal migration to a southern town, explained, 'As relatives, they always treat them fairly, for they are bound by custom to give them the same quantity of food that they themselves eat'.

Not all northeners agree that this is in fact what happens; in one of the Chiana villages, a man and his two wives agreed, in the presence of their eight children, 'They [the relatives in the town] always exploit them'.

The truth of the matter may depend on the circumstances. In Enyinasi in the Western Region, it was explained that migrants established in the town treat new arrivals from the village well, 'especially when they are well-to-do, for they would like to be spoken of well in their own village'. Much depends on what is demanded; near Kpandu in the Volta Region, a household pointed out, 'Some treat fairly up to a time—that is, you are expected to find some work of your own after a month or two (it is not a joke feeding a person in the town)—and then withdraw this fair treatment; others—the selfish—never treat them fairly'. In Dwinyama, Ashanti, it was argued that individual cases differ in both town and country, for 'it depends on what sort of child or relative they are; this [differentiation in liking and treatment] can happen in the village too'.

There were no statistically significant differences in the pattern of response by major migration region.

Most urban responses to the question set out in Table 5:9 were that help was given, but it was frequently explained that this was difficult—often much more difficult than the new migrants or the villagers credited. A rural-urban migrant, established in Accra's wealthy Ridge area but with twelve children to support and educate, explained, 'There are some difficulties in helping some of them, since the demand from the village is always greater than one can meet'. In the coastal cities the cost of extra food was a sore point, but in the forest at Kumasi it was more common to be told, 'There are no great difficulties because there is not much difference in chop [food] money'.

Financing the journey

Travelling to the town costs money. A major anomaly in Ghana is that relative distances mean that it costs comparatively little from the richer south and a considerable amount from the poorer north. Lorry fares alone can absorb £2 or more per person for a journey from the further flung parts of the Upper Region to Accra, an amount representing almost one-tenth of the annual national income per head there and a considerably greater fraction of cash incomes. In addition, there are the costs of establishment in the town, especially if the migrant is the first member of his extended family to go there. A series of questions, set out in Table 5:10, were framed to investigate the source of this finance. Those in the rural survey were directed to all households, as this is a matter of general village knowledge and concern.

Table 5:10 Responses to the questions, (a) [rural survey] 'How do people going to the town get the money to go with?' [urban survey] 'When you first came from your village to Accra (or Kumasi, Sekondi-Takoradi, or Cape Coast), how did you get enough money to be able to do it?' (b) [if money borrowed] 'What kind of arrangement is (was) made for paying it back?' (c) [if money borrowed] [rural survey] 'Do they always pay it back?' [urban survey] 'Did you pay it all back?'

Responses	Rural survey		Urban survey	
	Number	Per cent[a]	Number	Per cent[a]
(a) [rural survey] 'How do people going to the town get the money to go with?' [urban survey] 'When you first came to Accra how did you get enough money to be able to do it?'				
Own money, worked and saved	763	43	241	48
From relatives (loan or gift)	667	37	177	36
From non-relatives in village (loan or gift)	116	7	6	1
From friends (loan or gift)	15	1	7	1
Borrowed (or advanced from employers or future employers)	328	18	29	6
Total: responses	1,889	106[b]	460	92[b]
respondent households	1,782		500	
(b) [if money borrowed] 'What kind of arrangement is (was) made for paying it back?'				
Repay when able to do so or on return	331	42	6	16
Repay by instalments	315	40	17	46
No arrangement	149	19	14	38
Total	795	100	37	100
(c) [if money borrowed rural survey] 'Do they always pay it back? [urban survey] Did you pay it all back?'				
Yes	537	65	18	53
No	283	35	16	47
Total	820	100	34	100

[a] Percentages in (a) are of all rural survey households and of 500 eligible urban survey households containing migrants, in (b) and (c) of the number of respondents.

[b] Adds to nearly or more than 100 per cent because of multiple responses.

The pattern of rural household response is probably similar to the pattern of sources tapped by migrants, for the great majority of households discussed cases known to them, usually cases within the household itself. Thus both surveys suggest that, although the most important source of finance is the migrants' own exertions, this accounts for less than half the total. But this source, together in many cases with other money raised within the family, accounts for the great majority of finance. Some village entrepreneurs, usually the migrant's own employer, will advance some money, but no well established loan system exists. An important new category covered by advances or loans from future employers is the increasing numbers of educated young who apply for government or semi-official positions or sometimes jobs with large firms. The only other source of money which is now becoming more important is that of loans within the village, a sign of the increasing penetration of villages by the modern economy and of growing amounts of available cash, sometimes seeking investment.

Far more money is given than lent, although, of course, the net effect is often much the same. The migrant who has been given money by relatives feels he must spend some of his urban earnings on them. In one sense this might be one of the most profitable ways of investing rural money—a point established in terms of money spent on the education of children (Caldwell 1965; 1966). This is not meant to imply that all such gifts are carefully planned; most are spontaneous, and tradition and family sentiment play major roles.

There is little formality about most loan arrangements; so little, indeed, that many even of the relatively few urban respondents who had borrowed money could not recall clearly what the exact arrangements for repayment had been. Often it is suggested that repayment be discussed after a job has been found, or, indeed, if a job is found.

The informality of much of the borrowing and the fact that most of it is done through relatives means that there is a good deal of uncertainty about repayment. Almost half the urban respondents who answered the question had not made full repayment, at least formally. However, it is probably true that most rural-urban migrants do return to relatives, in the form of goods, money, and board for later migrants or children coming to the town for education, many times the money lent them. Nevertheless, it is this uncertainty, together with the small size of many of the necessary loans, which makes lending money to migrants as a commercial venture a risky undertaking.

In most traditional areas the whole discussion of formal lending and repayment to relatives was regarded as being in rather poor taste. In Wa, in the far northwest, a 50-year-old man only temporarily returned from Kumasi explained how in the subsistent north, where cash is relatively scarce, aspiring migrants raise the necessary money: 'They sell shea butter [made of a vegetable oil from the fruit of a tree], crops from their farms and so on;

those who borrow are few indeed—a larger number rather steal from parents; if they do borrow at all, repayment is rare because a man would always like to borrow from a near relative'. In another Upper Region household it was said, 'They earn it; while they are in the village people have some jobs to do that can earn money—they may sell crops. Borrowing is not common because it is not proper to lend money at interest and so this is not encouraged'. The latter remark was obviously made by a Moslem; the view would not be general because most northerners are not Moslems.

Further south, in much more transitional societies and economies, these scruples about making loans do not apply. Nevertheless, the 52-year-old father of nine children, some of them migrants to the town, reported in Akuse, Eastern Region, 'Some do pay; others don't bother to and indeed may not be expected to'. In the Akwapim Ridge area near Accra, the oldest cocoa farming area in Ghana, it was stated that loans from even close relatives may be secured 'by giving a promissory note that the money will be paid back after starting work', but nevertheless only 'some do so'. In New Offinso, Ashanti, it was claimed, 'They are given money by members of the family; they pay after they have work, else they will be taken to court'. Some migrants in the town described loans or gifts from outsiders. A 30-year-old Ashanti migrant in Kumasi from Jamasi, which he never visits, reported, 'A master [lorry driver] paid everything so I needed no money'.

There were different statistically significant patterns of response from the major migration regions. It is in the North, where potential migrants are undoubtedly most wanting for cash, although admittedly their relatives may be in an equally bad position, that they are most likely to raise all their money by personal exertions. This was reported in over two-thirds of all households in the North compared with an average of less than one-third elsewhere. The ease with which money could be secured from relatives varied directly with the wealth of the region, being greatest in the South and Ashanti, not so great in Volta, and least in the North. Thus, while almost half the migrations are financed in this way in the South, only about one-eighth are in the North.

Summary

The broad outlines of the mechanics of rural-urban movement are clear enough, the salient features being set out in summary form in Table 5:11.

Ghana is, by African standards, a small, rich country with a highly mobile population. No part of the country is further than about 350 miles from Kumasi or 500 miles from Accra, even the latter distance no more than two days' (or £2-£3) journey by lorry. The main roads of the country teem with lorries; the 1960 census showed that almost 60,000 persons

Table 5:11 Summary of certain responses to questions on migration (percentages)

Responses	Rural survey	Urban survey
Had some idea of town life before migration	78	63
Acquired this idea from a visit (percentage of those with some idea)	65	36
Idea approximately correct (percentage of those with some idea)[a]	—	63
Some town earnings to be saved or remitted	84	80
Some town earnings to be used on village house or farm	69	31
Will (or did) go by lorry	89	74
Will (or did) stay with relatives or friends	68	55
Migrants already established in town are always happy to help relatives	77	—
Migrants already established in town always treat relatives fairly	62	—
Migrants already established in town are prepared to help other villagers	—	54
Migrants already established in town are always pleased to help relatives and other villagers	—	48
Migration financed by own earnings	43	48
Migration financed by relatives	37	36

[a] The total number answering this question was slightly higher than the number claiming some idea in the first response listed.

worked in transport, of whom about 30,000 were lorry drivers and perhaps 10,000 drivers' mates.

In these circumstances over three-quarters of aspiring rural-urban migrants claim a reasonably good idea of what living in the town is like. In fact almost two-thirds of them have acquired this by visiting the town, a phenomenon which has apparently been rapidly on the increase. This finding can be related to the earlier one that it is almost exclusively those villagers with town relatives who visit the town.

The position appears to be as follows. Village families without relatives in the town are unlikely to send members to visit the town. Almost certainly they are also unlikely to migrate, for the penchant for commencing a migration by joining a relative in the town is very strong. But if some determined member of the family does break precedent by establishing a beach-head in the town, he is likely to be followed at intervals by a wife, either from a pre-migration marriage or a marriage arranged on a return to the village, children if any, and, for temporary accommodation, by siblings, nephews, nieces, or others. This is chain migration in quite an extreme form.

This form of migration does establish very strong links between the village family and the town. It allows the flow of information and permits easy and cheap visits to the town. There is little evidence in Ghana that problems of communication delude villagers about the real nature of the town, or that rural-urban migration is based largely on false hopes. On the other hand there is very little evidence that mass communications play a significant role in stimulating the migrant flow, although it is not impossible that this position will change with the spread of television.

A major purpose of migration is to be able to earn more than is necessary merely for town subsistence, and so to be able to save, and perhaps remit to the village, some of the surplus. The great majority of migrants do manage to do this. At first a major objective of most is to buy a house or farm in their village area, but although many persist with this project, others become more absorbed in town life. In time many migrants spend an increasing proportion of their earnings on town entertainment and pleasure. They help support the multitude of little bars, often ramshackle places, found in and around the towns.

For the actual journey the great majority of migrants squeeze into a lorry, ultimately to alight in a town lorry park and make their way to the home of a relative or friend. Usually they are given board for a period. They are expected to use this period in a reasonably vigorous search for a job, but they are often given valuable assistance in the search.

Most migrants believe their relatives are happy to help them in this way, although a minority claim that the town household gets more than its outlay back in the form of cheap domestic labour and in the extra graciousness of life that this can provide. Town families sometimes complain that they provide costly board in return for very inefficient and 'bush' labour. There is little doubt that townspeople often feel under uncomfortable pressure from village migrants, not so much because of individual obligations, but because of the sum total that such obligations may assume. The village often has little real appreciation of the limits of a town income, or of the inroads which providing temporary accommodation or hospitality for visitors can make. There is little doubt that many townsmen are prepared to help relatives but draw the line at spending on assistance to other villagers. Only just over half said that they helped other villagers, and many of these made it clear that such help was often limited to helping in the search for a job.

These arrangements reduce the amount of money needed to render migration possible; indeed sheer poverty is not a major brake anywhere in Ghana on the movement from the country to the town. Almost half of all aspiring migrants can save enough money to cover their needs and other assistance can often be obtained fairly readily from relatives. Most of this help is given rather than lent, but there is no doubt that the maintenance of such family relationships and traditions facilitates a kind of return on the gift. There is a parallel here between family expenditure on migration and expenditure on education. In both cases the expenditure allows the recipients to earn more and to return more to their relatives. In only a minority of cases do the recipients regard the return expenditure as a specific obligation arising from the original expenditure; it is a much more basic aspect of Ghanaian family relationships and of patterns of mutual obligation.

6

Urban-Rural Links

When the migrant has reached the city, found a job, and established himself in reasonably satisfactory housing, he has usually not completed a once-and-for-all operation. Very few migrants begin a new life and forget the old. On the contrary, for most there are continuing links of all kinds with the village; very often the town is regarded as a kind of stopping place, and the stay there as a kind of sojourn. The roads are thick with mammy lorries full of rural-urban migrants temporarily returning to the village or coming back to the town from a visit to the village. The migrant makes not one journey but many, and provides the lorries with their chief custom.

It is this which makes African rural-urban migration in some ways potentially far more significant for social and economic change than has been the case with similar movements in the West. The new attitudes and artifacts which flow into the Ghanaian towns, especially the coastal cities, from the outside world are readily carried on to the village. So is the money from the more modernised economy of the towns. There is no clear division between urban and rural population. One can sit in a Ghanaian town discussing rural life, and find that most participants preface nearly every observation with 'In my village . . . .' Similarly, a conversation about the country's towns will, in most villages, draw in very considerable numbers of persons with their own urban experiences to relate. In the villages the view is widespread that the towns will continue to channel to the villages ever more knowledge of modern things and of 'civilised' modes of life.

This condition provides the possibility of rapid social and economic change; indeed it helps to explain the degree of change which has occurred in southern Ghana this century. In order to investigate these continuing urban-rural connections, a series of questions was framed on various aspects of the relationship.

Visiting the village

The strongest contacts which the migrant maintains with the village are his or her revisits. These are often arranged for holidays or periods of leave from work; at Easter, for instance, the mammy lorry system is strained to move the migrants from town to village and back again. Sometimes migrants manage to get away from work and the town to attend special ceremonies in the village, especially those with which they have some personal connection, such as the marriage or funeral of a relative. Often, too, migrants return for consultations at the village fetish shrine.

In Table 6:1 an attempt has been made to measure the frequency and duration of such visits.

Table 6:1 Responses to the questions, (a) [rural survey] 'How often do they come back to the village?' [urban survey] 'How often do you go back to the village?' (b) 'How long do they (you) usually stay in the village each time?'

Responses	Rural survey		Urban survey	
	Number	Per cent[a]	Number	Per cent[a]
(a) 'How often do they come (you go) back to the village?'				
Once or more a month	203	13	89	18
4-11 times a year	68	4	44	9
1-3 times a year	915	61	213	42
Less than once a year or 'rarely'	159	11	83	17
Don't know; no response	163	11	71	14
Total	1,508	100	500	100
(b) 'How long do they (you) usually stay in the village each time?'				
Up to 2 days	209	14	140	28
3-7 days	602	40	171	34
8 days-1 month	395	26	136	27
More than 1 month	152	10	32	7
Don't know; no response	150	10	21	4
Total	1,508	100	500	100

[a] Percentage of 1,508 eligible rural survey households and 500 eligible urban survey households.

The general pattern is fairly clear, although the 'no response' category contains respondents whose behaviour is irregular or who cannot generalise about it. In the urban survey there are quite a number of respondents in this category who come to the town when young, or whose whole family has come, and who do not expect to retain contact with the ancestral village.

Probably one-fifth of migrants or slightly more tend to break close contact with the village by visiting it less often than once a year or never at all. Once a year was frequently mentioned as the least often that return journeys could be made without the village or village family feeling that a discourtesy had been done them.

Probably four-fifths of migrants who have left the village later than their infancy, and who have some relatives left in the village, do manage to make annual visits. Many do no more, for a very big fraction of the 1-3 visits a year category are in fact annual visitors; perhaps half of all migrants who ever return to the village do so once a year. The rest do so more frequently; probably around one-sixth at least once a month. Those predominating in this category are short-distance migrants, especially if they have left spouses or children in the village; they are almost commuters.

This group contains a large number of transitional migrant families who are still in the process of transferring the whole family to the town. It also contains a disproportionate number of very young migrants.

The majority of migrants spend no more than a week on each visit. The very short stays are in most cases attributable to migrants who return frequently; the majority of annual visitors manage to stop for around a week. Thus, although the links with the village are not broken, most rural-urban migrants do not spend more than about one-fiftieth of their time in the village. One reason is the difficulty of getting more time off work. Another, as the years pass, is undoubtedly that the town dweller becomes bored by a longer period in the village and becomes restless to get back to the fury and excitement of the city.

As might be anticipated, there are very large regional differentials in the answers (statistically significant). Distance, with its accompanying high costs in money and time, dictates that only a negligible number of migrants return to the North more often than once a year, and one-third of them cannot even manage that. Most Volta migrants also return only once a year, but all but a handful can achieve that. The more frequent returnees, 93 per cent of those in the first two categories in part (a) of Table 6:1, are found in the South and Ashanti, most of them in districts reasonably close to a large town, the very districts from which the large towns draw a disproportionate number of migrants.

One type of migrant might be under-represented in the rural survey responses in Table 6:1. That is the migrant who belongs to a household which has migrated in its entirety to the town. Hence in each survey area interviewers listed such absent households and subsequently asked questions about whether their members ever visited the village. Rather surprisingly, it was established that even in these families visits to the village, although often infrequent, do occur in about two-thirds of all cases. A similar figure was obtained in the urban survey from households of this kind.

Another aspect of rural-urban links is the seasonality of migration movements, especially in the case of movements described as seasonal migration. However, short-term migration could be shown to be controlled by the seasons in only something over three-fifths of all cases. Seasonal control is still the prevailing pattern amongst short-term migrants from the north, where life is largely determined even now by the cycle of subsistence agriculture, but in the more developed areas to the south the timing of much short-term movement is determined by individual factors rather than by the economy.

Respect in the village

There is often some apprehension of town life in the village, and some feeling that good-for-nothing girls go there or that all girls might come to no good there. Nevertheless, preliminary trials had shown too that there is also immense respect for towns and especially town life—a belief that new, worthwhile, modern ideas flow from the city, and a widespread conviction that 'civilised' manners are to be learnt there. Accordingly, in the main survey a question, in rather extreme form, was asked, as set out in Table 6:2.

Table 6:2 Responses to the questions, [rural survey] 'Do village people see the people who live in big towns as more important and show them more respect?' [urban survey] 'When people who have come from the villages to work in Accra (or Kumasi, Sekondi-Takoradi, or Cape Coast) go back to their home villages, do people there see them as more important and show them more respect?'

Response	Rural survey Number	Rural survey Per cent[a]	Urban survey Number	Urban survey Per cent[a]
Yes	1,173	78	376	75
No	280	18	65	13
No response	55	4	59	12
Total	1,508	100	500	100

[a] Percentage of 1,508 eligible rural survey households and 500 eligible urban survey households.

Although the proposition was put rather uncompromisingly and dogmatically, in each survey over four-fifths of those who gave a response said 'yes'. This is clear evidence of a viewpoint which seemed to be commonly agreed upon throughout most of rural Ghana. It is evidence too that there are obvious non-economic reasons for migrating to the town; it is a way of winning respect and increasing one's prestige amongst one's own people. As long as such a viewpoint prevails, not only is rural-urban migration likely to continue, but a ready rural reception is likely to be given to ideas and modes of behaviour flowing from the town; there is very little sign of village resistance to such flows. Sometimes the responses were qualified, often in a pragmatic way, as in the case of the Upper Region household who answered, 'Yes, when they come back richer'. But, on the whole, it was the 'no' responses which were most often qualified.

There were significant regional differences in response. In the traditional emigrant areas, Volta and the North, 'yes' responses outnumbered 'no' ones by ten and thirteen times respectively; in the more sophisticated South, where towns are common, the ratio dropped to a little over four times; while in Ashanti, with its strong rural family traditions, it was not much higher than double.

The transmission of skills to the village

The problem of the transmission of acquired skills from the town to the country is rendered complex by the earlier finding that villagers learning skills are more likely than those not so equipped to try their fortune in the town. Nevertheless, they sometimes learn these skills from persons in the village who have themselves acquired them in the towns.

When rural households were asked if they knew cases of persons who had learnt to do jobs in the town and then had come back to do the same kind of job in the village, 76 per cent said that they did, 23 per cent that they did not, and 1 per cent failed to respond. The need for such persons in the village, and the profitability of returning, depends on the extent to which skills are lacking in the rural area. Thus 86 per cent of households in the North knew of such cases, but only 81 per cent in Ashanti, and just over 70 per cent in Volta and the South (differences significant). In Dwinyama, Ashanti, it was pointed out, 'It depends upon the type of work; if they will profit more by working in the village, they will come to work here'. Near Chiana in the Upper Region a man being interviewed related, 'A friend of mine learnt carpentry in town and he's now the village carpenter'.

On the other hand the rural survey indicated that many skilled persons merely retire to their home villages with no desire to continue working. Others find that the village can support very few artisans and that most jobs of this type are being done by people who have plied their trade in the village for a long period. In the urban survey respondents were asked about the extent to which they practised their job in the village or expected to do on retirement, as shown in Table 6:3.

Table 6:3 Responses to the questions, [urban survey only] (a) 'Do you ever go back and do the job you have learnt in the town in your home village?' (b) 'If you ever return to your village for a long time, or for good, do you hope to do this job there?'

Response	Number	Per cent[a] Respondents[a]	Per cent[a] Responses
(a) 'Do you ever go back and do the job you have learnt in the town in your home village?'			
Yes	28	6	8
No	310	62	92
No response	162	32	—
Total	500	100	100
(b) 'If you ever return to your village for a long time, or for good, do you hope to do this job there?'			
Yes	114	23	33
No	235	47	67
No response	151	30	—
Total	500	100	100

[a] 500 eligible households where one or more respondents were migrants.

The most meaningful percentage column in Table 6:3 is that of responses, for most respondents who failed to reply visited their village for very short periods or not at all and were unlikely to return to settle. The pattern is the one expected from the rural survey findings. Comparatively few migrants practise their trades during short visits back to the village. However, around one-third of the long-term or permanent returnees expect to employ their skills if only for part-time or irregular work. The great majority of the remainder, and this is the real limitation on the urban-rural flow of skills, either have no real skills, for they have worked as labourers or night-watchmen for instance, or have skills, such as that of telephone operator, which cannot be used in the village. There are some other skilled persons who are determined to retire on their earnings merely into a kind of gracious village life.

It is probable that the flow of skills will not be as great as part (b) of Table 6:3 indicates. Some migrants will decide not to return to the village after all, while others will die unexpectedly before they can do so. Some who do return will find the existing village tradesmen hostile to encroachment upon their work. Nevertheless, the flow of skills with returnees, even with these qualifications, is substantial, and is a very important aspect of the country's social and economic fabric. It helps to explain the change actually taking place in what might on casual observation be taken to be remote, rural fastnesses.

Building a house in the village

There is a close connection between the growth of the urban labour market in Ghana (in addition to the growth of cash-cropping) and the very great investment in substantial housing in the smaller towns and villages. In Chapter 5 we observed that housing forms by far the largest item of specific expenditure in the village by the rural-urban migrant. In turn the building of these houses employs a good deal of skilled and non-agricultural labour in rural areas. Many of the larger village houses, often built at least partly with town money, are large family structures. They are frequently of two storeys surrounding a courtyard which may contain a sunken water reservoir. The walls may be faced with cement, or may consist, as has been the case more recently, of concrete blocks. The roofs are usually of corrugated iron, which rusts rapidly. Other houses built with money from the town may be more modest.

A large majority of rural households replied to questions that a great number of migrants to the town do build village houses for their retirement, and a somewhat smaller number added that others build rooms on to their families' houses in the village or repair existing parts. Others still, but apparently fewer, commence building after their final return. There are those, as pointed out in Dwinyama, Ashanti, 'who think to build for their old mother and father even if they will not come back'.

These patterns occur throughout the country and there are no very substantial differences by major migration region. The building of whole houses in the village while continuing to work in the town is probably somewhat more common in the South, where the houses are most usable during this

Table 6:4 Responses to the questions, [urban survey only] (a) 'Do you own a house in your own village?' (b) [if 'no' for (a)] 'Are you building one here now?' (c) [if 'no' for (b)] 'Do you hope to build one there before you finally return to the village?' (d) [if 'no' for (c)] 'Do you hope to build one there after you finally return to the village?' (e) 'Have you built any rooms on to your family house in the village?'

Response	Number	Per cent[a] Respondents[a]	Responses
(a) 'Do you own a house in your own village?'			
Yes	97	19	23
No	329	66	77
No response	74	15	—
Total	500	100	100
(b) [if 'no' for (a)] 'Are you building one there now?'			
Yes	30	9	9
No	299	91	91
No response	—	—	—
Total	329	100	100
(c) [if 'no' for (b)] 'Do you hope to build one there before you finally return to the village?'			
Yes	218	73	73
No	81	27	27
No response	0	0	—
Total	299	100	100
(d) [if 'no' for (c)] 'Do you hope to build one there after you finally return to the village?'			
Yes	53	65	65
No	28	35	35
No response	0	0	—
Total	81	100	100
(e) 'Have you built any rooms on to your family house in the village?'			
Yes	47	9	16
No	239	48	84
No response	214	43	—
Total	500	100	100

[a] Percentage of 500 eligible respondents in (a) and (e), 329 in (b), 299 in (c), and 81 in (d).

period, for, on the whole, they are closest to the towns. It is least common in the North, possibly for the converse of the reason given above, as well as for the reason that northerners tend to be the poorest town residents with the least surplus money. The latter observation is supported by the fact that the building-on of an extra room to existing houses is far more commonly done in the village by migrants from the North. Similarly, and here it is the distance factor which is operating, northerners are relatively more likely to commence initial building after retirement, and Ashanti least likely.

In order to obtain a quantitative picture of the process, urban households were asked the series of questions set out in Table 6:4.

There is clear evidence in Tables 6:4 and 6:5 of very considerable

Table 6:5 Summary of responses in urban survey to the building of housing in home villages

Category of respondents	Percentage of respondents: Recorded by questions (a) to (d) in Table 6:4		Recorded by questions (a) to (d) plus (e) in Table 6:4	
	500 'eligible' respondents	Respondents answering (a)	500 'eligible' respondents	Respondents answering (a)
Owning a village house (or rooms)	19	23	29	35
Owning a village house (or rooms) or currently building	25	31	35	42
Owning a village house (or rooms) or currently building or hoping to build before return	69	83	78	94
Owning a village house (or rooms) or currently building or hoping to do so before or after return	80	96	89	107

building activities in the villages supported by town earnings and even more anticipated activity.

Analysing a multiple response from an urban household is not difficult because in nearly all cases such responses represented an adult couple and were recorded as the household response. There is much greater difficulty in determining the universe for such questions. Not all households containing persons of village birth include persons old enough at the time of migration to feel sufficient link with the village to consider returning. Those who were not old enough probably form a substantial fraction of the 'no response' category in part (a) of Table 6:4. On the other hand this category undoubtedly also contains migrants who decided quite early during their urban residence that they would live their lives out in the town and had no need to establish village housing.

Therefore, if the question is confined to the building of a house, the truth about genuine rural-urban migrants, excluding those who made the journey as infants or very small children, probably lies somewhere between the two left-hand columns in Table 6:5. That is that just over one-fifth of migrants in the town have already built a house, and well over one-quarter possess either a completed house or one still in the course of construction. Fully three-quarters expect ultimately to return to the village and to possess a house there by the time they do so, while perhaps eight-ninths expect to live in their own house in the village before they die.

The response pattern is rendered more complex by including the answers to the supplementary question about adding rooms to the family house in the village. In the two right-hand columns of Table 6:5 these responses have been added to those about houses. This procedure is probably almost correct for the first line, but incorporates ever greater double-counting for subsequent lines, as the figure 107 per cent, purposely included, shows, for some migrants begin by building rooms while intending ultimately to replace them by a house. It is probably reasonable to suggest that over one-third of the migrants had at the time of the survey invested in the construction of some form of accommodation in their home villages and that before their death well over 90 per cent expect to do so. Even if we discount heavily these expectations as arising from undue optimism, this urban-rural relationship has very great implications for social and economic change in rural Ghana. It is unlikely that fewer than half the migrants will ultimately undertake such construction.

This spreads the cash economy to the villages and in turn sets up demands there for other products to be bought with the cash earned; it stimulates the production of building materials in the village and gives direct employment on house-building or indirect employment in the procurement and making of the building materials; and, because of the frequent equipment of the house with such superior facilities as a water reservoir or even electric light, it brings urban modes of living to the rural areas.

The reluctance to come back

One should not overstate the indestructability of the rural-urban link. There are in Ghana, as in the West, rural-urban migrants in the town who shudder at the mention of rural life and who have almost completely broken with it

Table 6:6 Responses to the questions, (a) [rural survey] 'Do any people go to the town and dislike coming back to the village even for visits?' [urban survey] 'Do some people who have come from villages to live in Accra (or Kumasi, Sekondi-Takoradi, or Cape Coast), dislike going back to their home villages even for visits?' (b) [if 'yes' for (a)] 'Why do you think this is so?'

Response	Rural survey Number	Rural survey Per cent[a]	Urban survey Number	Urban survey Per cent[a]
(a) 'Do any people go to the town and dislike coming back to the village even for visits?'				
Yes	969	65	344	69
No	533	35	156	31
No response	6	0	0	0
Total	1,508	100	500	100
(b) [if 'yes' for (a)] 'Why do you think this is so?'				
They prefer town life	462	48	170	49
There has been trouble in the village	197	20	91	27
They are ashamed of their failure in the town	176	18	86	25
They think themselves superior to villagers	62	6	48	14
They have no relatives or friends left in the village	72	8	25	7
Total: responses	969	100	420[b]	122[b]
respondents	969		344	

[a] In (a) percentages of 1,508 eligible rural survey households and 500 eligible urban survey households; in (b) percentages of 969 and 344 respondent households respectively responding 'yes' to (a).

[b] Adds to over 100 per cent of multiple responses.

and with their rural relatives. These people place much emphasis on being townsmen and on the joys of town life. In order to ascertain the reasons for their behaviour, a question was asked to identify them and a further one about their motives, as shown in Table 6:6.

Most households know of specific cases of persons who are reluctant to return to the village for even short visits. The only regional difference of significance is that fewer people of this type are known in Ashanti.

In Akuse, Eastern Region, a 52-year-old widower with nine children, some of whom had gone to Accra, explained, 'Some have no relatives left and others find life in the village dull'. On the Akwapim Ridge near Accra a rather specialised problem was discussed, although it may indeed be an example of a much wider range of problems: 'They are satisfied with the town life and feel they cannot live in the village any longer, as they may have bought things using electricity, which is not available in the village'. It is certainly true that the migrant in the town usually comes increasingly to feel the disadvantages that lack of electricity poses in the village, particularly the darkness at night.

While it is clear that the chief reason for not wishing to return to the village is preference for town over village life, a preference which is sometimes felt with almost neurotic intensity, there is a range of other reasons. One emphasised strongly when mentioned was that many migrants are avoiding specific trouble in the village. Sometimes these problems arise from family dissension. A 39-year-old migrant in Takoradi, who had given up returning to his native town of Apam, although it was only about eighty miles eastwards along the coast, explained the reluctance as 'in order to avoid family troubles and be self-supporting'. A husband and his four wives in a Brong-Ahafo village drew on their experience to explain, 'Perhaps they were troubled in the village and were leading a peaceful stay in the towns'. Sometimes the difficulties were a good deal more serious, especially in the traditional villages of the North where real physical danger was something which might well have to be faced by some returnees. The reply of a family in a small village of the Upper Region was typical of many: 'Yes, if they committed a crime in the village before going to the town'. It might be noted that such crimes are rarely known to the national police force, and often are not crimes by their definition. Sometimes, too, especially in the North, witchcraft is a factor. Near Chiana, Upper Region, a household replied, 'Yes, if they are bewitched'. Yet it is the accusation of practising witchcraft and the fear of retaliation that is most likely to inspire migration.

Whilst the failure to succeed drives many migrants back from the town to the village, it seems to others to make it more difficult for them to return. They have departed the village boasting of their coming success and good jobs, or their relatives have done it for them, and instead have met with unemployment or menial employment; far from raising the living standard of their relatives in the village, they have barely been able to support themselves. Many try to hold on in the town in the hope of finally achieving the desired success—a success which is thought of largely in terms of income but which also includes type of job and style of life.

Some town migrants think themselves superior to villagers, partly because they were self-elected to break from the village bonds, but largely because of the changes wrought by town life. Others may have lost their village links because of the death or migration of many of their relatives in the village. Many households, especially in high mortality areas, explained that older migrants in the town might feel little continuing connection with their area of origin, because, in the words of an Upper Region household, 'their direct relations might have died'. There may be real problems of ease of movement, and these might arise from urban or rural causes. In distant households in the north this response was typical of quite a number: 'They may be unemployed and not have the money to come back'. On the other hand, the returnee may feel real apprehension about his stay in the village; one such returnee from Accra, intending to go again to the town at some uncertain date, explained, 'They feel, when they visit the village, they may not be allowed to go again'.

Table 6:7 Responses to the questions, (a) [rural survey] 'Do some people come back from working in the town and not want to live in the town again?' [urban survey] 'Are there some people who come from the villages to live in Accra (or Kumasi, Sekondi-Takoradi, or Cape Coast), but, after some time, go back to their home villages and say they do not want to live in Accra (or Kumasi, Sekondi-Takoradi, or Cape Coast) again?' (b) [if 'yes' for (a)] 'Why do you think this is so?'

Response	Rural survey		Urban survey	
	Number	Per cent[a]	Number	Per cent[a]
(a) 'Do some people come back from working in the town and not want to live in the town again?'				
Yes	1,052	70	339	68
No	456	30	144	29
No response	0	0	17	3
Total	1,508	100	500	100
(b) [if 'yes' for (a)] 'Why do you think this is so?'				
They preferred village life	403	38	174	51
They did not succeed in the town	367	35	192	57
They had made enough money	182	17	53	16
An opportunity had offered itself in the village (e.g. inheritance of farm, availability of job)	77	7	40	12
They had no relatives or friends in the town	35	4	4	1
Total: responses	1,064[b]	101[b]	463[b]	137[b]
respondents	1,052		339	

[a] In (a) percentages of 1,508 eligible rural survey households and 500 eligible urban survey households; in (b) percentages of 1,052 and 339 households respectively responding 'yes' in (a).

[b] Adds to over 100 per cent because of multiple responses.

Regional differences in response were not great. Interestingly, northerners, who come from rural areas which are in most marked contrast to the towns of the south, are least likely to feel superior to the village people, and are least likely to be suspected by the villagers of harbouring such sentiments. They are the least likely to prefer town life for its own sake, but the most to fear trouble on their return to the village or to lack surviving close relatives to whom to return. As might be expected, the Ashanti, with their smaller propensity to migrate, are the migrants who most rarely lack close relatives in the village.

The reluctance to stay in the town

While some rural-urban migrants are reluctant to forsake the town for even brief visits to the village, there are others who flee the town for the security of their native areas. The questions set out in Table 6:7 were framed to investigate this.

The migrant who has once been bitten by town life and is now twice shy, is also a well-known figure. This is particularly the case in the North, where only one-tenth of respondent households could not recall a specific example well known to them (significant difference between the North and other major migration regions). The differences between urban and rural response patterns were explicable almost entirely in terms of greater volubility in the towns, although, when account is taken of this, it might be noted that there is a slightly greater tendency in the village to offer explanations in terms of having achieved a financial sufficiency or being repelled by anomie.

The questions of preference for town life and the financial success or failure of the migration are often intimately connected. For the northerner the question of preference may lie between harsh alternatives; an Upper Region household pointed out, 'They might have suffered more in the town'. In the south things may be less grim; a migrant from Mpraeso, Eastern Region, in Tema but on the point of returning, explained of the hypothetical returnee, 'He didn't find life as pleasant as he thought it would be'.

Financial success and failure were often contrasted in the discussions. In Fete, Central Region, a fishing village offering no new opportunities and located only twenty miles in a straight line from Accra (although further by road), it was said, 'Some fail to get jobs; others come back with enough money to open their own business'. Almost identical sentiments were echoed from Bawku in the far northeast: 'Some acquire money sufficient enough to enable them to settle comfortably in their village, but others are completely disappointed in the town and ultimately decide that they were better off in their village'. Some migrants, such as pensioners, have achieved, from past urban employment, a fixed income which will go further in their home village than in the city; in Mampong, Eastern Region, an area with long-established schools from which many migrants have gone to responsible positions in Accra, it was said of the returnees to the area, 'Some are pensioners and others have lost their jobs'.

Although a good deal of emphasis is placed, especially by the educated, on the joys of town life compared with the dullness of the village, the majority of explanations are in economic terms. It is interesting to note how many respondent households assume that the coming into being of economic opportunity in the village will attract many migrants back, even if, according to a considerable number of the replies, equal opportunity exists in the town.

The only significant differences in regional patterns of response were those between the North and the other three major migration regions. Northerners place much more emphasis on preference for village life, over half responding in this way, in spite of the fact that village life in the North is much harder in terms of deprivation of goods and facilities than it is anywhere further south. Northerners also place a good deal of stress on having secured enough money to return; admittedly a modest sum is often sufficient to make them considerably better off than their neighbours and may allow the payment of bridewealth or the purchase of cattle for this purpose. On the other hand few northerners hide in the town because of financial failure; this is a characteristic of migrants from more economically developed areas.

Rural dependence on town money

In economic terms the most important aspect of rural-urban migration is the counter-flow of remitted money and of goods which characterises the migration stream. Such flows of wealth are undoubtedly important, not only to the villagers but also to the migrants. Evidence of this has been pro-

Table 6:8 Responses to the questions, [rural survey] 'Does this household receive any money from people working in the town?' [urban survey] (a) 'Do you send any money back to your village?' (b) 'Did you send any money back to your village when you first came to Accra (or Kumasi, Sekondi-Takoradi, or Cape Coast)?'

Response	Rural survey			Urban survey Question (a)			Urban survey Question (b)		
	Number	Per cent All respondents	Per cent Eligible respondents	Number	Per cent All respondents	Per cent Eligible respondents[a]	Number	Per cent All respondents	Per cent Eligible respondents
Yes	596	33	40	317	54	63	234	40	47
No	1,067	60	—	52	9	—	215	37	—
No response	119	7	—	216	37	—	136	23	—
Total	1,782	100	—	585	100	—	585	100	—

[a] 1,508 rural survey households with some migrant member in the town and 500 urban survey households containing at least one rural-urban migrant.

vided by the very real distress felt by international migrants in West Africa, as the new national states have made it more difficult to remit earnings out of the country (Caldwell 1967a: 119). More wealth than money flows from the town to the village, for returning migrants bring presents and also goods of their own. But money flows are easier to measure, and hence the questions analysed in this section will confine attention to them.

The sending of money. As shown in Table 6:8, rural households were asked whether they received money from the town and urban households were questioned on whether they were sending or had sent such money.

At least one-third of rural households claim to receive money as such from the town, as do at least two-fifths of those from which someone has migrated to the town, even if that migrant has long since established his own town-based family and household. When all rural households are analysed, it is revealed that rural Ashanti is less dependent on urban remittances than any of the other three major migration regions. This is, of course, a reflection of the fact that rural Ashanti produces fewer rural-urban migrants, but this in turn probably indicates that the rural economy has less need of urban remittances. When the analysis is confined to rural households which have sent forth rural-urban migrants, it is found that two-thirds of northern households of this type do receive money from the town, compared with around two-fifths in the South and Volta and just over one-third in Ashanti. There is undoubtedly far greater pressure on the northern migrant to send money, not merely because the North is poor, but also because many northern households have no other way of earning cash. Without it such imports as kerosene or sardines cannot be bought and lorry fares cannot be paid. Conversely the low figure for Ashanti is not an indication of weak family sentiment, for the Ashanti family is still remarkably strong; it is the product of lesser need and weaker pressure on migrants.

There is no inescapable incompatibility between the rural and urban figures. Over half of all urban households and nearly two-thirds of those containing migrants do claim to send some money to rural areas, compared with the figure of two-fifths for rural households with migrants in the town claiming to receive such money. Almost certainly some urban respondents somewhat guiltily exaggerated the help they gave; they probably counted very infrequent gifts or money long since sent as money provided for the village, while rural households were undoubtedly more reluctant to consider this as receiving money from the town. But the major explanation seems to be that urban households often contain more than one migrant, frequently husband and wife, but do not remit money to each rural household from which they come. Thus the money might go to the husband's family in the knowledge that the wife's brother was making adequate payments to the wife's family.

Table 6:8 also confirms the pattern described in the last chapter. Migrants are least likely to remit money during the initial settling-in period, when they are still unemployed or perhaps working for very low wages. In fact they are more likely to be sending money to the village years after their arrival than they are immediately afterwards.

These money flows are a very significant aspect of the country's economy and society. Probably one-third of all rural households are recipients and the fraction is almost certainly growing quite rapidly. It is not so easy to calculate the urban outflow, because the urban survey selected a high proportion of immigrant suburbs. However, the 1960 census showed that the proportions of the populations of Accra, Sekondi-Takoradi, Kumasi, and Cape Coast Municipalities who were born elsewhere were 42, 55, 62, and 31 per cent respectively, and of their aggregate 53 per cent. Such figures should be treated carefully because some of the population born elsewhere may have come from somewhere in the vicinity; on the other hand this is outweighed by the fact that children predominate amongst the locally born. Possibly three-fifths of the adult population of the four towns are rural-urban migrants and in probably over two-thirds of the households at least one spouse is a migrant. If around 63 per cent of these households, the level suggested by Table 6:8, pay out some money to rural families, then about four-ninths of all urban households are doing so. This is a financial movement of considerable magnitude.

The frequency of remittances. Rural and urban respondent households were cross-questioned about the frequency with which money was sent to families back in the villages, the responses being classified as accurately as the data allowed in Table 6:9.

Table 6:9 Responses to the question, 'How often is the money sent?' [rural survey 'yes' responses in Table 6:8; urban survey 'yes' responses in Table 6:8, part (a)]

Response[a]	Rural survey		Urban survey	
	Number	Per cent[b]	Number	Per cent[b]
Once or more a month (or 'very often')	273	46	168	53
4-11 times a year (or 'often')	54	9	37	12
1-3 times a year (or 'occasionally')	167	28	21	7
Less than once a year (or 'rarely')	32	5	17	5
'When needed' or 'when asked for'	13	2	16	5
'When there was some money to spare'	16	3	39	12
No response	41	7	19	6
Total	596	100	317	100

[a] Such responses as 'very often', 'often', etc. have been equated with numerical responses in accordance with the most commonly observed relationship in those schedules where both kinds of response were recorded.

[b] Percentage of 'yes' responses in Table 6:8 rural survey and question (a) of urban survey.

There is a good deal of correspondence between the two surveys. The major discrepancy is more apparent than real. The first four responses attempt to estimate the frequency of remittances, while the next two do more to explain the mechanics of the money movement. Needless to say the migrant in the town knows that money is sent 'when there is some to spare'; the recipient knows only that it comes 'occasionally' and hence this is his response.

The table bears adequate witness to how frequently money flows from town to village; more frequently, for instance, than Table 6:1 shows returning migrants do. In half of all cases money is paid at least monthly. In these cases it is usually passed on from each wage payment. Such remittances are probably received by one-sixth of all rural households, and are probably made by one-third of all urban households which contain any migrants.

The frequency of remittance varies inversely with distance (statistically significant). Where the village is no great distance from the town, the migrant may often take money back or a relative may visit him to collect it, and there is much more likely to be a lorry which visits both places so that a single driver can be trusted to pass on the money. Thus in the two major migration regions where towns are found, the South and Ashanti, almost two-thirds and over half respectively of the remittances are received by rural households at least monthly, but the fraction drops to less than one-third in Volta and to one-sixth in the North. In the latter areas money is most often received once to three times a year, very often on the annual revisit to the village of the migrant. This is especially the case in the North, for three reasons. First, a greater proportion of migrants are illiterate and find it impossible to avail themselves of postal or banking facilities; second, the visits of relatives are very infrequent; third, lorry runs usually terminate at Kumasi, where new runs begin for the North, so migrants further south cannot entrust money to a single driver.

The initiation of remittance. Responses tending to show why money was sent were recorded in preliminary trials, and prompted the inclusion of a supplementary question in the main survey asking urban respondent households directly, 'Do you send the money regularly, or when you have some to spare, or when your family in the village say that they need it?' Of those households which did remit money, 56 per cent replied 'regularly', 27 per cent 'when there is some to spare', and 17 per cent 'when needed or asked for'.

There was a very high correspondence, almost an identity, between those households which send money at least monthly and those which send it regularly. Where there is a regular arrangement, it usually takes the form of sending a certain amount of money from each pay packet. In the remainder of the cases there is usually some kind of understanding that money will be sent from time to time. In about three-fifths of these cases it is the migrant who takes the initiative, although he might frequently have been reminded of the general need in the village household; in the remaining two-fifths the village household asks for it. Thus money flows fairly freely without a great deal of begging for it; of all village households which receive money probably only about one-sixth have to ask for it specifically each time.

This pattern was confirmed by the rural survey, there being complete agreement on the one point where both urban and rural are in the position to know all the facts—about one-sixth of the money is sent as a result of specific appeals from the village. Of the remainder most is sent regularly. There are significant regional differentials. The two traditional emigrant areas, the North and Volta, are most likely to have the kind of household crisis which can be solved only by money being sent from the distant town. Migrants from the North are much less likely than are those from any other region to make arrangements for regular remittances; there is usually an understanding that money will be sent when it can be spared.

The volume of remittances. Rural and urban households were questioned on the approximate size of each remittance, as set out in Table 6:10.

Table 6:10 Responses to the question, [rural survey 'yes' responses in Table 6:8; urban survey 'yes' responses in Table 6:8, part (a)] 'About how much money is sent each time?'

Response	Rural survey	Per cent		Urban survey	Per cent	
	Number	Respondents[a]	Responses	Number	Respondents[a]	Responses
Less than 10s	22	4	5	5	2	2
10s-19s 11d	65	11	14	26	8	10
£1-£1 19s 11d	82	14	18	71	22	27
£2-£9 19s 11d	259	43	56	140	44	54
£10 or more	35	6	7	18	6	7
No response	133	22	—	57	18	—
Total	596	100	100	317	100	100

[a] Percentages of 596 eligible rural survey respondent households and 317 eligible urban survey households.

The findings are essentially compatible, although there is probably some reluctance amongst urban respondents who send very small amounts to state the fact. On the other hand most of the 'no responses' are not a sign of reluctance, for the great majority of the respondents in this category send irregular amounts, many of them sending money on request—often the amount said to be needed.

The overall picture is fairly clear. If we exclude the payments of irregular amounts, over half the remittances are £2 or over, but less than £10. Very many are in fact two, three, four, or five pounds in notes. But close to two-fifths of all remittances are of smaller sums still, and these amounts often go a surprisingly long way in the village. The large amounts,

£10 or more, are almost entirely annual remittances, usually taken home personally by the migrant.

The only significant regional differential is that between the North and the other major migration regions. Because of distance and infrequent remittance over three-quarters of all sums of money received in the North are between £2 and £10; in the three other regions two-fifths or more are smaller than £2. On the other hand the North does not figure any more conspicuously in the really large remittances, £10 or more, because these are usually sent by 'white collar' workers, amongst whom are numbered very few northerners indeed. In the North a typical emigrant household is one where a male returns once a year from Kumasi, stays a week and enriches the household by some goods and perhaps £5 or £6 in money.

The method of remittance. Respondents were then asked, as shown in Table 6:11, how the money was sent.

Table 6:11 Responses to the question, [rural survey 'yes' responses in Table 6:8; urban survey 'yes' responses in Table 6:8, part (a)] 'How is the money sent?'

Response	Rural survey		Urban survey	
	Number	Per cent	Number	Per cent
Through the post office	356	60	140	44
With relatives or friends	159	27	89	28
Taken personally	83	14	57	18
By lorry drivers	57	10	55	17
Through a bank	4	1	12	4
Total: responses	659[a]	112[a]	353[a]	111[a]
respondent households	596		317	

[a] Adds to over 100 per cent because of multiple responses.

Some of the discrepancies in Table 6:11, especially in the use of the post office and lorries, seem to arise from the different incidence of the second method suggested in multiple responses. However, the major patterns are certainly comparable.

The most important single method of remittance is the post office, although it may not be more so than all personal methods, relative, friend, self, and lorry driver, combined. The use of the post office does not mean that pound notes are mailed from one address to another. It means that migrants go to the town post offices to send money, often in the form of money orders. Their money orders or their letters then go to the nearest rural post office to their place of origin and in due course their relatives come to hear that it has arrived. The latter may expect it, of course, because of some regular arrangement or because they have just appealed for assistance. Even if this is not the case, they soon learn of the arrival of money, for the post office staff tell people who might pass the message on and they tell others. Money is important and there is often great earnestness in seeing that those for whom the remittances are destined are contacted, especially if the money is meant for a specific purpose or is due before a specific date, as in the case of school fees for the approaching term. Although banks are prepared to remit money in a similar way they are much less commonly employed, partly because they are much more infrequent in rural Ghana.

Money is frequently sent back to the village with relatives returning from short visits to the town; often, indeed, such visits are made in order to point out a family crisis and to ask for assistance. Sometimes it is a fellow villager who performs this role. Frequently, too, it is the mammy lorry drivers who take money. They regard it as part of their job and are completely trustworthy. Respondents were often quite surprised when we queried the matter, and pointed out that a driver could hardly continue his run if there was any suspicion that he could not be completely trusted with the passing on of money.

There are significant differences between the major migration regions. Money is most frequently carried personally or by friends or fellow villagers to the North and least in the South. The post office is used to all areas but most frequently to villages in the South and Volta, as is also the case with the use of lorry drivers. There is, of course, a scarcity of lorries plying to the furthest parts of the North and even Ashanti (i.e. the outlying parts of Brong-Ahafo).

The changing pattern of remittance. In order to probe further the changing pattern of remittance with length of residence in the town, urban households containing migrants were asked a series of six questions comparing the period immediately after their arrival with the time of the survey.

Only 40 per cent of the migrants sent money back to the village during the first hectic period of finding a job and often of working on lower wages than was subsequently the case. Later the number feeling themselves securely enough settled to send money rose to a plateau from which it slowly descended over the years. The reasons for this slow decline were many; in some cases it could be attributed to the final transfer of all wives and children to the town, in others to the death of parents remaining in the village, in a few cases to the growing to adulthood of various nephews and nieces for whom help towards their education had been sought, and in others to a gradual weakening of all emotional ties with the village. This decline should not be overstated; in terms of the amount of money sent it applies to only a minority of migrants. Two-thirds of all migrants in the town claimed that at the time of the survey they were sending to the village as much money as they had ever done, or even more. It is of course true that inflation, which probably amounted in Accra to about 25-30 per cent over the four years preceding the survey (Omaboe 1966: 414), may have meant that the real value of some of the remittances fell. But in other cases, rising salaries meant that more, even in real terms, was sent. There is little doubt that social and economic change in the countryside, and an enormous expansion in educational opportunities, meant that rural households felt a much stronger need of money than they had previously.

Those respondents who specifically stated that they had once sent money back to the village but had discontinued doing so (only one-sixth of all migrants in the town) were questioned about the length of time they had kept sending remittances. About one-third said a year or less; these were mostly migrants who arrived married and spent a period transferring members of their own nuclear families to the town. Almost two-thirds of the remainder gave periods of less than five years, but this was more than anything a measure of the recency of most migration with its acceleration during the last few years. Some replied in terms of the cessation of some specific obligation or need, and this would appear to be the case also for most of the others.

To whom specifically has all this money been sent? Of those migrants who have sent remittances while working in the town, 77 per cent have sent money to one or both parents. This, we have found from other surveys (Caldwell 1965: 190-3), is the most critical of all obligations, even when the parents could not be regarded as having reached a kind of retiring age. Money had been sent to relatives other than parents, wives, and children by 22 per cent, most of it going to siblings, nephews or nieces, most often to help with education, or to uncles or even aunts. In 12 per cent of cases it had gone to wives and in 11 per cent to children, sometimes prior to their transfer to the town and sometimes as an almost permanent arrangement. Some migrants have, of course, more than a single obligation and hence the percentages just quoted add to over 100.

The employment of remittances. The respondent households in both surveys were asked to explain the use to which these remittances were put. A careful distinction was kept, usually successfully, between the migrants'

Table 6:12 Responses to the question, [rural survey 'yes' responses in Table 6:8; urban survey 'yes' responses in Table 6:8, part (a)] 'What is the money, which is sent to persons in the village, used for?'

Response	Rural survey Number	Rural survey Per cent	Urban survey Number	Urban survey Per cent
Maintaining the village household, gifts to individual members, etc.	438	73	221	70
Education of children (other than migrants' own)	56	9	52	16
Funerals, weddings, festivals	15	3	9	3
Helping with building, securing a farm, trading	80	13	37	12
General village welfare	37	6	0	0
Total: responses	626[a]	104[a]	319[a]	101[a]
respondents	596		317	

[a] Adds to more than 100 per cent because of multiple responses.

own savings, which they might well employ in the village to build a house, meet the cost of bridewealth, or any of the other purposes listed in Table 5:2, and money sent specifically to their households of origin or other relatives or persons in the village. Table 6:12 suggests that this aim was largely achieved.

The major use of all remittances is merely to help maintain the migrants' household of origin in the village. This is particularly the case with regard to the migrants' parents. The migrant often helps with specific projects such as helping the family build a house or secure a farm; or he might assist his mother or sister get together some capital to buy stock for a small trading business—she might even become a kind of wholesaler (there are many levels of wholesaling, especially in the marketing of cloth) if he can supply enough money. A constant source of appeal, and one of which the migrant can appreciate the wisdom, is assistance to allow brothers or sisters or nephews or nieces to stay at school to acquire more knowledge and improve their earning power, especially for town jobs.

Three points about Table 6:12 should be noted. First, there was, for accidental reasons, a slight difference in the instructions to rural and urban survey workers, the main effect of which was to leave a residual 'general village welfare' response in the former, a category which is merely scattered throughout the other responses in the latter. Second, the categories are not mutually exclusive. The 'maintenance of the village household' category undoubtedly contains some money meant primarily for educating related children, and the apparent discrepancy on the latter matter between the rural and urban surveys is probably to be explained in this way; it may also contain, as may the 'general village welfare' category of the rural survey, some money ultimately spent on village ceremonies. Thus, such ceremonies may absorb more money than appears from the table, but still much less than many of the town-born claim—most of the money that flows to the villages is undoubtedly spent on mundane necessities. Third, expenditure on the education of the migrants' own children was taken to be part of normal consumption expenditure, and was excluded from this examination of remittance.

Once again the only significant differences between the major migration regions were those between the North and the three more southern areas. In the former only 2 per cent of the remitted money is earmarked specifically for education, compared with 10-12 per cent in the latter, but this is probably largely both a reflection of differentials in the attitudes towards education of the societies in general and a commentary on the relative lack of school places in the North. Conversely, far more of the money (18 per cent of responses) going to the North is intended for helping to establish a farm, or set a woman up in trading, than of that going elsewhere. In this sense migration and subsequent remittance is more a force for economic development in the North. However, this may merely reflect level of development; its equivalent further south may be the money invested in furthering schooling.

The balance of rural-urban earnings in the village

Interviewers attempted to help village households to calculate the origin of the various incoming cash flows to determine, as set out in Table 6:13, whether the gross flow from the town exceeded that derived from rural areas.

Table 6:13 Responses to the question, [rural survey 'yes' responses in Table 6:8] Does this household receive more money from the town than from the villages?'

Response	Number	Per cent: Respondent households[a]	Per cent: All rural survey households[b]
Yes	143	24	8
No	453	76	25
Ineligible (no money received from the town)	—	—	67
Total	596	100	100

[a] Percentages of 596 eligible rural survey households.
[b] Percentages of all (1,782) rural survey households.

It appears that about one-twelfth of rural households actually receive a majority of cash income from the town; thus, in about one-quarter of the cases where town income is received it exceeds money income from local and other rural origins. These figures obscure the important differences by major migration region; in the South, Volta, and Ashanti from 6 per cent to 8 per cent of all households derive the majority of their money income from the town, the regional differences between the three not being significant, while in the North over 14 per cent do. These differences are partly a reflection of the scantiness of other cash income sources in the largely subsistent North. For instance, of those households that do receive some money from the town, this forms the majority of cash income in only one-sixth of the households in the three more southern regions, compared with almost one-third in the North.

An attempt was made to calculate the actual cash inflow into the rural households. Of the 596 households which claimed some inflow, 553 (93 per cent) were able to provide estimates of the average frequency of remittances and the average size of each remittance, which appeared to be sufficiently definite to warrant further calculation. These households received on average from the town about £50 per year, a sum which formed approximately one-sixth of all cash income. This fraction was higher in the North. The sum calculated may be too low, as there appeared at times to be confusion in the answers between all remittances received and extra remittances sent in answer to appeals for help—some of the latter have almost certainly been excluded. Nor does the calculation include goods sent from the town, which is often the best place to buy them, or other goods, or sometimes possibly even money, distributed by migrants on temporary or permanent return.

Many of the comments recorded from the interviews help to explain the need for and the operation of the remittance system. In the South school fees, especially for brothers and sisters, were frequently mentioned. A Volta Region household explained that the money was needed 'for buying food, meat and other small needs of the home'; the question of meat arose quite frequently for it is a foodstuff that subsistence crop-farming does not produce. A typical list of the most urgent cash outlays in the North came

Table 6:14 Responses to the questions, (a) [rural survey] 'Do people coming back on visits to the village from the town bring presents?' [urban survey] 'When you go back to your village, do you take back presents?' (b) [if 'yes' for (a)] 'What are the common types?' (c) [rural survey] 'Do they bring money?' [urban survey] 'Do you take money?'

Response	Rural survey			Urban survey		
	Number	Per cent Respondents[a]	Per cent Responses[b]	Number	Per cent Respondents[a]	Per cent Responses[b]
(a) 'Do people coming back on visits to the village from the town bring presents?'						
Yes	1,461	82	94	327	56	88
No	90	5	6	45	8	12
No response (usually 'not relevant')	231	13	—	213	36	—
Total	1,782	100	100	585	100	100
(b) [if 'yes' for (a)] 'What are the common types?'						
Cloth or clothing	847	58		203	62	
Food	691	47		173	53	
Other non-durables (e.g. soap, seeds for the farm etc.)	151	10		95	29	
Durables (e.g. radios, bicycles, farm implements etc.)	70	5		22	7	
Total: responses	1,759[c]	120[c]		493[c]	151[c]	
respondents	1,461			327		
(c) [rural survey] 'Do they bring money?' [urban survey] 'Do you take money?'						
Yes	1,085	61	83	257	44	78
No	223	12	17	74	13	22
No response (usually 'not relevant')	474	27	—	254	43	—
Total	1,782	100	100	585	100	100

[a] Percentages of total (1,782) rural survey households and total (585) urban survey households.

[b] Percentages of households responding in (a) and (c).

[c] Adds to over 100 per cent because of multiple responses.

from Wa; the household needs money for 'salt, kola and marriages'. Kola nuts, it might be noted, are imported from the southern forests, and, especially in Moslem areas where alcohol is forbidden, are chewed as a mild stimulant. Another northern family pointed out that, when money was available, it was usually sent to them by post, but 'if the sum is large, somebody is invited from the village to come'.

Bringing goods and money to the village

However, a good deal of the wealth that flows from town to village does not do so in the form of money; a great deal is brought back in the form of goods by permanently or temporarily returning migrants. The questions set out in Table 6:14 were constructed to examine the nature of this flow.

In part (a) of Table 6:14 the apparent discrepancy between rural and urban responses arises from the different forms of the question asked, that in the rural survey being more general, although most households did in fact answer it with reference to their own position. Perhaps nine out of ten migrants do return with presents. Those who do not tend to be either short-distance migrants who frequently zig-zag between village and town, or young migrants from relatively prosperous rural households, such as those found in cocoa-farming areas, who regard themselves as the poorer members of the family. This is brought out clearly by a comparison of the major migration regions. In the three southern regions one rural household in fifteen claims that the migrants do not return with presents, indeed in Ashanti the fraction reaches one in eleven, but in the North this was the case in only one household in almost forty.

The most common kind of goods to receive from the town are cloth and clothing, especially the former. This is so because, apart from the making of some rough cloth in the north, there is no manufacture of textiles in Ghana. Hence cloth is imported and then distributed through the major towns where it can usually be obtained more cheaply and always in greater variety than elsewhere. Since in the tropical climate of the country most clothing is made of cotton cloth, often not extensively made up, there is a relatively great demand for the material. In addition migrants often bring back a length or roll of cloth so that their female relatives may trade with lengths of it. Another item of clothing which frequently comes with the migrants is shoes or sandals, often the kind of sandals made out of old lorry tyres. The food brought back, especially over short distances, is often of the type not grown in the village and attracted to the larger market of the town in a way that it is not attracted to the smaller and more infrequent market of the village. Non-durables frequently include soap and seeds, and less frequently salt, kerosene, and sardines, which now seem to reach most village markets or shops. On the other hand the more precious durables, such as the transistor radio or bicycle, are usually bought in the town, finding their way back by lorry, and, in the case of the larger items, often occasioning some argument with the driver and his mate about transport costs.

Cloth is taken back to the village to a similar extent in all the major migration regions, and food to the greatest extent in the South and the least in the North, but this is little more than a measure of distance and hence of difficulty in undertaking the transport. However, it is above all the northerner who takes other goods back home, for his relatives live too far from the town to visit it and buy their own. He is at least five times more likely to arrive from the town bearing a transistor radio or bicycle, and much more likely to appear with a hoe or a bag of seeds.

In the South, a well-off family in Aburi, on the Akwapim Ridge near Accra, an area which has for long diverged from traditional rural society, explained that returnees brought them 'provisions, clothes and toys for the children'. However, a female trader in Cape Coast took back, on frequent visits to her husband and children in the village, staple foodstuffs that came into the urban market from more distant rural areas, 'plantain [the non-sweet banana from the forest further north], yams [tubers from further north still beyond the thick forest] and kenkey [made from ground maize]'. A household in the southern part of the Volta Region received from Accra 'clothing, tobacco for the aged, bread and biscuits'. In Odumase in Brong-Ahafo, returnees usually were encouraged to bring from Kumasi 'soap, clothes, tobacco, and bread'. An Upper Region household at Bawku, from which emigrants had earned quite good wages in Kumasi and Accra, had received 'clothes, footwear, bicycles, and money'.

The bringing home of money was also checked, although the practice had been discussed earlier in the interview when examining all forms of money flow from town to village. Perhaps four-fifths of migrants give away some money on their return home, but the proportion is lower than is the case with the disbursement of goods. There were no significant regional variations in the practice, and hence it should be noted that, whilst the northerner feels greater pressure than others to return home to distribute goods, this is not so in the case of money; he may, of course, take the reasonable attitude that the limited number of retail outlets in the North makes it better to do any necessary purchasing while still in the southern part of the country.

Urban respondents were questioned further about what was done in the village with the money they gave away on their return, but the pattern of response was almost identical with that shown in Table 6:12 for all remitted money. Perhaps a little more is spent in the case of distributed money on festivals or parties, as might be expected, for these are sometimes occasioned by the return of the migrants themselves. A 38-year-old male migrant in Takoradi, who does not average even annual visits to his home village not much more than 100 miles away in the Central Region, nevertheless said that when he did manage a trip, usually because of a funeral, he made presents of money, which 'is used to cover my obligations to relatives and clansmen and for death ceremonies'. A younger man in Kumasi, who manages to go back to the village more frequently, said his monetary presents were expected to cover 'drinks for father and money for family care'.

Living standards in emigrant households

How important to the individual households is this income increment from the town? It is clear that it does not merely provide luxuries; indeed the majority is spent on subsistence. The respondent households were questioned on the point as set out in Table 6:15.

Table 6:15 Responses to the question, [rural survey] 'Is a family very poor if none of its members work in the town?' [urban survey] 'Would your family in your home village be very poor if none of its members worked in a town?'

Response	Rural survey			Urban survey		
	Number	Per cent Respondents[a]	Per cent Responses[b]	Number	Per cent Respondents[a]	Per cent Responses[b]
Yes	516	29	31	155	27	32
No	1,161	65	69	312	53	68
No response (usually 'not relevant')	105	6	—	118	20	—
Total	1,782	100	100	585	100	100

[a] Percentages of total (1,782) rural survey households and total (585) urban survey households.

[b] Percentages of 1,677 and 467 responding rural and urban survey households respectively.

It should be noted that the question in Table 6:15 did not merely ask whether the town money helped; in effect it asked whether it was critical in terms of an accepted minimum standard of living by putting the emphasis on the words 'very poor'. In about one-third of the relevant cases it was agreed that this was indeed so. It may be that families that demand more from the world are more likely to encourage emigration or at least to produce an atmosphere of restlessness and dissatisfaction that does so. It is true, as seen in Chapter 3, that emigrant households are on the whole better off, but the relationship here is probably complex. Undoubtedly, emigration and the consequent flow of goods and money from the emigrants does raise living standards in the village household; but it is also probably true that wealthier households educate more of their children, and educate them further, so increasing the likelihood of emigration.

An analysis of replies by major migration regions produces some surprises. Rural Ashanti, especially the booming new cocoa areas, as might be expected, tend to be sceptical of the thesis, and the whole area recorded only 23 per cent of 'yes' replies amongst the responses. However, the traditional North, although relatively very poor, and although continuing to export emigrants to the South for income-producing work even at the cost of the wholesale separation of husbands and wives as well as fathers and children for long periods, is very reluctant to admit its dependence on the southern economy. Only 22 per cent of the responses were 'yes'. It is in the more developed area further south that there is real restlessness for higher incomes and an awareness of relative poverty. In the South, where income per head is much the same as in Ashanti (Szereszewski 1966: 93), economic opportunities have been increasing relatively slowly, and consequently 'yes' answers made up 36 per cent of all responses; while in Volta, poor, but with long contacts with the outside world and a traditional emigrant area, the 'yes' response was 49 per cent of the total. Felt poverty obviously depends not only on relative conditions but also on relative expectations.

In their further comments on the position in general of villagers most respondents qualified their observations. On the Akwapim Ridge to the north of Accra one household replied, 'Yes, if there are no jobs in the village', and another said rather similarly, 'It is not necessarily so if farms are available'. The same views were widespread; it all depended on access to land and the type of farming which could be undertaken. In the swampy parts of the southern Volta Region it was said, 'Not if they are farmers and fishermen'. Such attitudes were especially common in the new cocoa-farming areas. Thus in Dwinyama, Ashanti, a household observed, 'Not necessarily, not in all cases; most families can support themselves all right in the village'. But even here this view was far from universal. In Fiapire, Brong-Ahafo, it was said, 'Yes, they would be very poor, unless they have fairly large cocoa farms'. Such viewpoints can even be heard in the north; near Wa a household consisting of a 50-year-old man, his three wives, and his three surviving children observed, 'Yes, they will be very poor, unless the family has some livestock for sale'.

Various other special qualifications were put forward. In Accra's crowded immigrant squatter section, an old migrant from Zabrama, in the inaccessible and nearly deserted north of the Eastern Region, summed up the position on one of Ghana's frontiers of settlement, 'If in terms of money —yes; otherwise, no; there is plenty of food and meat'. Many respondents pointed out the seasonal nature of poverty. This occurred even in the south; in Tema a migrant from Agona Abodom, near Swedru in the Central Region, commented on his own area, 'Yes, they may become very poor; they get money from the cocoa farms but this is only seasonal'.

Sometimes the determinants were seen more in terms of fate or personal capacity. In Adutor, Volta Region, a 65-year-old widower, who had himself returned from a long period in Accra, believed it "all depends on God's Will; some [families] may be rich even if none of their members work in the town'. In the cocoa country of Brong-Ahafo, a young (30 years) polygynist, father already of seven children, a non-migrant, determined to remain one and not given even to visiting the town, maintained, 'No, because if one works hard, he can obtain money no matter where he stays'.

Summary

It is possible to gain some general idea of urban-rural links by extracting from the tables of responses the most frequently encountered replies, as has been done in Table 6:16.

Most rural households have sent at least one member to the town as a migrant, although the links between the migrant and the household have in many cases become weak because he or she has established an urban household or because the migrant's parents in the village have died. Even in the latter case the migrant is likely to continue to visit the village and even to bring gifts, but the visits will probably be less frequent and the probability of remitting regular money much less. Similarly, most urban households contain at least one migrant harbouring some feeling of obligation to the village.

The most obvious manifestation of these obligations is the periodic

Table 6:16 Summary of certain responses to questions on urban-rural links (percentages)[a]

Response	Rural survey	Urban survey
The migrant revisits the village at least once a year	78	69
The migrant's visit is no longer than a week in duration	54	62
The migrant is seen as more important and given more respect than those who did not migrate	78	75
The migrant hopes some day to practise his skill in the village	—	33
The migrant owns/is building/hopes to build a house in the village	—	80
The household receives money from migrants	33*	—
Money is remitted at least once a month	46	53
Remittances average £2-£9 19s 11d each	56	54
Some remittances are sent:		
through the post office	60	44
by a person (self, relative, friend, lorry driver)	51	63
The remittances are used chiefly for maintenance	73	70
The village household receives more money from urban remittances than from all rural sources	8*	—
The migrants bring back:		
presents	94	88
money	83	78
Village families would be 'very poor' without remittances	31	32

[a] Responses, except those asterisked, are given as percentages of 'eligible' households (i.e. in most cases the 1,508 rural survey households with one or more migrant members in the town and the 500 urban survey households containing one or more migrant members from rural areas); asterisked responses are percentages of all 1,782 rural survey households and 585 urban survey households.

visit to the home village, an undertaking which prevents town dwellers in Ghana from becoming too urban in their outlook and which keeps on the roads an extraordinarily large and ramifying lorry system. Most migrants make such trips at least annually but stay no longer than a week, there being inverse relations between journey distances and the frequency of visits and between the frequency of visits and the length of stays. During these visits the migrant may find compensation for those aspects of village life which are frequently beginning to irritate him in the high respect in which he is undoubtedly held. This respect stems not merely from the fact that he can provide money and goods, but is related also to his courage in migrating, his successful adjustment to town life, and the extra knowledge and polish he has acquired from urban living.

Many migrants retain even firmer contacts with the village. Some on their return visits can stay in houses they already own, which may indeed already contain their wives and children, others supervise work on houses which they are building, while most envisage the house they hope to build. Around one-third of the migrants hope, on their final retirement to the village, not only to live in their own house, but to practise, at least part-time, the trade they learnt in the town. Most of the rest either have acquired no very saleable skill or have been in employment for which there is no demand in the village.

In economic terms rural-urban migration is much more important to the countryside than is the same phenomenon in most of the developed world. Probably one-third of rural Ghanaian households receive some money from the town, and one-third of these households believe that they would be 'very poor' if they did not. Poverty is, of course, a relative and subjective concept; emigrant households are on the whole economically better off than non-migrant households but their economic aspirations are probably greater still.

The writer has attempted elsewhere to calculate the actual money flows occurring within the country as a result of rural-urban migration (Caldwell 1967a: 142-3). All the incoming money that could be recorded by the rural survey averaged only £15 17s 4d per year for each village household, but amounted to about £1 per week in the case of those households which were receiving money and which could provide what appeared to be reasonably satisfactory figures. It was calculated from these figures that in 1963 cash receipts in rural areas from the town were probably running at over £8 million or 1½ per cent of the national income. The true figure is certainly higher, for these calculations exclude the value of a good deal of the distributed goods and some of the spontaneous gifts of money or the amounts sent as a result of unexpected emergencies. In total value all wealth flowing from town to countryside, including the migrants' own savings and investments, may easily total £16 million per year. However, even the former figure represents much more of the country's cash income than 1½ per cent, for a good deal of the national income estimate consists of the imputed value of subsistence economic activities.

In urban areas those immigrant households which were remitting money to rural households and could provide reasonable statistics averaged about £43 per year each in such payments, or between one-twentieth and three-quarters of the stated incomes of the household heads. Probably those in greater doubt about the exact size of remittances paid considerably less. Nevertheless, the calculations referred to above showed that it is possible that about £5 million per year, or about one-tenth of the income earned in Accra, flows out of that city as remittances, savings, and goods, and that most of it finds its way to rural Ghana.

In some ways the most illuminating findings do not appear in the summary table at all, for they do not refer to aggregate results but to the different patterns observed in the rural survey between the major migration regions. The most distinctive divisions were those between the North and the rest of the country. These undoubtedly arise largely from the fact that the regions are being observed at different stages of development; powerful external influences have moved in from the coast to the interior in such a way that the former has been exposed to some influences for generations longer and even now much more intensively. Such contrasts explain the major north-south regional differences to a much greater extent than do age-old ethnic and related cultural differences, some of which certainly exist. Most of the features noted in the pattern of migration from the North undoubtedly characterised migration in the past from other areas. Social and economic conditions persist in the North which have largely passed further south. Thus, only in the North do most people still live hundreds of miles from the nearest town with more than 50,000 inhabitants; only there does cash agriculture still not form a significant part of the agricultural economy; only there does the number of persons over 6 years of age with schooling fall to 6 per cent and the number of 6-9-year-olds currently at school to 12 per cent compared with 29 per cent and 40 per cent respectively in the next lowest major migration region, Ashanti (data from 1960 census); only there does income per head, both cash and imputed, sink to £23, compared with double that amount in the next poorest region, Volta; only from there has the net migration of the native-born reached 157,000 compared with 95,000 in the nearest comparable region, Volta; only from there are there still 196 males per 100 females outside the region compared with 122 in the next nearest major migration region, Ashanti (Szereszewski 1966; calculations from 1960 census; Caldwell 1967a: 122-4).

It is these rather grim facts of life which explain why those from the North, and to a lesser extent those from Volta, less frequently return home, but why northerners stay longer when they do manage to do so. The need for emigration explains, too, why it is more widely assumed in the North, followed again by Volta, that the returning migrant will be regarded with above average respect. It helps explain why northerners more rarely send money back, but why, when they do, it is more likely to be a fairly large amount and why it is more likely to be taken personally or entrusted to some other person. It is also understandable that a greater proportion of northern migrants are apparently under pressure to send money back. The poor, subsistent nature of the region also leads us to understand why this money or these goods form a larger part of total income in the North and why it is more likely there to be used as a productive investment either in the acquisition of a farm or the setting-up of a woman in trading. On the other hand it is the more unchanged, traditional nature of northern society which makes it easier for families to understand why some migrants cannot adjust to town life, and, in all probability, why disproportionately more northerners cannot manage to do so.

Conversely, it is precisely those characteristics which have already developed furthest in the southern parts of the country which denote the way social and economic change are likely to go with regard to migration. Migrants are increasingly likely to migrate with their families or be joined by them shortly afterwards; they are likely to pay more frequent return visits but for shorter periods; on the other hand they are probably less likely to take presents, remit money, or even build a home in the village to which to return; when they do send money, the post office will probably be more frequently used.

Thus the rural-urban relationship will probably become more important socially and less urgent economically. Even if the income differential between town and countryside fails to close, the spread of cash-earning activities in the latter will almost certainly reduce the fraction that remittances from the town form of all household cash income and hence the degree of need for such remittances. However, some of these trends may not yet have begun; it is possible that in some respects, even economic ones, the high-water mark of rural dependence on the town still lies ahead. Almost certainly the total volume of money flowing is still climbing.

7
Living in the Town

Rural-urban migration is more than anything a search for money, and indirectly for the things that money can buy, and that can be more easily acquired in the town. Some migrants, however, are unduly optimistic about how much they can earn, and most underestimate the calls upon those earnings. Expenditure patterns in the town are usually very different from those in the village, and some traditional ways of life in rural areas are found to be ruinously expensive if persisted with in the new urban environment. Thus the town imposes new social and economic conditions upon the migrant, and may in time accustom him to these conditions and change his viewpoint in accordance. These matters were probed in the final sections of the interviewing schedule.

The acquisition of money in the town

Largely as a result of the mobility of the population, urban-rural communications in Ghana are good; Table 5:1 shows that for two-thirds of the migrants town life approximated their expectations and that for a considerable fraction of the balance it was better than they had hoped. Nevertheless, there are disappointments on the financial side. Some town wages quoted in the village are not the kind that unskilled migrants get, and wages that seem huge by the standards of village costs and needs dwindle when faced by the necessities and temptations of the town. The respondents were asked, as shown in Table 7:1, about their financial expectations and subsequent experience.

Thus, though the city may live up to and indeed exceed most expectations, it does not provide all the anticipated money. Nearly three-quarters of all migrants felt this way. The fundamental reason is that no amount of explanation in the village (and in any case few potential migrants receive much explanation on the point) can drive home the lesson that the city is an entirely acquisitive, cash society. It is hard for the villager to realise that there are places within his own country so different from the village, where there is no food just for the growing or even picking, and where often there is not even any cheap food; it is equally hard to realise that cheap housing usually cannot be built even for the labour, and that in such places

Table 7:1 Responses to the question [urban survey only], 'Have you had as much money and been able to buy as many things as you hoped when you first came here?'

Response	Number	Per cent[a] Respondents	Per cent[a] Responses
Yes	128	22	26
No	368	63	73
No response	4	1	1
Ineligible[a]	85	14	—
Total	585	100	100

[a]Non-migrants.

one often has no close relatives to join by moving in with them or by building rooms on to their houses. Thus the expected surplus money, which should have provided clothing, savings, and pleasure, is often less than was expected.

Sometimes the lack of money was recognised as being merely something less than perfection; a 32-year-old migrant from the Eastern Region, living with his wife and two young children in Accra's squatter quarter, Nima, observed, 'Yes, partly, but not as much as I would have liked'. Sometimes purchases were merely postponed; a 45-year-old artisan, living with his wife and five children in Takoradi, where he was employed on the docks, reported, 'I am now preparing to build a house which I had planned to build about four years ago'. Even for those who qualified their responses, most hopes had often been subsequently achieved; a young surveyor in Cape Coast, father of two children, pointed out, 'Yes, I have bought clothing, furniture, a wireless set, a record changer and a bicycle'.

Rural-urban contrasts

Worrying about money. Some of the leads in the question in Table 7:1 were pursued further. For, if the village is pitifully poor, but the more

Table 7:2 Responses to the question, 'Where do people worry most about not having enough money to care for themselves and their families—in the town (Accra, Kumasi, Sekondi-Takoradi, or Cape Coast) or in the village?'

Response	Rural survey			Urban survey		
	Number	Per cent Respondents	Per cent Responses	Number	Per cent Respondents	Per cent Responses
In the town	1,282	72	75	408	70	79
In the village	352	20	21	53	9	10
In both	65	3	4	56	10	11
No response (mostly ineligible[a])	83	5	—	68	11	—
Total	1,782	100	100	585	100	100

[a] I.e. in rural survey households with no knowledge of the town and in urban survey households with no knowledge of the village.

affluent town also imposes strong financial demands, where do people worry most about expenditure on necessities? The replies to this kind of query are shown in Table 7:2.

There is no question that most Ghanaians, even three-quarters of the villagers, see the town as the place of financial worries and of domestic financial crisis. Life in the village might be desperately poor, or even deprived, but its residents are rarely faced with demands they cannot meet. The exception, apart from the paying of taxes, a recent phenomenon, is the problem of schooling costs, which is now being felt in quite remote rural areas.* It is hardly surprising that, in Table 7:2, a somewhat greater proportion of town responses stress urban costs and a somewhat greater proportion of village responses stress rural costs. Nor it is unexpected that, in the town, where large numbers of rural-urban migrants were being interviewed, this group, who had left the village because of the shortage of available money and who were now struggling to make ends meet in the town, were often prone to emphasise the financial problems of both locations.

The difficulties of the town were widely cited. A seasonal migrant to the southern towns, interviewed while back in the Upper Region, had no doubt where one worried most—'in the town where everything has to be bought'. This was repeated even by those villagers who had never migrated or had much contact at all with urban life; a 50-year-old household head in Brong-Ahafo had no doubt that most worrying occurred 'in the town, because of the high cost of living'. There were exceptions; a 48-year-old man in Wa, Upper Region, who admittedly had never been to the town, maintained that the greatest worries were 'in the village—there are odd jobs to be done in the town for a living, but money is difficult to get in the village'. However, in the same location, a 64-year-old permanent returnee from Kumasi said his financial difficulties had been 'in the town—money is needed in the village only for taxes'. Some were beset with problems in either place; a 30-year-old miner in Aboso, who had already acquired two wives and eight children, understandably retorted, 'in both places there is a great need for money'. Similarly, a rural-urban migrant in Cape Coast, father of eight children, reported, 'You do not find any difference; you will get worried in both places depending on your earning capacity'. Finally there were a few who had a greater capacity for acceptance, like the Moslem migrant in Accra's Nima, who replied, I don't know because I don't worry; God will provide anywhere you are'.

There were statistically significant differences between all major migration regions except the South and Volta. Money worries are not felt to be greater in the town by the residents of the most affluent villages. Rather, this view is held where villages are most traditional and where their in-

* This problem and its potential effect on family size is discussed in Caldwell 1967b.

habitants are least likely to have become accustomed to the kind of strains met in the city. Thus, while in Table 7:3 only two-thirds of households in the South and Volta are seen to feel that money worries are greatest in the town, this is close to being a universal conviction in the much poorer northern villages. Northern rural-urban migrants to southern towns face enormous problems of adjustment, for they pass not merely from a poor society but from a largely subsistence one to a way of life where everything has a money value and decisions usually have to be weighed in terms of relative cash costs. It is this transition to a total cash society which is the fundamental cause of strain, even though migrants more frequently describe the problem as one of outrageously high urban costs.

Table 7:3 Responses to the question about where people most worry about money, by major migration region (rural survey only)

Region	Response (percentages of all responses)			
	In the town	In the village	In both	All responses
South	64	31	5	100
Volta	68	25	7	100
Ashanti	81	16	3	100
North	97	3	0	100

The burden of the large family. The money problems of the town are so much those of maintenance, especially high food and rent costs, that it would seem inevitable that they must vary with household composition. We had learnt in other investigations that children are least likely to earn their own keep in those parts of society where the greatest socio-economic change has taken place (Caldwell 1967b), and that in towns parents may be under very great pressure to keep children at school and to make asso-

Table 7:4 Responses to the question, 'Where do you think people can most easily afford to have a lot of children, in the town (Accra, Kumasi, Sekondi-Takoradi, or Cape Coast) or in the village?'

Response	Rural survey			Urban survey		
	Number	Per cent Respondents	Per cent Responses	Number	Per cent Respondents	Per cent Responses
In the town	207	12	13	38	7	7
In the village	1,362	76	84	392	67	76
No difference, or 'difficult in both'	53	3	3	89	15	17
No response (mostly ineligible[a])	160	9	—	66	11	—
Total	1,782	100	100	585	100	100

[a] I.e. households in rural survey with no knowledge of the town or of rearing children in the town and households in the urban survey with no knowledge of the village.

ciated expenditures (Caldwell 1968b). Accordingly, respondents were questioned, as set out in Table 7:4, about the relative pressures exerted by large families in urban and rural areas. There is little doubt that the conditions of town life do mean that large families are subjected to greater difficulties than they meet in the village. Of those respondents who expressed their answers solely in terms of one or the other, in the urban survey over ten times as many stated it was easier in the village than the number averring this about the town, while in the rural survey the preponderance was almost seven times as great. There are probably pressures in the whole country towards a reduction in family size (Caldwell 1967b), pressures which are certainly already quite considerable amongst the economically better-off group in the town (Caldwell 1968b). There was by 1960 a rural-urban fertility differential, fertility apparently being about one-tenth lower in the towns than elsewhere, as well as a socio-economic differential within the towns (Caldwell 1967c; 1968b).

Most respondent households, arguing that it was more difficult to afford large families in the town, saw little point in explaining the obvious—more food and housing was required, both of which increased in cost with rise in amount needed. In addition children earned little, largely because there were personal and social pressures to keep them at school and a shortage of suitable employment.

It was those who felt some qualifications had to be made who spelt out the position. Much depends on what kind of income can be earned in the town. A widow in Akuse, fifty miles to the northeast of Accra, said that it was cheaper 'in the village; though, in the town, if you get a good job, you might find it easier'. A 67-year-old, once a migrant to Kumasi, but long since returned to Abesem in Brong-Ahafo to settle down with two wives and, according to his somewhat vague reckoning, twenty-four children, believed, nevertheless, that the ability to rear a large family in the town 'depends on the kinds of work the parents will have there'. In the Eastern Region an aspiring migrant and his wife and two children believed, while planning to move to Accra, that the answer was, 'In the town, where income is more regular'. Often town facilities were stressed, particularly schools and hospitals. A permanent returnee from Accra, living with his wife and four children in Kpandu, Volta Region, thought over his experience and concluded, 'I can't answer this neatly, for, although as regards food, this is easier in the village, yet, thinking about medical facilities, things are obviously better in the town'. A restless household head near Bolgatanga in the Upper Region weighed the whole matter and decided, 'perhaps in the town because of the better medical care'. Some respondents mused on the paradox that, although children are more expensive to raise in the town, urban families are often sent their rural relatives' children because of the greater provision of schools in the towns. Finally, some northern households, almost always non-migrant ones, replied complacently, as in this response from Salaga, 'Every place is suitable for getting many children, if by the grace of God they come'.

Once again, as shown in Table 7:6, there were significant differences in the pattern of responses from the major migration regions except between South and Volta. In these two areas about one-sixth of respondent rural households believed that the large family could be more easily reared in the town, but the fraction fell to one-tenth in Ashanti and one-sixteenth in the North. There is not much doubt that the large family is little strain in fully subsistence conditions, where the extra products needed can partly be produced by their own labour. But such conditions hardly exist in a pure form any longer anywhere in Ghana. Another investigation showed that even in the North a majority of persons feel that the large family suffers more economic strain than the small one (Caldwell 1967b: 224). The villagers do feel the need of some cash purchases and the arrival of schooling is radically altering traditional expenditure patterns. Nevertheless, the northern villages, and to a lesser extent the Ashanti villages, still have enough of their own resources, and few enough of the consumption temptations of the town, to make the rearing of children in them markedly cheaper than in the town. The villages of the South and Volta differ in several ways. First, they are found in the coastal areas with a longer period of development, more entrenched cash expenditure patterns, and with a greater density of shops of one kind or another. Second, more developed education facilities in the Eastern, southern Volta, and Central Regions mean that there is greater pressure to send and keep children at school, with all the direct and indirect attendant costs, as well as the total or partial withdrawal of the children from the labour force. Third, a longer history of education in these areas has meant that migrant adults tend to earn more in the towns than do Ashanti, and often very much more than northerners. Nevertheless, Table 7:6 leaves little doubt that it is only the exceptional migrant, even from these areas, who can so considerably increase his earnings in the town that he actually finds the burden of a large family lighter there.

The practicability of polygyny. The traditional family has not only usually been large, it has also frequently been polygynous. In fact polygyny often helped to explain its size. In the subsistence village the system often worked well enough, probably better than any alternative. Where land was available, the many hands of the wives and children did sufficient work to support themselves, and, where there were more than the usual number, probably sufficient to raise the economic condition of the patriarch to an above average level. In other ways his standard of living had also been raised; there were many relatives to give him attention and see to his wants, and their very number was evidence to all of his worldly success and brought him proportionate community honour. Furthermore, the form of polygyny which demanded that a deceased brother's widow be added to one's wives provided a badly needed form of social security in a community that had little place for an unmarried woman. Nor, on the whole, were wives hostile to the acquisition of extra spouses, for their work was lightened and they gained in relative seniority in the prestige scale from its high point with the first wife down to the most recent.

There seemed little reason for all this to change. Many missionaries campaigned against polygyny, but were accused fairly enough of preaching the values of the West rather than those of the Old Testament, and often succeeded in splitting their followers, so that the pro-polygyny faction was encouraged to form its own splinter sect. But the cash economy, the school-orientated society, and the town way of life have all introduced new conditions incompatible in many ways with polygynous marriage. It was on the last point that respondent households were questioned, with the response shown in Table 7:5.

The answers are more clear-cut with regard to the inhospitality of the town to polygynous marriage than even to the large family. Of those who replied unequivocally in terms of one or the other, the preponderance of answers for the village in contrast to the town was eight times in the rural survey and, in the urban survey, where presumably respondents had greater experience of town conditions, thirteen times.

Table 7:5 Responses to the question, 'Where can a man most easily afford to have more than one wife, in the town (Accra, Kumasi, Sekondi-Takoradi, or Cape Coast) or in the village?'

Response	Rural survey			Urban survey		
	Number	Per cent		Number	Per cent	
		Respondents	Responses		Respondents	Responses
In the town	177	10	11	33	6	6
In the village	1,432	80	86	420	72	81
No difference, or 'difficult in both'	56	3	3	67	11	13
No response (mostly ineligible[a])	117	7	—	65	11	—
Total	1,782	100	100	585	100	100

[a] I.e. households in the rural survey with no knowledge of the town or of polygynous marriages in the town and households in the urban survey with no knowledge of the village or of polygynous marriages in the village.

The polygynous family does in fact encounter many problems in the town, especially physical and economic problems. Accommodation costs can be ruinously expensive, especially if the wives have to be housed separately. The same is true of food. The fact that the wives were willing to enter polygynous marriage probably shows that they are not educated enough to earn the kind of wages paid in the town for professional or skilled work. The emotional problems may be greater. There is an increasing tendency in the town to regard polygyny as evidence of an ineradicable 'bush' background, and often as evidence of low educational levels. It is becoming very difficult, for instance, for a professional man to practise overtly traditional, formal polygyny. Furthermore, educated wives, and the families of educated wives, are becoming far less tolerant of the institution, and a middle- or upper-class townsman might well lose one wife by taking another (Caldwell 1968b: 56-8).

Most respondents spoke of the high cost of necessities in the town. A household in a village not far from Accra pointed out, 'You can get a lot in the town, but you can afford it better in the village', while a migrant in Accra, in a good job but hard pressed to support his wife and six children, replied, 'In my home village maintenance is easier'. Accommodation was frequently mentioned: a polygynously married woman in Akuse, Eastern Region, said it is cheaper 'in the village—in the town you have to grapple with the problem of accommodation'. The profitability of using a workforce of wives for farming in rural areas was often mentioned, but the views were held most strongly by the town-born. One Accra-born household living in the wealthy Ridge area explained that polygyny was cheaper 'in the village, where the wives help in working on the farm, and the more the number the larger the farm, [for] women get a lot from their farms'; and another similar family maintained, 'In the village some marry so that many can help in the farming'.

Such views were not universal. An aged polygynist in one of the Bolga villages in the Upper Region, who admittedly had not experimented with migration himself, nevertheless echoed the feelings of many who saw merely the possibility of women finding in the town a bigger market for their petty trading, when he said, 'In the town, because there the women can trade and so support themselves'. Some answered tangentially to the point at issue, by discussing where it was most likely that one could find a second or third wife. For instance, a 34-year-old household head in the Upper Region, as yet with one wife but planning to stay in the village and apparently aiming at polygynous marriage, replied, 'In the village, because it is easy to marry'. There is some point in his remark; in his local government area the 1960 census apparently recorded a sex ratio in the 15-44 age range of 59 males per 100 females, a ratio probably attributable to age misstatement as well as predominantly male emigration, while it recorded for the same age range a ratio of 131 males per 100 females in Kumasi, the destination of many of the migrants. It is the very shortage of women in the larger towns which has catalysed changing attitudes towards their roles, especially in the marriage situation. Women did not always feel this way; a widow who had not remarried, and who lived in an Eastern Region local government area, which, although rural, exhibited a sex ratio amongst 15-44-year-olds not far short of parity, complained, 'The question is pointless—you can get wives everywhere and look after them'. Sometimes it was pointed out that there are still traditional groups even in the large towns;

in Cape Coast a migrant from Keta, Volta Region, believed polygyny more economically practicable 'in the village, but sometimes among the fishermen in the large towns'.

Once again there were significant differences by major migration region, except between the South and Volta. The pattern was very similar to that found in responses to the question on large families, and so the two have been set out for comparison in Table 7:6.

Table 7:6 Responses to the questions about where it is cheaper (a) to rear a large number of children and (b) to support a polygynous marriage, by major migration region (rural survey only)

Response[a]	Region			
	South	Volta	Ashanti	North
(a) Rearing of children				
In the town	16	18	10	6
In the village	79	78	88	93
No difference	5	4	2	1
All responses	100	100	100	100
(b) Supporting polygynous marriage				
In the town	14	18	8	4
In the village	81	77	90	96
No difference	5	5	2	0
All responses	100	100	100	100

[a] Percentages of all responses.

It is clear that polygyny probably still occasions little economic strain, and probably little social strain as well, in the North, and this may well still be largely true in rural Ashanti. But further south socio-economic change is probably narrowing the urban-rural gap in the impracticability of polygyny as measured both in economic and social terms.

The success of rural-urban migration

Ultimately many of the questions asked in this study lead to the central one, whether the migration, decided upon as it usually was on imperfect knowledge, has been a success. As the reasons for migration are many, and there is usually an intermingling of economic and social motives, the assessment of this can usually only be provided from the migrant's own opinion. Accordingly respondents were questioned on this point, as shown in Table 7:7.

The urban survey responses are of particular interest in that they record the personal reactions of migrants. Of those migrants who have stayed on in the town, around five in every nine have found that urban conditions have lived up to their expectations. Thus, in spite of all that has been recorded here of unexpectedly high urban costs and of the pressures urban life exerts against a continuation of traditional family forms, the larger

Table 7:7 Responses to the question, [rural survey] 'Do people who go to live in the town generally find town life as satisfactory as they had hoped?' [urban survey] 'Has life in Accra (or Kumasi or Sekondi-Takoradi, or Cape Coast) been as good as you thought it would when you first came here?'

Response	Rural survey Number	Rural survey Per cent Respondents	Rural survey Per cent Responses	Urban survey Number	Urban survey Per cent Respondents	Urban survey Per cent Responses
Yes	669	38	43	281	48	57
No	898	50	57	216	37	43
No response (mostly ineligible[a])	215	12	—	88	15	—
Total	1,782	100	100	585	100	100

[a] I.e. households in the rural survey which have no close knowledge of migrants going to the town and households in the urban survey containing no migrants.

towns of Ghana are not made up mainly of the bitter or discontented.

Nevertheless, the rural survey answers do supply a necessary corrective. The migrant population living in urban areas is not an unbiased sample of rural-urban migrants. On the contrary, most of the more dissatisfied migrants have probably returned to the village. This does not mean that the returnees living in the village are all failed rural-urban migrants; many of them are, in fact, very successful migrants who have saved as much in the town as they desired and have returned to the village to live comfortably with the assistance of these savings. Nevertheless, one can hear in the village more about the disappointed migrations than is usually possible in the town.

It is instructive, therefore, to note that, even in the village, four out of every nine households having some contact with migration regard these movements as generally being successful. Weighing both surveys, and taking into account the biasing effect of disappointed migrants, under-represented in the town and over-represented in the village, it would be a reasonable estimate to say that about half of all rural-urban migrants find that the towns measure up to their expectations.

At Alakpeti, a moderately prosperous village in hilly country between Ho and Kpandu in the Volta Region, an area of cocoa and coffee farms, a cocoa buyer with an interest in figures estimated: 'As far as this area is concerned, it is only about 45 per cent [of all migrants to the town] that find town as satisfactory as they had hoped'. This observation is interesting, because many of the migrants are unusually well prepared for occupational success. For historical reasons, this area has the largest proportion of educated persons in rural Ghana; at the time of the 1960 census over half the population over 6 years of age had been to school and two-thirds of the 6-14-year-olds were currently there (Census 1960: Atlas, 19-20).

Those who had been disappointed were far more vocal than those who were satisfied. Many once again told tales of unexpected financial difficulties. A young husband with one child in Dwinyama, Ashanti, while planning migration, nevertheless mused over the fact that 'many regret; their work and their living expenses are usually more than they calculated'. An Ashanti in Accra's Nima replied, when asked whether he was as satisfied as he had expected, 'No, I thought it would be cheaper but that's not true'. Some had specific complaints; a migrant in Takoradi's Effiakuma felt that he could make the adjustments needed, but observed, 'I change according to the changes in the conditions of living; only the compulsory savings [additional to taxation] make life somewhat difficult'.

Some explained the differential effects of these difficulties, especially in terms of lack of preparedness for securing an urban job. A teacher in Accra who had come from the Volta Region said, 'Yes, generally', he was as content as expected, for 'those who have a good education and are employed are satisfied', but, he continued, 'illiterates often are disappointed with town life, especially when they are not employed'. That these adjustment strains can be very great, and can lead to various kinds of psychological reactions, was reported, particularly in the North; a Chiana Asunia, Upper Region, household said that satisfactions often fell far short of expectations, and, when the jolt was too great, 'sometimes they fall sick or are out of employment for a long time on arrival'. Rural parents are often apprehensive about what their migrant children might do in these circumstances: a household in Enyinase, Western Region, reported that there was often dissatisfaction, and that 'some find life so hard that they resort to robbery'. Even after a period of residence there may be regrets; a migrant settled in Nima, Accra, with his wife and four children, said he had made a mistake, for 'life in Accra is too fast these days'. Sometimes dissatisfaction because of unemployment spills over into general grievances about the towns. In Cape Coast a female migrant from the Western Region said she was discontented because 'there is a shortage of work and the public facilities and recreation are poor', while a male migrant from Saltpond, fifteen miles eastward along the coast, also thought reality fell well short of his expectations, for 'there is a shortage of work, the life is very dull, and the cost of living is very high'.

It is clear from the pattern of responses what the pattern by major migration region is likely to be. Those who are dissatisfied are those who cannot easily get jobs or adequate jobs, usually because of their lack of qualifications, including the ability to read. Those who do not expect this are the migrants who knew least about the town because they had not even been able to pay it a visit prior to migration. These are all characteristics found to a much greater extent among migrants from the North. Thus it was not unexpected that, while there were no significant differences in response patterns between the South, Volta, and Ashanti, where about half the rural households reported that the migrants had found the town as satisfactory as they had hoped, these reactions were in marked contrast with that found in the North, where only 18 per cent of households reported satisfaction.

Summary

The lure of the town is strong, but urban life also produces its dissatisfactions and discontentment. Many migrants are so disillusioned that they quickly return to the village, while some exhibit various kinds of emotional reactions. Nevertheless, others find the town either lives up to expectations or, although falling short of expectations, provides some advantages that the village cannot. Some reactions to the town and some evidence on why changes in way of life are often enforced on rural-urban migrants are summarised in Table 7:8.

Table 7:8 Summary of certain responses comparing town and village life[a]

Response	Rural survey		Urban survey
	All respondents	Northern respondents	
Migrants earn as much and can buy as much as expected	—	—	26
People worry most about money in the town	75	97	79
People can most easily afford to have a large family in the village	84	93	76
Men can most easily afford to practise polygyny in the village	86	96	81
Migrants find the town generally as satisfactory as they hope	43	18	57

[a] Expressed as percentage of respondents answering each question.

Several points stand out in the summary. First, the town disillusions many whose expectations have been placed too high, either because of poor urban-rural communications or, perhaps more frequently, because of unwarranted optimism about the prospects for migrational success. Nevertheless, partly because the most discontented usually return to the village, close to three-fifths of the migrants in the town live much the kind of life they expected.

Second, the aspect of town life which most frequently fails to live up to expectations is the money which can be earned and more particularly just how far that money will go. Even amongst the residual migrants in the town expectations were reached in only one-quarter of all cases. It is interesting to note that this failure of the town does not lead to more general dissatisfaction. The reason seems to be that there are other, previously underestimated, compensations. The migrant, especially as time passes, usually appreciates more and more the town diversions, the bars and the dancing and the varied swirl of life. He often also appreciates the lack of village constraints and even the relative anonymity of urban residence.

Third, the cost structure of town life is very different from that of the village; it incessantly demands cash for necessities, and questions whether more is not available for tempting luxuries and diversions. Certainly the townsman has to have a very good income if he is not to be plagued by financial worries on a scale that even the more poverty-stricken villagers rarely know.

Fourth, these financial strains militate against some of the most traditional aspects of Ghanaian family life. In the age-old subsistence village economy, prestige and even wealth flowed from the possession of several wives and a multitude of children. If extra land could be farmed the tribe could provide it, and extra hands could help build the additional *swish* (earthen) houses. But the modern town is not so accommodating. Houses, except in squatter areas, are built of expensive, manufactured material on high-cost urban land, and scarcity produces often exorbitant rents even in shanty-town areas. Extra space costs money and the large family can rarely be housed as cheaply as the small one. Similarly, nearly all food must be bought, for there is little space for growing it and available farming land is often far away. There is increased pressure and temptation to send children to school, which, even when it is fee-free, often means expenditure of all kinds, for not only are there books and better clothes to be bought, but educated children can successfully demand all kinds of costly things. The position is more difficult still if polygyny is practised, for the number of children is usually greater, and women who were content to live in adjoining rooms with external doors in the village can often not be so accommodated in the town, and, in the new intellectual atmosphere, may not regard such accommodation so tranquilly. However, the unkindest cut is that the extra financial strain is not rewarded by a proportionate increase in prestige; on the contrary, the polygynous migrant in the town may find himself looked upon as one who has not succeeded in transforming himself into a townsman at all.

Such aspects of the urban environment produce not merely strain within the family but actual change. Polygyny is markedly less common in the towns and the average number of children borne per woman at every age is lower than in the villages (Caldwell 1967a; 1967c; Tetteh 1967). The latter is achieved largely by means of another basic change in traditional family life; the average age at marriage for both males and females is higher in the urban than in the rural areas. In the Northern Region only 8 per cent of females of 15-24 years of age had never married at the time of the 1960 census, but in the Accra Capital District over one-third had not done so (Tetteh 1967: 202). Some of this can be attributed to a differential in the migrant stream itself, for the ambitious who have delayed marriage or postponed parenthood are probably most likely to try their luck in the town. However, there is no doubt that most must be explained by very different living conditions in the towns and by urban-rural differences in outlook on life.

Fifth, the degree of disappointment with town life, of error in estimating town costs, of worrying about urban financial commitments, and of contrast in the economic ease with which large numbers of children or wives can be supported, is proportional to the socio-economic distance the migrant has to move from traditional to more modernised, urbanised society. Such strains are greatest when the migrant moves from largely traditional, subsistence, poor, lowly educated areas, such as are now found in Ghana chiefly in the north.

It is probable, therefore, that in the country as a whole some of these strains are lessening. As the cash economy penetrates more deeply into rural areas and new forms of cash-cropping are found, and as the schools spread to the remoter villages, the emotional ease of migration will undoubtedly increase. Migration itself, with its tendency to change the village economy by bringing more cash into it and the village society by bringing back urban manners, plays a role. The migration process is thus self-reinforcing. There is little doubt that the volume of rural-urban migration will increase even faster than the growth of rural population.

8

Return to the Village

To most West Africans the ancestral village always remains 'home'. This is true not only of the recent migrant to the town, but also of the long-standing migrant, and, even in rural areas, of families who have migrated for some generations to new farming areas.

Very few migrants to the town assume during their first journey that there will be no final homecoming, and almost none that a complete break is being made. Although they may have some relatives or friends in the town, these are usually of less significance than the many personal links they have forged since birth in the village. For everyone born in the village has a pre-ordained place in its society; and, except in very large centres, everyone knows everyone else.

The personal links

Most rural-urban migrants make friends in the town, usually amongst their own ethnic group with a considerable proportion from their own or neighbouring villages. Nevertheless, many close friends remain in the village and revisits help to maintain these links. In the urban survey, as shown in Table 8:1, respondents were asked about the balance of these friendships.

Table 8:1 Responses to the question [urban survey only], 'Have you as many good friends in Accra (or Kumasi, Sekondi-Takoradi, or Cape Coast) as you have in your home village?'

Response	Number	Per cent[a] Respondents	Per cent[a] Responses
Yes	232	40	46
No	267	46	54
No response	1	0	—
Ineligible[a]	85	14	—
Total	585	100	100

[a] Non-migrants.

Thus, for about five-ninths of the migrants the friendship links with the village remain the strongest. There was some evidence that the number of friends in town did increase with duration of urban residence. However, it was often the young, perhaps more orientated towards town life than their elders had been, and showing an increasing tendency to arrive in the town about the same time as several of their friends from the same rural area, who claimed the highest proportion of town friends.

Much depended on the extent to which the rural background had already prepared the migrant for town life. Thus, after three years in Accra, a migrant from Bimbilla in the Northern Region said he had 'no friends in Accra—all in the village'; but after the same period, another of approximately the same age from the southern Volta Region, an area which has experienced a good deal in the way of external social and economic influences and related internal changes, reported, 'Almost all my friends are here'.

Migrants are often insecure and may be emotionally upset. Nevertheless, survey workers were surprised at how frequently migrants warned of the dangers of trusting affection to anyone, or at least to any non-relative. Some migrants are persons who are psychologically rather unstable, who have left the village bearing resentments, and who are no more likely to come to easy terms with the town. A clerk from Mampong, twenty miles north of Accra, explained after eighteen years in the latter town and after he had ceased all visits to the former, 'I have only one friend whom I can trust in Accra—none in my home town'. A woman working as a postal agent in Cape Coast said that, twenty-three years after migrating to the town from a small village in the Brong-Ahafo Region, her friends in the town were 'only a few; friends could be dangerous'.

Remaining in the town

When leaving the village few migrants envisage living their lives out in the town. But, with the passage of years, and with the strengthening of urban bonds, sometimes in the form of married children settling down in the town, the position may change. Some migrants who intend to return to the village may fail to do so because they postpone it for so long that they are overtaken by sudden death. Rural survey respondents were questioned on

Table 8:2 Responses to the questions, [rural survey] 'Do many people, who have gone from the village, stay in the town when they are old, and die there?' [urban survey] 'Do you mean to stay in Accra (or Kumasi, Sekondi-Takoradi, or Cape Coast) all your life?'

Response	Rural survey: Number	Rural survey: Per cent Respondents	Rural survey: Per cent Responses	Urban survey: Number	Urban survey: Per cent Respondents	Urban survey: Per cent Responses
Yes	526	30	30	38	7	8
No	1,256	70	70	462	79	92
No response	0	0	—	0	0	—
Ineligible	0	0	—	85[a]	14[a]	—
Total	1,782	100	100	585	100	100

[a] Non-migrants.

the general position and urban survey respondents on their own intentions, as set out in Table 8:2.

This table should be interpreted carefully; there is, for instance, no necessary conflict between the rural and urban survey patterns of response, although this might not at first sight appear to be the case.

The urban responses show what is taken for granted in most West African large towns, namely that rural-urban migrants regard the town as a place for work but certainly not a last resting place. Fewer than one in twelve of the urban survey rural-urban migrant respondents were so much townsmen that they could envisage no ultimate move back to the village.

The proportion who do stay in the town until death is almost certainly considerably greater than the 8 per cent suggested by the urban survey. There are apparently two main reasons for this failure to undertake the anticipated return. One is a growing number of links with the town with longer duration of residence, a fact which is partly submerged in the average figure of 8 per cent. By the time a man has worked much of his life in Accra and is about to retire, he will often have more close relatives in the town than the village. The chances are that his parents who remained in the village will both be dead, as may be some of his brothers and sisters, while there is a strong probability that he has married children living in the town rearing some of his grandchildren.

Even so, a large majority of migrants still intend to return home. Perhaps the main reason that many of them do not is that death comes suddenly and unexpectedly; they die in the town although they had intended to return to the village soon, often after another year's work or after a certain sum had been saved.

The rural responses cannot be interpreted quantitatively, by assuming, for instance, that three-tenths of migrants fail to return. Of course, such a figure might not be wildly out, for in a surprising number of households responses to this kind of question evoked a report on the one or two appropriate cases best known to them. But it is almost certainly evident that the fraction caught by death in town is well above the one-twelfth of urban respondents who imagined that they would be tempted to stay.

Death is in one sense a cause of return migration. Frequent mention was made during interviews of widows returning to the village after the death of their husbands.

The pattern of response in the rural survey displayed no significant regional differences. This probably arises at least partly from counterbalancing factors. Thus the migrant from the traditional North to the southern towns crosses a wide cultural, social, and economic gulf, and, on his first arrival in the urban area, often feels an urgent desire to return to an area which he understands and where he is understood. But his final return also presents greater problems. For, although the Accra-born may never have regarded him as a townsman, he has experienced great change and is often hesitant about returning to a society so very different from the town. This is not lessened by the fact that the distance of his home area will have on average meant less frequent trips home than has been the case amongst rural-urban migrants originating further south. Even in the case of the final return the distance factor can be important; the return is more expensive and more final—the temptation to stay on in town a little longer to save a little more is often very strong.

The time to return

Whether a return is accomplished at all is obviously dependent to a considerable extent on its timing and on what kind of a goal has been set. Respondent households were questioned further on these points, as shown in Table 8:3.

Table 8:3 Responses to the questions, [respondent households answering 'no' in Table 8:2 only] [rural survey] 'When do they finally come back to the village to stay for good?' [urban survey] 'When do you mean to go back to your village and not come to Accra (or Kumasi, Sekondi-Takoradi, or Cape Coast) again?'

Response	Rural survey		Urban survey	
	Number	Per cent	Number	Per cent
In terms of age:				
old age, specified age over 60, at retirement, when sick, etc.	836	67	145	31
specified age under 60 (expressed either in terms of age or specified period of time)	206	16	45	10
In terms of a target:				
enough money earned, house in village completed, etc.	68	5	54	12
present job finished, training or education completed	103	8	24	5
Non-specific:				
fairly near future, soon,	0	0	33	7
when needed at home	21	2	8	2
Don't know, not sure	22	2	153	33
Total	1,256	100	462	100

The most important point to note about Table 8:3 is that the questions asked in the rural and urban surveys were different sorts of questions, not in any sense comparable. In the former respondents were asked to generalise about the past experience of themselves or others, while in the latter the inquiry was about intention.

In the town, immigrants, or, in the case of immigrant households, the household heads and spouses, divided themselves by their reactions into roughly three equal groups. About one-third did not know or were not certain, although many made the point that this did not preclude them from making a decision at some later date in accordance with events. Another one-third had definitely come for a working lifetime, and would return when work became impossible, difficult, or unpleasant because of age or premature illness. The remaining one-third had targets unrelated to age or likely to be achieved before the onset of old age. Some intended to return in the near future, the great majority of them being short-term migrants. Most of the rest fell into two groups, each of which had set some kind of target unrelated to specific jobs: for one-eighth of the respondents that target was one of money saved and/or money spent on a village house, while one-tenth intended to stay in the town only for a certain period or to a specified age. Finally, a few were kept in the town by uncompleted training of some type, after which they expected to take their skills elsewhere.

In Accra an unmarried male migrant from the Volta Region explained that although he had ceased making temporary visits to his home area, he nevertheless assumed that eventually he would return permanently, 'when I feel I can no longer work'. This is often so even with educated migrants holding senior positions who would seem to many to be fully adjusted only to the conditions of the capital; a public servant, living in Accra's exclusive Ridge area, from which he had almost completely ceased visiting his native village in the swamps of the southern Volta Region, was still certain that 'when I am very old and have reached pensionable age, I would like to go back to my village'. An unskilled northerner living temporarily in Tema's Ashaiman, an outer suburb with a good deal of squatter-type settlement, and working in the dock area, explained that he would return to his wife and five children, 'when much money has been saved'.

Ultimately the final return, if it takes place at all, is probably decided in most cases, as two-thirds of rural households aver, by age or sickness, often both in association. Such a return may follow a single long period or several shorter periods of residence in the town. In the rural survey most respondent households described the timing and reason for the final return much as did a teacher in Logba Alakpeti in the Volta Region, who said it occurred 'when they are very old and pensioned and can't do any more work'. A few made estimates of the usual age of returnees, often naming ages which seemed to the outsider low in view of repeated references to the fact that those who found they could work no longer were 'very old'; a cocoa farmer in the Brong-Ahafo Region claimed, 'few do this [i.e. stay in the town]—most return when they are between 55 and 65 years old'. Some answers specifically discussed the strong desire to die in the ancestral village; a household in Dwinyama, Ashanti, claimed that very few rural-urban migrants from that district stayed in the town until the end of their lives, for they came back 'when they are old and are nearing death'.

Money was quite frequently mentioned as determining the time of return. Sometimes it was cited with no particular reference to age; a teacher said that, in the southern Volta Region village to which he had been posted, migrants seemed to return 'after 10 to 25 years in the town and [in addition] at any time they feel they have sufficient money to establish themselves in the village'. Usually age and money were coupled together, as by the members of the farming household in Chiana Asunia in the Upper Region, who said that the migrants return 'when they are old and have enough money to enable them to come back'. But the role of money is complex; sufficiency or insufficiency can mark the end of the period in town. It was reported from Birifo, in the extreme northwest of the country, that the migrants usually come back finally 'when they have no more income or when they are sick or pensioned'. However, even with this type of response, the emphasis was usually placed on the drying up of sources for obtaining more money rather than on money itself. It is clear that a migrant faced by dwindling savings invariably feels he can eke them out further during his declining years in his native village, where housing in free, cheap, or already provided for, where food is easily obtained, and where the society makes few demands for a heavy-spending way of life.

The only significant difference between the patterns of response for the major migration regions concerns age targets for retirement to the village. In the three more southern regions appreciable numbers of persons return to the village in mid-career convinced that they can continue to earn some income there and that the period in town has sufficed to give them some advantage, for it may have built them a house, piled up some savings, or added to their skills. But return to the North usually means return to near-subsistence conditions. There are many northerners who are largely satisfied with these conditions but who come to the town seasonally, although not necessarily every season, to earn cash incomes. However, those who come for longer periods usually share the same philosophy. They will stay on in town as long as they are in reasonably continuous employment. If they face what appears to be a substantial or indefinite period without work, and this is by no means uncommon for illiterates such as they usually are, they will return, perhaps permanently, to the North. If, on the other hand, they remain in work, they will stay in the town indefinitely until old age or sickness renders their continued employment uncomfortable, difficult, or impossible. When this is recognised, they will return to the home village.

Accommodation for the return

Probably the major concern in the reabsorption of returning rural-urban migrants is their housing. Most of the long-term absentees left when they were young and single and had no claim to any housing other than that they had shared with relatives. Once, when population growth was slower than now, the death of relatives often freed existing housing. But declining mortality, with a consequent rapid natural increase in most villages except in the far North, makes this less likely. Once the returning migrant would have been content with a *swish* hut of the traditional type, but long residence in Ghana's largest towns is making this increasingly unlikely.

The rehousing of the returnee is now of much personal concern to those involved, and the reason for a major transfer of capital from the towns to the villages. Building materials may be sent from the town; and so may money, which employs local craftsmen and buys local products. In this way the cash economy spreads, and rural-urban migration creates some job opportunities for the non-migrants.

Urban survey households containing intending returnee migrants were questioned on the provision of village housing for the final return, as set out in Table 8:4. Some questions on this matter had already been asked when urban-rural links were examined, and have been discussed in Chapter 6 and set out in Tables 6:4 and 6:5. This second approach was justified because it approached the matter this time in the context of the discussion

Table 8:4 Responses to the questions, [urban survey only, restricted to respondents answering 'no' in Table 8:2] (a) 'Do you expect to own a house in the village when you finally go back there?' (b) [if 'yes' for (a)] 'How do you expect to get this house?'

Response	Number	Per cent Respondents	Per cent Eligible households[a]	Per cent Responses[b]
(a) 'Do you expect to own a house in the village when you finally get back there?'				
Respondents giving answers other than 'no' in Table 8:2:				
not eligible (i.e. non-migrants)	85	14	—	—
migrants intending to stay in town	38	7	8	—
Respondents answering 'yes' in Table 8:2 and answering question in Table 8:4:				
Yes	317	54	63	90
No	36	6	7	10
No response	109	19	22	—
Total	585	100	100	100
(b) [restricted to respondents answering 'yes' in (a) above], 'How do you expect to get this house?'				
All respondents except those answering 'yes' in (a) above]	268	46		—
Respondents answering 'yes' in (a) and answering question in (b):				
house already built, purchased, being built, or otherwise acquired	70	12		22
will build house before or at return	199	34		63
will purchase house before or at return	36	6		11
will take over all or part of family house	12	2		4
no response	0	—		—
Total	585	100		100

[a] In (a) only, percentages of 500 respondent households containing one or more migrants.

[b] In (a) percentages of 353 households responding, and in (b) of 317 households responding.

about the possibility of return. It also served as a check on the previous question, a check which, as explained below, raised some perplexing issues.

Table 8:4 shows that almost two-thirds of rural-urban migrants in the town stated that they expected eventually both to return to the village and to have made housing arrangements by the time they did so. However, it would be unwise to assume that the 'no response' category in part (a) consists largely of those who were evading answering 'no'; a recheck of the schedules against earlier responses to the question set out in Table 6:4 suggests that most would answer 'yes'—probably some believed that they had already answered the question, while others were perplexed by the use of the verb 'expect'. Thus, a fair estimate would be that the great majority of returning migrants expect to own their own housing, and most attribute their ability to achieve this to their work in the town.

Of those who intend to own a house, other than a pre-existing family house, fewer than one-quarter apparently were already owners or were in the process of building at the time of the survey, although if we accept the figures of Table 6:4 this proportion may approach one-third. This does not necessarily discredit the rest as builders of 'dream castles', although it does suggest that the figures should be treated with some caution. Because of the rapid increase in rural-urban migration, many of the migrants are still young and are fully engrossed with establishing themselves in town; later, nearer the time of return, they will face the problem of village housing. The figures also reflect the fact that many migrants who do complete the building of a village house return home soon afterwards, the main purpose of their labour in the town having been attained.

Two other points should be noticed. The first is that the taking over of a family house, as distinct from being allowed to crowd in with relatives already in such a house, is not now an important way of rehousing returning migrants. The second is that most migrants are personally involved with the making of their own houses, and do not purchase either old houses or ones specially built for the market.

The use of migrant earnings to build houses in the 'home' area is not a feature solely of rural-urban migration. The very great investment in housing on the Akwapim Ridge to the north of Accra originally came almost entirely from migrant cocoa farmers (Hill 1963: 190-1), although it has since been supplemented by town earnings and other money, such as that from diamond concessions in the Birim Valley.

Finally, it is necessary to consider the origin of discrepancies between Tables 6:4 and 6:5 on one hand and Table 8:4 on the other. The former suggest a higher proportion of house-building in the villages by migrants in the town than does the latter. A minor reason has already been discussed in Chapter 6, namely the fact that the categories in Tables 6:4 and 6:5 were not mutually exclusive and that when categories were added some doubling up occurred. But the major reason would appear to be the faulty construction of the question shown in Table 8:4. Firstly, it contained the verb 'expect', describing a mental response which another survey has shown to produce difficulties in translation to Ghanaian languages and to yield a very high 'no response' rate (Caldwell 1968b). Translation and retranslation have shown that there are linguistic and cultural problems in separating translations which imply 'anticipate' from those which imply 'hope'. Confusion on the part of both interviewer and interviewee, on a scale not suggested by the original trials, led to almost one-quarter of the respondents questioned in Table 8:4, part (a), taking refuge in silence. Secondly, the question set out in Table 6:4 was a well-constructed series of simple, straight-forward inquiries, while that in Table 8:4 attempted to find out too much in a single bite. There are other explanations too, all of which have validity for some interviews. In Table 6:4 attention is paid to all migrants, while in Table 8:4 it is restricted to those who intend to return to the village; but those who intend to stay on in the town are on average atypically wealthy and many of them own village houses to which they will never return permanently. In Table 8:4 those who will take over a family house are shown separately from those who own a house they have built or purchased; in fact many of them have already acquired possession of the family house. Similarly the table makes no attempt to inquire about the building on of rooms to an existing family house. Finally, and apparently not unimportantly, the question set out in Table 8:4 was the last one on the schedule; tired interviewers and interviewees were only too anxious to get it over with.

Nevertheless, migrants in the town are very much concerned with the whole quite complex problem of building in their 'home' villages. Those with higher incomes are particularly interested. A male nurse in Accra from a southern Volta Region village, although only 31 years of age and expecting to spend many years in the town, and supporting a wife and five children in Accra, said of the village that he had all but ceased visiting, 'Yes, I am already making plans to build a new house'. A surveyor in Cape Coast, supporting with him a wife and two children, nevertheless expected to build back 'home' when he had the means, 'a cement two-storey building'. Sometimes the main purpose was to provide a *pied à terre*; in Accra's wealthy Ridge suburb a wife from Odumase, 100 miles away in the forested cocoa-growing country on the main road to Kumasi, ruminated, 'I'd like to have a weekend home there where I can go occasionally'. Frequently such a house was no mere luxury, but a good investment; in Accra a 53-year-old police officer from Winneba, forty miles along the coast to the west, reported that, although he had a wife and twelve children in the capital, in his 'home' town 'I have already built one [house] and have sublet rooms to tenants'. Many migrants had to be more modest. A clerk from Mampong, a little over twenty miles to the north of Accra on the Akwapim Ridge, reported that although he hardly ever visited 'home' he had inherited his 'father's property, which I hope to improve upon', while in Takoradi a 43-year-old watchman, living with his wife and two children who were all from Navrongo in the Upper Region, an area so remote from the coast that they had not visited it for years, stated, 'I shall repair my own father's house'.

The reality of return

One should not too readily equate the expressed desire of rural-urban migrants to return 'home' in old age, if not earlier, with the likelihood of their actually doing so. Town links may become stronger than anticipated, while unexpected and sudden death may upset other plans; the former possibility is probably becoming ever greater with each successive wave of immigrants, as urban life becomes a more accepted Ghanaian pattern of living, while the latter is becoming less likely as modern medicine brings capricious death more under control. No-one can be certain about the present genera-

Table 8:5 Ghanaian-born population enumerated in the Accra Capital District by region of birth, sex, and age, 1960
(percentage distributions in each sex-age group)

Birth region	Age (years)					
	Male			Female		
	15-24	25-54	55+	15-24	25-54	55+
Census Regions[a]						
Accra Capital District	44·7	44·8	79·3	52·8	62·1	85·5
Eastern Region	21·1	19·0	6·0	20·3	16·8	7·0
Western Region	12·0	12·1	5·0	9·0	7·1	2·7
Volta Region	10·9	11·9	5·1	10·5	8·8	3·2
Ashanti Region	5·6	4·4	0·7	3·2	1·9	0·3
Brong-Ahafo Region	0·8	0·4	0·1	0·3	0·2	0·0
Northern Region	4·9	7·4	3·8	3·9	3·1	1·3
Total	100·0	100·0	100·0	100·0	100·0	100·0
Major Migration Regions[b]						
Accra Capital District	44·7	44·8	79·3	52·8	62·1	85·5
Southern Region	33·1	31·1	11·0	29·3	23·9	9·7
Volta Region	10·9	11·9	5·1	10·5	8·8	3·2
Ashanti Region	6·4	4·8	0·8	3·5	2·1	0·3
Northern Region	4·9	7·4	3·8	3·9	3·1	1·3
Total	100·0	100·0	100·0	100·0	100·0	100·0

[a] Administrative Regions in 1960; for administrative purposes the Accra Capital District is separated from the Eastern Region. Subsequently the Western Region was subdivided into the Western and Central Regions and the Northern Region into the Northern and Upper Regions.

[b] With the exception of the Accra Capital District, the major migration regions employed in this study. The Southern Region is identical with the Census Eastern and Western Regions and the Ashanti Region with the Census Ashanti and Brong-Ahafo Regions. The two other regions are identical in both analyses.

Source: Census 1960: *Advance Report*, Table 13.

tion of migrants, but we can gather together some evidence about their predecessors.

The 1960 census published one table showing the Ghanaian-born by region of birth and region of enumeration, which allows a separate examination of the Accra Capital District, of the population of which about five-sixths was found in Accra-Tema. In Table 8:5 the population in each sex and adult age division is shown by place of birth.

When the major migration regions are examined separately, the table shows very similar proportions of males born there in the 15-24 and 25-54 age groups in most cases. This is not the case with Ashanti, where the higher proportion in the younger age group is probably a sign of a recent steep rise in the volume of rural-urban migration, especially that directed at the national capital, and with the North, which is so far from the southern towns that migration has long been thought of as something more suited to growing men than to adolescents.

The contrast between the percentages in the 25-54 and 55+ male columns suggests a good deal of permanent return to the villages, although this contrast is also a product of increasing rural-urban migration over the last generation. Nevertheless, the steep fall in the older emigrant census regions, Eastern, Volta, and Northern, is sufficiently great to suggest that increasing migration is not the only reason for the contrast.

Three other features should also be noted. The first is that 55 years is too low a limit for the oldest age group to register all returns to place of birth. The second is that there is apparently some confirmation for a suggestion made earlier in this chapter. The steeper fall in percentages for the Eastern than for the Northern Region supports the view that rural-urban migrants are more likely to return prematurely to home villages in the former than in the latter region, because their skills can often be employed to some extent in the villages, because they are not entirely leaving the cash economy or more modernised society, and because the decision is not so final or difficult to implement, since the distances are much shorter. Against this, the shorter distances may well have encouraged a greater proportion of temporary returns for enumeration in the census. The third is that the proportion which migrants enumerated in the Accra Capital District make up of all persons over 55 years there, is much greater than the proportion these same migrants make up of all persons born in their home regions of this age.

The female section of the table is broadly similar. It shows that the volume of female migration has been smaller than that of males. However, a comparison of the first two columns suggests that such differentials are passing; female migration appears to be growing more rapidly than male migration, although part of the reason for the high proportion of emigrant females in the 15-24 column may be that wives tend to be younger than husbands. The phenomenon of return in old age is just as pronounced for women as men.

Because of the use of 55 years as the lower limit of the older age group, little can be done to estimate the ultimate volume of return migration. However, the rural survey can be used to compare proportions of village population ever away for long periods in urban areas and the return flows from such migrations, as has been done in Table 8:6.

Table 8:6 Percentage of population of rural origin[a] in each age group on long-term absence[b] in urban areas or permanently returned from such absences, by sex, Ghana, 1963

Sex	Category	Age group				
		20-24	25-29	30-44	45-64	65+
Persons:						
	ever long-term absentees	21	23	24	21	14
	currently long-term absentees	16	15	16	9	3
	permanently returned from long-term absence	5	8	8	12	11
Males:						
	ever long-term absentees	24	29	30	28	18
	currently long-term absentees	20	20	21	13	4
	permanently returned from long-term absence	4	9	9	15	14
Females:						
	ever long-term absentees	19	16	19	14	9
	currently long-term absentees	13	10	12	6	2
	permanently returned from long-term absence	6	6	7	8	7

[a] I.e. persons belonging to rural households examined in the rural survey.

[b] I.e. absence for more than a year (includes persons visiting village at the time of the survey).

Source: Rural survey households.

The proportions of those who have ever been long-term absentees continue to mount through the first three age groups, as there are some rural-urban migrants who do not make their first journey to the town, or at least their first one with the intention of settling down there, until after 30 years of age. The subsequent fall in older age groups is evidence of the increasing incidence of such migration. Over twice the proportion of females in the 30-44 age group had permanently migrated to the town as had been the case amongst those a generation older. The volume of rural-urban migration is much larger again because of the growing population; possibly four times as many women aged 30-44 had participated in such migrations as had been the case in the same age group a generation earlier. This roughly agrees with what we know of urban growth during that period (Caldwell 1967a).

The proportions of all persons who have migrated for considerable periods to the town, but who have returned with the intention of never going again to town to settle, continues to mount with age. Even in the 20-44 age group it is considerable, amounting to 5 per cent, and rising to 7 per cent if persons are included who have gone to the urban areas for shorter periods but intend never to go again. In these age groups at least, most of these returnees can be regarded as 'migration failures' who found town conditions too uncongenial. By 25-29 years of age there are almost as many permanently returned males from long-term rural-urban migration in the North as there are long-term absentees away in the southern towns. Such return flows of unsatisfied migrants are probably a feature of most of the world's migrant streams; they are certainly a conspicuous feature of West African rural-urban migration, as a study of the movement into and out of Lagos, Nigeria, has shown (Ejiogu 1968).

For the two age groups between 25 and 45 years of age the proportion the returnees make up of all long-term absentees remains at about one-third, a little lower for males and a little higher for females. After that it climbs rapidly, passing half in the 45-64 age group, and reaching almost four-fifths in the over-65 group, with no very marked sex differential.

There is, then, clear evidence that a very large proportion of surviving past rural-urban migrants have fulfilled the proclaimed intention of returning 'home'. It is difficult to estimate the impact of mortality on this picture—to guess whether death prematurely caught disproportionately more migrants still in the town than was the case in the village with migrants who had returned home early because of symptoms of approaching fatal illness.

Table 8:6 should, however, be interpreted with caution for four reasons. Firstly, it does not represent different stages in the history of the same migrants. It is a simultaneous picture of different age groups participating in a process which is very far from static. Thus, the cohort that was 30-44 years of age at the time of the survey will ultimately produce about twice the proportion (and possibly four times the number) of long-term migrants in the town as did the cohort that was over 65 years of age when surveyed. For this reason alone, one would expect a survey of the former in the year 1998, when they were 65 years of age and over, to show not 3 per cent still in town but 6 per cent.

However, and this is the second point, the reality is probably more complex than this, and accordingly 6 per cent is probably too low an estimate. The urban way of life is undoubtedly becoming a much less alien intrusion into the culture, if only because many more Ghanaians are living in such conditions. In the thirty-nine years between 1921 and 1960 the number of Ghanaians living in centres with over 5,000 inhabitants multiplied almost nine times. In the last twelve years of that period the number in such centres trebled and the proportion of the total population found within them almost doubled, reaching almost one-quarter of all Ghanaians. In those twelve years the six largest centres absorbed almost two-fifths of all the increase in urban population (Caldwell 1967a: 131-6). Many other features of the society which were likely to orientate persons increasingly towards an acceptance of urban life and even an acceptance of living one's life out in an urban setting were changing very rapidly. For instance the number of school pupils enrolled, in a country where the subject matter of lessons often seems to relate only to those local conditions which are urban, had multiplied by over five-and-a-half times in the thirteen years prior to the survey (Hurd 1967: 225); between the 1948 and 1960 censuses the number of persons in the community who had ever been to school or who were still there had increased over eight-and-a-half times, and the proportion of the population in this group over five times. It is hard to imagine such convulsive changes not leading to a weakening in the belief that a return to the home village is either necessary or desirable in old age.

The third point urges caution in interpretation in an opposite direction to the previous two comments. The ultimate residue of migrants in the town in the cohort which was over 65 years of age at the time of the survey might easily fall well below one-fifth, especially if many of them have decided to return home at the onset of what appears to be mortal sickness.

The fourth point modifies the third. The one-fifth of sometime long-term absentees in the town who are still there after 65 years of age does not mean that only one-fifth of those who spent much of their working lives in the town are still there. Many of the returnees spent only a limited time (often no more than a year or two) in the town before returning to the village years earlier; some of these returnees could certainly be described as unsuccessful migrants in that they had not achieved all their hopes in the town and had not adequately adjusted to life there.

Summary

The anticipation of ultimate permanent return to the home village is an integral part of most rural-urban migration and of most subsequent urban residence in Ghana. It plays a major role in determining saving and spending patterns and the maintenance of personal relationships, as well as deciding the need for journeys to make periodic revisits while living in the town. It helps to explain all kinds of aspects of urban society, for rural-urban migrants form a substantial part of such society; in 1960 those born in the locality formed less than half the total population in Accra-Tema, less than two-fifths in Kumasi, and less than one-third in Sekondi-Takoradi, while of the immigrant balance two-thirds, four-fifths, and three-quarters respectively originated within the country. In one sense the urban population is not as durable as it might first appear, although it should be noted that it is generally accepted that the urban-born children of rural-urban migrants are much more likely to see their days out in the town than are their parents.

Some of the more notable features of this return to the village are summarised in Table 8:7.

Over nine-tenths of the migrants living in the town ultimately intend to return to their home village. Most will probably succeed, as there is evidence that four-fifths of the older migrants have done so, evidence that is rendered less than fully satisfactory in that it includes amongst the re-

Table 8:7 Summary of certain responses about the return to the village (percentages of responses[a])

Survey	Response	Percentage
Urban	Still have more good friends in home village than town	54
Urban	Intend ultimately to return to home village	92
Rural	Proportion permanent returnees form of all persons over 65 years of age who migrated to the town for long periods	79
Rural	Cause of return to village is age or sickness	67
Urban	Returning migrant expects to own a house in home village	90
Urban	Returning migrant already owns a house in home village	22

[a] Expressed as a percentage of respondents answering each question.

turnees those who spent only a small fraction of their younger lives in the town but excludes others who might have returned subsequent to the survey at very advanced ages. These figures understate the contribution of rural-urban migration to permanent urban settlement, for the rural-urban migrants do bear and raise children in the town, who are very much less likely than their parents ever to return on any permanent basis to the ancestral village. It is probably also true that, with the passage of time and the greater absorption of urban ways into the Ghanaian culture, an increasing proportion of rural-urban migrants themselves will choose to see their lives out in the town. Thus, one can speak of the increasing permanency of the Ghanaian town.

Although the migrant may have always regarded the town as a kind of temporary working sojourn, nevertheless there is a good chance that he will have remained there until old age or sickness, or both, dictate his return home. However, he usually does not return to the village as a stranger. So constant have been the links he has kept up with the village, through visits to it or by the hospitality he has shown to relatives or friends visiting the town, that the majority of migrants living in the town report that they have fewer 'good friends' living there than in the village. Nevertheless, there is a substantial minority who have been prevented by distance or other factors from visiting the home village except perhaps over long periods. Even in this group most seem to have retained contact through relatives and friends visiting the town or migrating to it; most plan to return ultimately to the village, although the proportion is somewhat smaller than amongst those who frequently go 'home'; and hardly any would anticipate being treated as a stranger or an unexpected returnee when moving back to the village.

Many, in fact, return better equipped for village residence than those who have never been away. Work in the town has probably paid for a house; perhaps not for the 90 per cent who expected to own one, but almost certainly for a proportion much closer to that figure than to the 22 per cent of migrants in the urban area who owned a village house at the time of the survey. Many have also earned a good deal of respect during their absence, not only because of their urban experience, but because of the remittances and gifts to the village and the help extended to villagers arriving in the town. Many come home also with savings and considerably more belongings than are possessed by most people who have never left the village. Many villagers would say, with a classical interpretation of the word, that the migrants were more 'civilised' than when they left.

For many rural-urban migrants such a return to a substantial house, and perhaps another wife, marks the completion of a successful migration.

9

The Role of Migration

The movement of peoples has long been of importance in Africa. Much of the continent is too grudging in its support of either crops or stock to allow sedentary farming to be carried on indefinitely in the one place. Shifting cultivation, usually involving movements over comparatively short distances, and nomadic herding, which may range over hundreds of miles, have been age-old features of Africans' lives.

Such movements were not individual movements in the sense that one man could decide upon a very different destination from his fellows. Indeed, until well on in the nineteenth century it was dangerous in most parts of tropical Africa to go beyond the bounds of one's own ethnic group. This did not always prevent persons from seeing distant parts. Whole segments of an ethnic group were often mobile, and in the savannah country nomadic peoples often moved quite quickly if climatic conditions proved unsuitable in the area in which they were found; many habitually moved with the seasons. The migration of agricultural people in the more forested lands also took place more slowly but often over considerable distances; one example is the arrival three or four centuries ago of the Ewe people in what is now Ghana's Volta Region, as well as in Togo, from a previous homeland further to the east.

Individual migration, admittedly often in groups in the case of earlier movements towards the coast from the savannah lands, began on a large scale at the end of the nineteenth and the beginning of the twentieth century when the colonial powers in their extending domains could guarantee the stranger greater personal safety. The first half of the present century was the heyday of long-distance migration. Much of the movement was the seasonal labour migration of adult males occurring during the slack farming season. The extent of the French and British territories, and the lack of restriction on movement within them and usually between them, meant that migrations of hundreds of miles were common and movement of over a thousand miles not unknown.

This position began to change during the 1950s, and changed more rapidly during the 1960s as country after country secured independence. At first most of the new nation states lacked the apparatus to impose strict checks at all points on their long land frontiers, but it was inevitable that they should aspire to do so to a greater degree than had the colonial régimes. The new states had to look after themselves; the persons over the border were not merely other subjects of the same empire. They often faced balance of payments problems which were aggravated by the remittance of money across the borders by migrants in a sense that was not the case in empires with a single currency or with fully convertible currencies. They faced increased pressure from the home electorate to safeguard job opportunities against foreigners. For these and more bureaucratic reasons they had an increasing tendency to introduce immigration requirements to which foreigners did not always adhere but which deterred some of them from trying to enter the country to take up residence there. Thus, in much of tropical Africa, international migration is becoming more difficult than internal migration, although the two are often indistinguishable in terms of motivation and other socio-economic characteristics.

In other ways the migration streams have also been undergoing change. Sub-Sahara migration has long been equated in official and other reports with 'labour migration' and has often been explained almost entirely in terms of the needs of mines and plantations. The descriptions have never applied neatly to West Africa. The mines are few and in much of the area even tree-crop agriculture has been largely in African, small-holder hands.

In Ghana European estates have been almost unknown. The cocoa industry, which has played such an important role in the economic development of the country, spread as a result of successive, relatively small-distance migrations of entrepreneurial cocoa farmers (Hill 1963). These farmers have used migrant seasonal labour for many of the more onerous and menial tasks such as clearing and weeding. Gold, from which the old Gold Coast derived its name, developed earlier this century a considerable mining industry, which preferred to attract labour for longer terms than a mere season. Like cocoa, the industry attracted migrants from the south, the north and from other countries. Other migrants came to work on the diamond fields or in the timber industry.

The migration was little organised by the employers and carried no responsibility to work only in a certain specified industry. For many migrants the journey to southern Ghana was a migration to a place of very considerable social and economic change, and such rural-rural migration bore many resemblances to the kind of rural-urban migration discussed here. Some rural-urban migration seems to have been an important feature of urban growth for at least half a century, judging by the urban returns in the censuses. Nor has the pure type of male labour migration had a monopoly of movements of southern Ghanaians for at least two generations. Women and even children moved in the early cocoa migrations, and have been following or accompanying men into Accra, Kumasi, and Sekondi-Takoradi since at least the early 1920s.

Rural-urban migration should not be regarded as the antithesis of rural-rural migration; both have been movements from the less developed to the more developed parts of the country, from the more traditional to the less traditional, and often from the largely subsistence to the largely cash economy. The interrelationship has been closer even than this, for migrants have often stopped, and sometimes worked, in the towns in the course of a rural-rural migration, either on the way from 'home' or back to it or on both occasions.

Nevertheless, the scale of rural-urban migration is new, and Ghana seems to have witnessed a more rapid revolution in this respect than most West African countries. Much of the contemporary movement even from northern Ghana southward is different—in destination, in that towns are a common attraction; in period, in that long-term absences are becoming increasingly important; in mode, in that most of the movement is now by lorry; and in manner, in that wives and even children increasingly accompany or follow the migrant—from that described by Prothero in his study of northern Nigerian migration a decade earlier (Prothero 1958). Much of the movement in southern Ghana, as Prothero implies has probably been the case in southern Nigeria, has long been of a different pattern. It certainly is no longer impelled by the same grim harshness of life, even of real hunger, as has often been the case with migration from savannah areas. It is decided more by ambition or whim than dictated by necessity, and much does not involve the long-term breaking up of families.

The scale of rural-urban migration in Ghana and the proportion it makes up of all migration will probably increase. There are several reasons. Perhaps the most potent is that practically all the forces shown in Chapter 3 to be related to the propensity to emigrate from the villages are on the increase, particularly education and other aspects of socio-economic change. The second is that much rural production has the capacity for becoming less labour intensive and more capital intensive as wages rise; this is certainly true of the cocoa industry. The third is that there is little sign of a slackening in town growth and little evidence of a sudden and prolonged fall in the rate at which urban employment can be increased. A medium projection of urban population growth suggests that such population will multiply by five between 1960 and 1985 and double again between that date and the year 2000. Thus in the last forty years of this century urban population might multiply by ten while rural population only doubles; by 1990 it is likely that the country will contain more people resident in urban than rural areas (Caldwell 1967a: 190). By that time the culture of the country should possess a substantial urban component; perhaps only that of the Gas in Accra now does.

This very substantial shift of population is something that is already well under way, even if the absolute numbers are not as awe-inspiring as the projected ones. The urban population of Ghana, using the census criterion of inhabitants of centres with 5,000 or more population, rose from less than one-fifth of a million after World War I to half a million after World War II. Then the urban population trebled in the twelve years from 1948 to 1960, growing at an average annual rate of over 9 per cent, or three times that of rural areas. About two-fifths of all intercensal population increase was absorbed by the towns even though they housed only about one-eighth of the population at the beginning of the period. Three-fifths of the intercensal increase in the urban population occurred in the part of the country termed 'South' in this study. Less than one-quarter of this urban increase can be attributed to the natural increase of those inhabiting the towns at the beginning of the period, while perhaps a little over one-fifth can be explained by foreign immigrants and their increase. However, substantially more than half the growth has arisen from either rural-urban migration, together with subsequent natural increase, or, and this is the lesser factor, the increase in size of villages past the minimum criterion of urbanisation. By 1960, three years after independence, Accra-Tema had over 400,000 inhabitants and had probably passed the half-million mark by the time of the survey described here.

Such rapid urbanisation is probably partly the direct product of social change and economic development, and partly the indirect product in that rural-urban migration has been accelerated by high rates of population growth in rural areas following mortality declines there. Nevertheless, such urban growth has been of crucial importance for continued change and development. Urbanisation and rural-urban migration have been and will continue to be an integral part in economic and social transition; it may not be too much to say that they play the key role in such transformation.

The very size of Accra has played an important role in allowing Ghana to embark successfully on independent nationhood. By 1957 it contained about one-third of a million people and could provide a range of professional and artisan talents necessary to establish an independent administration and to build both the more abstract and the concrete apparatus needed in a national capital. Such efforts would have severely strained the city of 1948 with its 136,000 people or that of 1931 with 62,000. The relationship is, of course, not a one-sided one; part of the acceleration in population growth can certainly be explained by labour demands arising out of independence.

The development of manufacturing industry is similarly related to urbanisation. The growth of such industry attracts migrants from the countryside, as it has to Takoradi since the 1920s. In its turn the continued development of more industrial employment and of more complex manufacturing processes is certainly more likely where the urban population is sufficiently great to provide talent for the growth of all kinds of interrelated manufacturing. This appears to be occurring in the Accra-Tema-Akosombo (i.e. the location of the Volta Dam) triangle.

The obverse face of all this is that rural development may demand less, and not more, labour. The cocoa-farming areas have actually freed a good deal of local effort from farming, admittedly often by importing seasonal workers. Thus in the Eastern and Ashanti Regions, two areas with long established cash cropping in the form of cocoa holdings, 59 and 62 per cent respectively of the workforce were in 1960 employed in agriculture and only 28 per cent and 23 per cent in the growing of field crops and foodstuffs; in contrast, in the Northern and Upper Regions 86 per cent were in agriculture and no less than 84 per cent were producing locally consumed food. Rural-urban migration may be evidence of economic development in rural as well as urban areas.

Nevertheless, rural-urban migration usually provides more direct evidence of the development of urban-located production and of a continuing demand for labour to be engaged in that production. A substantial migration stream is more than likely to indicate a real differential, not merely in cash incomes, but in real incomes and living standards between town and country. Much has been said about migration streams arising from errors in village beliefs about town living standards; and urban unemployment and fringe shanty towns have been quoted to support the view that rural-urban migration is often based on fallacy. The evidence for Ghana seems to be that the differential in average incomes is substantial; in 1960 average income per head was £105 per year in the Accra Capital District, twice the level found in the South or Ashanti, somewhat more again than that found in Volta, and almost five times that found in the North (Szereszewski 1966: 92). It is true that the income in Accra may have been so distributed that the migrant did not increase his income as much as these figures imply, and that high costs in the city may have also reduced the real differential. Nevertheless, a considerable differential undoubtedly remained, although often narrower than the migrant had expected. It is not the absence of a differential which sends many migrants back to the village. The return is caused either by aversion to the social differential between village and town, or by inability, sometimes arising from the migrant's own attitudes, to secure a job during the initial period, or by widowhood, or by the accumulation of savings which can support a reasonably high standard of living in the village for a sustained period. Initial unemployment may be part of the investment one has to make to secure an urban income—although it may be true, perhaps increasingly so, that such an investment will not produce employment or sufficiently regular employment for some migrants, particularly those with a low level of education, skills, or application. The shanty town problem is more complex than it sometimes appears to outsiders. Housing may be impermanent and different from picturesque village housing, but most migrants do not seem to regard it as inferior. To many new migrants the very overcrowding of the shanty town vividly highlights the difference between the staid village and the exciting ebb and flow of town life.

In tropical Africa the town has a much more important role to play in economic development than the discussion above, on the predilection for large-scale manufacturing to settle in its search for low costs near other manufacturing or port facilities, might indicate. Traditionally the vast majority of Ghanaians have lived in villages and have been employed as subsistence farmers. The raising of living standards has been, and will be, intimately connected with a conversion of activities to cash production and the employment of an increasing proportion of the population in non-agricultural activities. But the ability of the society to undertake such a transformation rapidly and efficiently probably depends as much on continuing social as economic change. In the first industrial revolution the towns of Britain played an important role in that urban society induced the necessary parallel social revolution a good deal more rapidly than did rural society. This is true also in Ghana and the rest of tropical Africa. The age-old social relations of the village, and of course the production methods and exchange mechanisms of the village, just do not work in the town. The new attitudes and relationships which have to be invented, and which are described or implied in many parts of the present study, are almost always more suited to a cash economy and to the development of secondary industries in the country.

However, in Ghana and other parts of tropical Africa, and indeed in the whole developing world, towns have another, and perhaps equally important, role to play. It is almost certainly true that economic development can be speeded up if there is ready importation, not only of industrial plant and skills, but of many of the social mechanisms which have had to be developed in technologically advanced societies to fit in with such things. These include such tangible things as textbooks and syllabuses in mathematics and science, but, perhaps more importantly, they also include such intangibles as social attitudes which do not conflict with the kind of industrial activity and organisation of an economically advanced state. These may extend to the size of the family and the relation between parents and children over the latter's schooling (discussed elsewhere for the case of Ghana in Caldwell 1968b). The ports of southern Ghana have been carrying out this function for centuries, but importation and diffusion to the rest of the country have speeded up greatly over the last few decades.

Rural-urban migration plays an extremely important role in the diffusion process of both social and economic change generated in Ghana's towns by their very nature, and that brought in from outside. The process does not necessarily occur automatically, for, in some contemporary societies and many historical ones, town life little affects the great agrarian majority of the people. This is not so in Ghana. One reason is the relatively large volume of rural-urban migration. But this would not alone produce much diffusion of social and economic change. Such diffusion springs partly from the eventual return of most migrants to the village, but more significantly from the volume of 'home' visits made from the outset of residence in the town, and the volume of visits made by persons resident in the village to relatives living in the town.

Rural Ghanaians look upon the large towns as the sources from which the new patterns of living will come to an extent that would astonish rural residents in many developed countries. Such cultural flows are greatly assisted by the geographical and social mobility of the population. By world standards, Ghanaians, and possibly many other tropical Africans, almost certainly spend a disproportionate amount of their personal incomes on transport. In contemporary Ghana the prime factor in such movement is the lorries. They are the most conspicuous and the most common sights on the country's roads. Even on the most remote dirt tracks of the north one will rarely drive for more than a few hours without passing one, while the main routes into the large cities are covered by an endless chain of them. Nearly all carry passengers, although they frequently also carry goods. Well over half of all Ghanaians employed in transport work on the lorries; in 1960 almost 40,000 persons earned their incomes by driving the lorries and another 11,000 spent their time keeping them in repair. In most Ghanaian towns and villages the lorry park fills the role of the cathedral square of an older Europe; it was the large and important space in the centre of the town, in which exciting events are likely to occur, to which the stranger is inevitably attracted, and around which retailers cluster to sell their wares.

The degree of social mobility is a little less obvious, although it does bear some relation to the geographical mobility. There have for long been some wealthy Ghanaians, at first chiefs who often sold commodities such as land, that were strictly not theirs alone to sell, and later merchants and entrepreneurs with interests in diamonds or mahogany or general commerce. But a professional and administrative urban middle class has been largely a product of the years immediately before and since independence. During this period Ghanaians rose rapidly in the civil service, took high positions in political organisations, and were moved into positions of conspicuous responsibility even by the private, foreign firms. The inter-war boarding schools and the post-war university had been built just in time to supply the demand, although, even so, that demand has been strong enough to ensure some Ghanaians very rapid promotion.

There are two important points about this rapid promotion and the extended education that usually led to it. The first is that such Ghanaians have experienced an enormous infusion of imported culture, of cosmopolitan culture, and that they have led lives and accepted the kind of responsibility in which this new culture made sense (see Caldwell 1968). The second is that their rise in status has been so quick and so recent that most still have large numbers of poor and even illiterate relatives and friends. Furthermore, the Ghanaian social system has so far been largely successful in keeping these disparate groups in contact. Often very great pressure is put on successful men to go back to the village on visits to advise or assist the family or do the same for the whole village. Even more frequently are their relatives and fellow villagers likely to visit them in the town, on a scale that the poor rural-urban migrant never experiences or never could afford to experience. Usually he will find his contact strengthened with nephews or nieces whom he has agreed to help with the cost of education (Caldwell 1965). All these contacts serve as channels for cultural diffusion and prevent social change becoming isolated within an urban elite.

In fact, very great change has been occurring within the villages for at least two generations. This has been brought out in the study by the responses of the rural household, and perhaps more vividly by some of the comments made by the interviewers. Part of the cause is better communications and the spread of commerce. The widespread use of the lorry dates back only thirty years; good roads are a post-World War II phenomenon; mass reception of local radio in a range of Ghanaian languages is a product of the last decade: television has been received only since this survey. But a great deal, and perhaps the crucial part that allows radio and television to be meaningful, is a product of the circular flow of rural-urban-rural migration and of the smaller eddies between village and town which occur within the main flow.

Perhaps the most striking finding of the present study does not occur in answers to schedule questions at all. It was found in the remarks of chiefs and elders to the writer and to interviewers, and was repeated on a great number of occasions in the household interviews. Its essence was that migration is extremely important, and that individuals' decisions whether to migrate to the town or not were of the utmost significance. Again and again households were reported as saying that no-one (i.e. no-one from the outside world of government and university) had ever discussed a really important matter with them before. Rural-urban migration is no longer a subsidiary aspect of village life; it is a central concern, and for young adults raises questions of decision that few other matters raise.

To what extent, then, is this phenomenon adequately charted in the present study? For quantitative work on the exact volumes of flows, the representation of all parts of the country is not sufficiently exact and the survey suffered from being held too early to take advantage of the 1960 census frame for sampling. However, work of this type is probably best left to the massive organisation that governments can assemble; in Ghana there seemed no point in duplicating such efforts, for the 1960 census post-enumeration survey had concentrated on such aspects of migration and will doubtless publish the results in due course. What did seem necessary was to supplement this larger quantitative study with a smaller-scale investigation which could help explain the movements charted by the census by asking 'why?' and 'how?'.

The work was probably done on a sufficiently large scale and to an adequate depth to answer many of these questions. The problem of sufficiency of numbers arises in its most acute form when dealing with propensity to migrate, for some characteristics are represented by comparatively few respondents. Nevertheless, the broad pattern of associations between characteristics and propensity to migrate appears sound enough, and receives strong support from the fact that associations found in one area were usually confirmed in the others, even though, as would be expected, the intensity of the association varied. Even the direction in which that intensity varied from one area to another was almost invariably what one might have anticipated from knowledge of historical trends and contemporary conditions.

For the examination of propensity to migrate it was possible to subdivide the chosen ways of life into various categories of permanent and temporary rural-urban migrants and of rural residents by a technique which is not likely to be available to the mass census or even census sample. That technique might be described, if we somewhat whimsically borrow a term from the historical demographers who have used it to describe quite a different process, as 'family reconstitution'. The structure of the rural Ghanaian family, and its attitude towards itself, have allowed us to take a kind of census of the rural population which includes all living persons ever born there. There are some problems of loss or of marginal definition, but they do not obscure the general picture of migration movements and the part they play in the rural society.

These are fields where subsequent studies will inevitably redefine, modify, and debate approaches. What is probably less tendentious forms the bulk of the study—an attempt has been made to summarise the feelings, attitudes, and experiences of migrants and non-migrants in order to explain how the census figures of population movements and the survey findings on propensity to move came about. Such explanations provide the necessary link, probably the only link, between the transformation of the Ghanaian society and economy, which has been mentioned, and the rapid urbanisation which has been part of that transformation.

A very brief recapitulation of some of the major findings, so as to set them in perspective, is probably in order.

In Chapter 2 it was explained that rural areas and reasons for rural emigration to towns are more diverse than are urban areas and reasons for immigrating into them. The true urban heterogeneity occurs not so much between towns as within each, an internal contrast in economic well-being and way of life that many rural-urban migrants only appreciate fully when they have arrived in the town and find that they cannot easily share all that glitters there. For the glitter of the town is a real thing; there are both metaphorically and literally bright lights there, and the cosmopolitan population, gathered from both national and international origins, also adds a kind of colour which has excited many a rural-urban migrant. The bright lights are not the primary cause of Ghanaian rural-urban migration; the primary causes are much more down-to-earth economic facts; but they exert an important supplementary attraction.

The mobility of the population means that the towns strongly influence the countryside. Nearly half the rural population have at least seen and had brief experience of the larger urban centres, and most lorries arriving in the village bring some envoys from the town. Most of those from the town will probably be merely paying a visit, but amongst them will be some returning permanently. The latter will be of two types and the attitude of the village towards the town is partly constructed from their very different types of report. One is the successful migrant, usually returned after years away, pleased to be back, but not hostile to the town which has placed him in an advantageous economic and social position in the village and about which he will speak as an authority for the rest of his life. The other is the unsuccessful migrant, often young. He has seen the harsh side of urban life, and did not wait to complete the picture; frequently he failed to obtain consistent employment and sometimes he was far from well during most of the period in the town; towards the end his relatives or fellow villagers were likely to be obviously tiring of supporting him. His experience of the town has not been one to generate enthusiasm, and in any case he often feels obliged to paint the grey in darker colours still to justify his unexpectedly early return to the village.

Rural-urban migrants are of various types. In Ghana it appears that long-term rural-urban migration is gaining the ascendancy over seasonal migration. However, seasonal migrants still play an important role in the society, especially in linking largely subsistence agricultural areas with the town. For it should be realised that only some types of agriculture, and indeed only some kinds of climate, are sufficiently periodic in their annual cycle to induce large-scale seasonal migration; such forms of agriculture have been increasingly confined to Ghana's north. Migrants in the towns are also of various types. The contrasts used to be largely those between different ethnic or linguistic groups, in which Ghana and West Africa abound, and to a lesser extent between long-term migrants, often settled down with a family, and seasonal migrants who were usually single males. With independence, the demographer and the government official have become increasingly interested in the distinction between native-born and foreign-born, even though in Ghana's cities both are most likely to be rural-urban migrants and the latter may have travelled a shorter distance and have come from an area more like southern Ghana than the former. In the society as a whole this distinction will almost certainly be increasingly made, for the two groups are now treated very differently in regard to such important matters as the ease with which earnings can be remitted back to the village. In addition, the increasing extent to which all young Ghanaians are regarding themselves as Ghanaian nationals must ultimately render the contrast between the native-born and the foreign a major feature of society.

In Chapter 3 it was shown that there is no clear division between individual villagers who migrate and those who do not do so; the most unlikely people sometimes move to the towns. But there are clearly some characteristics which predispose people to rural-urban migration and which can be used for predictive purposes when dealing with substantial populations.

The long-standing tendency for the greatest mobility to occur amongst late adolescents or young adults has been maintained. With the extension of schooling to middle school and beyond, there is an increasing tendency for the decision to embark on rural-urban migration to be taken in the period immediately after the completion of formal schooling. This is, for a considerable fraction of the population, no longer a particularly young age; at the time of the 1960 census the median age in the last two years of middle school was almost 17 years in the whole country, and, in the Volta Region, for instance, higher still. Males are still more likely to migrate than females, but amongst the younger groups the margin has become small and is probably explicable entirely in terms of the lingering but diminishing educational differential between the sexes. It is quite possible, in spite of some hostility in many families to girls migrating to the city, that within a decade as many young females as males will be doing so—a phenomenon that has certainly been assisted by the very considerable growth of urban office jobs. Until mortality declines much further in rural areas, and parental survival to old age in good health becomes the near-universal pattern, it will probably continue to be easier for younger sons or daughters to migrate to the town and easier for them to stay there indefinitely.

The most significant relationship is probably that between education and literacy on one hand, education being the dominant and even the determining factor, and propensity to migrate on the other. This is so not merely because propensity to migrate increases so steeply with duration of formal education, but because the average duration of education being experienced by the nation's youngsters is itself increasing steeply. One can understand recent changes better and get a glimpse of the future if the propensities to migrate by education received, set out in Table 3:3, are applied to the population aged 25-54 and 15-24, for which we have education by age and sex figures for 1960 (Census 1960: Vol. III, Tables 3-5), adjusting the latter to compensate for uncompleted education. For two groups averaging a little less than twenty years' difference in age, the difference in education alone would have increased the propensity for rural-urban migration by over two-and-a-half times, approximately doubling in the case of males and effecting a nearly five-fold multiplication in the case of females. When the increase in the actual numbers in equal size age groups is taken into account, an estimate being made to take into account the effect of mortality, it becomes apparent that a single age group around 20 years of age would be likely to yield ultimately about four-and-a-half times as many rural-urban migrants as had an age group of the same breadth twenty years its senior. Furthermore, a projection of educational trends indicates that a single age group around 10 years of age in 1960 would probably ultimately yield almost two-and-a-half times the number of permanent rural-urban migrants that a similarly sized group ten years its senior would ultimately yield and about eleven times as many as the group thirty years its senior. These are the effects of increased education and a rapidly growing population alone, but they go far towards explaining why urban population had trebled in the twelve years preceding 1960 and why it was projected to multiply itself by four-and-a-third to five-and-a-half times in the subsequent fifteen years and eight-and-a-half to thirteen times in the subsequent thirty years. Such speculations help to explain the mechanics of change; the multiples themselves should not be taken too seriously. One of the reasons is that the propensity to migrate according to educational level as recorded in 1963 will itself vary with socio-economic change, not the least important of which will be educational change. Generally, higher educational levels will mean that a given level of schooling will not be in such demand in the city labour market, although no simple relation with expanding schooling can be determined because the town economy and its demand for skills is also altering with time.

The propensity of the educated to migrate to the towns may merely be an aspect, although the most important one, of a tendency for people to do so who have acquired skills fitted for survival in the non-traditional economy and society of the urbanised areas. There is, for instance, evidence that a young adult who has learnt a skilled trade in the village from an older craftsman, thereby equipping himself better than the untrained for earning a cash income in the village, is nevertheless more likely than the unskilled to try his luck in the town.

Much of the propensity for migration depends not so much on who the individual is, or what has been done to him, as on where his residence is and what has historically transpired in the area. Disproportionately more migrants come either from rural areas which are conspicuously poor or unable to offer non-subsistence employment or from areas which have experienced great socio-economic change which has radically altered both the traditional culture and economy. Related to the latter point, as well as to the pattern of school attendance which rises proportionately with the size of a centre, propensity to migrate to urban areas increases with the size of the place of residence, being least in small villages, greater in large villages, and greater still in what the census would describe as small towns. There is, in fact, some evidence that there is a good deal of movement between the large towns. Distance from a town proves an obstacle either to getting there or to such communications as allow it to exert an attractive force on villages; certainly propensity for rural-urban migration declines as the miles from the nearest large town grow.

Migration and family life affect each other profoundly. Once one member of a household, or of a larger family group, is lodged in a town the chances of others following rises very steeply; a process of chain migration has begun. In due course a town household of husband, wife, children, and perhaps some other relatives may assemble in the town. But family life there will not be the same as if the same separation from the ancestral families had occurred merely to another village house. The town household may well be smaller (often a nuclear family); there is a greater chance that the spouses will live together; there will be a stronger feeling that the important point in the upbringing of children is to keep them at school rather than teach them the ways of plants and animals. The whole range of effects on the family are very great and often subtle; in the long run they affect the whole social structure of the country.

Many families, using the term here in a broader sense than the nuclear family, are not now either fully rural or fully urban families. They are strung out between the village and town and have adapted themselves to this intermediate condition. The rural household depends to some extent on urban remittances and has come to enjoy a standard of living that rural exertions alone could not bring it; even to the outsider its way of life will obviously seem more comfortable than that of most villagers. It keeps in touch more than most with the society and politics of the town through visits from or to town relatives and sometimes through letters and other communications. Partly because of its better income, partly because of its more urbanised outlook, and partly because it has increasingly come to regard itself as producing adequately-prepared rural-urban migrants, the household is much more likely than village households that have not produced migrants to send the children to school as long as possible. Pressures are certainly building up to restrict family size. The urban household cannot be fully understood unless its relationships with the rural household, or with the rural households of both husband and wife, are appreciated. Good relations with the village maintain a kind of umbilical cord connection with the place where their existence is meaningful, where the ancestors lived and may still be contacted through the fetish, where they were known and where their activities are still watched with interest, and to which they will be able to retreat should they strike harsh times in the town. The visits to the village and even the sending of remittances give them a life outside the town. The links with the village are maintained by temporarily boarding newly migrated relatives or often by boarding young relatives for much longer periods during their education.

The essential point about these migrant urban households is this: they are a relatively new phenomenon, they are different, because of their rural links, from second and third generation urban households, but they are very much a feature of African urban life and not of its rural life. The migrant population in the towns has often been described as if it were essentially rural in its nature. This is not so; it is a distinct part of the urban population, but its way of life, even its remitting and its assistance with the education of young relatives and its reporting back to the village what has been happening in the town, is very different from that of the rural population. Its children will probably form urban households of more orthodox type. It is quite logical to argue that not only are the immigrant households a special subsection of the urban population, but the emigrant households of the village are a special subsection of the rural population. The latter are marked off from the rest of the rural population by their special relation with and dependence on the town; they are the rural counterpart of the town immigrant households.

The most portentous thing about the various factors that predispose rural population to migrate to the town is that most are markedly on the increase. In a society with a high birth rate and an infant and child mortality level that is believed to have fallen very considerably in the last two decades the number of young adults is probably increasing by at least 3 per cent each year, while the numbers that are educated, literate, or skilled is growing very much more rapidly. Rural-urban migration itself is hastening the change in socio-economic conditions in rural areas, and providing a greater proportion of rural residents with relatives in town so that new chains of migration can be forged. The process is already well under way; the 1960 census showed that the percentage of employed males working in agriculture fell from 86 per cent for those over 65 years of age by stages in each successively younger age group until it reached 52 per cent amongst the 20-24-year-olds. The younger adults are already living in an environment in which agriculture is not particularly dominant, an environment that average figures projected for the whole country suggest at first sight to be the lot only of a future population, perhaps 15 or 20 years hence.

In Chapter 4 it was seen clearly enough that both rural and urban areas exert 'pushes' and 'pulls', usually at the same time. It is clear that economic motives are dominant in encouraging the migration of some to the town, but they share place with non-economic motives in deciding that others should remain in the village. The attractions of the town for the migrant are, in order, work that will yield a satisfactory income and in particular a cash income, the availability of such facilities as hospitals, water, and street lighting, and entertainments beyond the traditional dancing or rituals of the village. What must be weighed against these attractions is the complexity and high cost of living in a society where all needs must be paid for, and the social problems that result from the absence of the strong social control of the village. Certainly, in both town and country it is believed by the great majority that village life is more 'manageable' and less corrupting. Ghanaians still judge the town; it has not been there long enough to become part of the unquestioned landscape.

There is no simple division in rural society between aspiring migrants, who want to go to the town, and the rest, who want them to stay. Many village households believe that their economic well-being depends at least partly on some of the members working for short or long periods in the town. There is somewhat greater apprehension about female than male migration, in the not altogether unfounded fear that girls may take up prostitution, but this is less strongly felt in rural areas where socio-economic change has been greatest, and may pass as female migration becomes commoner.

In Chapter 5 it was seen that, in Ghana at least, there is little support for the belief the migrants are lured to the town by fanciful and largely erroneous ideas of urban opportunities and urban life. Most aspiring migrants seem to have a reasonably good idea of what the town is like, increasingly from having already visited it. Two-thirds of the migrants living in the towns claimed that their pre-migration judgment of the town was largely correct, although the proportion would inevitably have been lower amongst the unsuccessful migrants who had already returned to the village.

Most migrations follow a similar pattern. Many migrants obtain some help from relatives to meet the cost of the journey and the initial lodgment in the town. At least nine-tenths now travel by lorry and two-thirds stay first with relatives or friends, the majority with the former. Most go with the idea of earning a surplus above daily needs and of remitting some money back to the village; around four-fifths succeed in doing so.

Chapter 6 showed that for most rural-urban migrants the link with the village remains strong. Over two-thirds of the migrants revisit the home village at least once a year, probably the longest period most migrants can be absent without giving offence, but even annual visits usually do not exceed a week in duration. The migrant is very much a town resident in his need to look to the retention of his job first. But he enjoys the respect he receives in the village, and there is widespread agreement that the successful migrant does receive it.

There are flows of money and goods as well as of people, but the former, unlike the latter, travel almost entirely in one direction, from the town to the village. Part of this is for the migrants' own eventual use, for four-fifths of all migrants, and perhaps a higher fraction of those intending to return to the village, hope to secure a house there. But much is to support relatives. In 1963 probably one-third of all rural households received some money from the town, although only one-twelfth claimed that the majority was of urban origin. Most migrants who remitted money did so at least once a month in amounts that usually varied between £2 and £10. Almost one-third of the rural households, mostly those that were receiving remittances, believed that village households would be 'very poor' without such money. The remittances are rarely assigned for specific purposes, except sometimes for educational expenses or for certain celebrations or ceremonies; mostly they are used to help meet the maintenance costs of the village family. The total flow of wealth is greater than the remittances, because visiting and returning migrants usually bring presents, more commonly in the form of goods than money. Cloth, which is more cheaply bought in the town, is a particularly common gift.

The urban-rural flow of wealth is a significant part of the Ghanaian economy. It is a demonstration that the development of the urban economy directly benefits very large numbers of people who do not take up residence in the towns. Calculations made elsewhere (Caldwell 1967a: 142-3) suggest that the flow might have amounted in 1963 to as much as £16 million or 3 per cent of the national income and a considerably larger fraction of that within the cash economy. It was also estimated that £5 million per year, or about one-tenth of the income earned there, probably finds its way out of Accra alone, and that most of this goes to rural Ghana.

This urban-rural flow of wealth appears to be playing a key role in the process of economic change within the country. One role is, of course, to ensure that rising productivity in urban industries does not result in rising living standards solely within a few urban enclaves. But experience within the country's remoter towns, which presumably reflects the position of less remote towns at an earlier date, suggests that the effect of cash remittances on rural areas is a good deal more important in causing fundamental economic change than is suggested merely by a rise in consumption levels.

A closed, fully subsistence agricultural village contains no money by definition; few services are likely to be offered, for it is practically impossible to make payments when everyone grows the same commodity, and farmers are inhibited from attempting to produce some goods for a cash market by their unfamiliarity with the market exchange mechanism. This situation in its pure form can probably be found nowhere in Ghana at the present time, but something close to it was certainly widespread in rural areas two or three generations ago and remnants linger in the Northern and Upper Regions.

In much of Ghana this system was first broken, and is still being broken in parts of the north, by money remitted back by migrants. At first the goldfields, cocoa-growing area, diamond diggings, and timber mills were more important than the towns as a source of remittances, but over the last fifty years this position has been changing, especially rapidly over the last two decades. The arrival of money in remote rural villages on a much larger scale than had earlier been the case (there had been a very limited supply of coinage and of cowrie shells) catalysed a great deal of activity. To some extent it merely made certain complex transactions, such as accumulating cattle for bridewealth, easier. But it also created new activity. Men who had the entrepreneurial vision and energy to import salt, kerosene, sardines, cloth, or later, bicycles and soft drinks, found a market. Lorries were more likely to ply to places where men could readily pay their fares in money.

The flow of cash ultimately affected not only services but production as well. In the north, for instance, millets were grown quite widely, and in somewhat more restricted areas yams were raised as well. But with increased money the local market became of more importance for exchanging even food crops, although by the time of the 1961-2 Inquiry into Household Expenditure nearly three-quarters of food consumed in the rural areas of the Northern and Upper Regions was still produced by the individual consumers themselves (Szereszewski 1966: 111). Experience with marketing made some farmers concentrate more on yam production, and with the advent of the lorry some tried their luck in the more lucrative southern markets. By 1961-2 the fraction of food consumed that was produced by the consumers themselves (i.e. subsistence production) had fallen to 60 per cent in Brong-Ahafo, around 44 per cent in the Ashanti, Volta, and Eastern Regions, and to 29 per cent in the Western and Central Regions.

The remittances are also having profound indirect effects on modernising the economy; the money makes it easier for parents to meet the dress and equipment standards necessary to send their children to school, and it is probably much less likely that an educated, literate farmer would be content to produce wholly or even largely within the subsistence sector than that an uneducated, illiterate one would.

Chapter 7 makes it clear that Ghanaians, like others of the present day and past, have to learn to live in towns. Where towns of a considerable size are appearing for the first time, the society has accumulated little experience in adjusting itself to urban life and has many social institutions which were fashioned for other conditions. Large families and polygyny have both been traditional in the country, but the great majority of the respondents, and nearly all those in the north, the region which still remains most like old Ghana, agree that such practices raise more problems in the large towns than they have done in the village. Polygyny is in fact on the wane in the towns and the large family may also be modified substantially in the years ahead.

Before they first reach the town, hardly any rural-urban migrants have ever lived in a fully cash economy or probably even imagined it. Most respondents, and nearly all northerners, feel that most worrying about money is done in the town. This is so in spite of the fact that few rural-urban migrants have ever before earned the kind of income they do in the town, or, taking costs into consideration, enjoyed the same level of consumption.

The mixed feelings of the migrants on the point seem to arise in four ways. First, they are somewhat shocked that everything has a price and that food is never given away or that unused rooms never seem to exist. Second, they find some of the urban prices outrageous compared with the rural areas. They rarely take into account the cost of transporting food into the city or the cost of acquiring land and erecting a building there; and indeed they are not wholly wrong, for some of the prices, especially in Accra, have reflected shortages in a fast-growing city much more than original costs. Third, they are often alone or nearly alone, and find that one has to be one's own book-keeper and keep money in hand, for some kinds of town payments cannot be postponed by the easy arrangements often possible in the village. The migrant faces the very real problems of default, or he finds that postponement or borrowing can be expensive. Fourth, they are faced by all kinds of temptations to spend money that they have never experienced in the village. In addition they often resent the very obvious inequalities in both earning and spending power that are a feature of the large towns.

Thus the town has its disappointments. It is very easy to underestimate necessary costs, and only one-quarter of the migrants managed to buy as much as they expected. This is not a measure of total dissatisfaction, for the town has other compensations. Some of them are the very temptations to fritter money which have prevented the migrants from acquiring all the possessions they had once envisaged. In fact over half the migrants questioned in urban areas had found the towns as generally satisfactory as they had hoped at the time of migration. Many of the rest were reasonably content even if some of their plans had proved dreams. However, it should once again be noted that such measures understate the extent of frustrated hopes, for the really disillusioned migrants are found back in the villages.

The rural areas which report a high rate of disillusion are in the north. This is only one example of a consistent pattern throughout the survey. Again and again those who had to make the greatest adjustments, or indeed who failed to make them because the demands were too great, were from the Upper and Northern Regions, the area designated in the study as the North Major Migration Region. It is unlikely that this has much to do with specific, traditional cultural patterns in the north. The whole tenor of the responses of the migrants from the area suggests that the basic problem is the gulf in ways of living that has to be crossed, supplemented to some extent by the sheer gulf in distance.

The necessary use of terms like 'urban', 'rural', and 'rural-urban' implies too simple an antithesis. Accra is much closer socially and economically to rural Akwapim, not far to its north, than the latter is to most parts of the rural north. Many rural-urban migrants from the north come from village cultures and agrarian economies that are not very different from those that their grandfathers and great-grandfathers knew. The journey south is a journey to towns which are in many ways not traditionally

Ghanaian at all, and which have features in common with cities in developing countries all over the world. It is always a journey across language barriers, a problem not faced, for instance, by the Ashanti villager who moves to Kumasi.

Much of rural southern Ghana has in many ways been partly urbanised in that it has shared in some of the social and economic change going on in the towns. Rural-urban migration has played its part in this. In much of the south commerce and cash production are widespread. Perhaps even more important have been the cultural and educational changes. Mission penetration, which has a Westernising effect, even a Westernising aim, as well as a Christianising one, has been going on for generations. At the time of the 1960 census more than half the Local Authority Areas in southern Ghana (i.e. South, Volta, and Ashanti combined) returned Christian majorities, while no areas in the north did so and in some of them almost the entire population was enumerated as adhering to the traditional religions.

Historically linked with mission activity has been education. The school curriculum is still largely imported, and, with increasing emphasis on higher educational levels, the curriculum is oriented towards cultures not traditionally Ghanaian. If its content describes activities of a type which are found in the country, they are largely non-traditional ones and to a very large degree urban ones. Thus the link between schooling and rural-urban migration is probably far more complex than the fact that education fits one better for urban jobs. Nevertheless, the migrant has less adjustment to make in the town when he comes from areas of similar educational and literacy levels. In 1960 the proportion of the population over 6 years of age who had been to school or were still there was in the 50-60 per cent range in Accra and the 40-50 per cent range in Kumasi, Sekondi-Takoradi, and Cape Coast. However, the former level was also reached in one rural area in the Volta Region, and the latter not only in two areas in the Volta Region, but in much of the heartland and old cocoa-growing area of the Eastern Region embracing the Akwapim and Akim districts. Rural areas where the proportion with schooling exceeded 30 per cent were found widely in the South, Volta, and Ashanti. In contrast, no rural areas in the North exceeded 10 per cent and some fell below 5 per cent.

The whole process is doubtless a continuing one. The towns will become in social and economic terms more unlike traditional Ghana, the southern rural areas will become more like the town today, and the north will become more like contemporary southern rural areas. The southern rural-urban migrant will continue to adjust more easily to the town, but the very size of the gulf between living conditions in the north and those in the southern towns will continue to send large numbers of rural-urban migrants southward from the Northern and Upper Regions. However, as schooling levels, type of agriculture, and a host of other social and economic factors in the north continue to change, some hastened by returning rural-urban migrants, it is probable that the northern migrant will experience fewer adjustment problems in the towns.

Chapter 8 shows that for most migrants adjustment never reaches the point where they decide to see their lives out in the town. Over nine-tenths intend to return ultimately to the village and nearly all expect to own a house there, most as a result of their activities in the town. This is not evidence that rural-urban migration does not build permanent urban population or that the Ghanaian rural population is so rural that it can never adjust successfully to town residence.

Permanent urban populations are certainly coming into existence in Ghana and elsewhere in tropical Africa. In 1911 Accra and the surrounding towns which are now incorporated within it had a population of 32,000 and in 1921 one of 44,000. Thirty-nine years later, in 1960, 416,000 persons were enumerated in Accra-Tema, of whom about 200,000 had been born locally. Rural-urban migration has played a major role in this transformation. Most rural-urban migrants do ultimately return to the village, but many have all or most of their children born and reared in the town. Since few of these children ever envisage forming closer links with the village than an occasional visit, they form the basis of the permanent urban population.

In the sense that most rural-urban migrants who work their active years out in the town are satisfied about what they have done, there can be no real question about their failure to adjust to the town. It could be said that they had failed to embrace town life so exclusively as to be adjusted to the town only; rather is their adjustment one to both town and village. They have a cyclical view of their lives which demands a beginning and an end in the village but which is satisfied and even happy to enjoy an extensive urban experience in the interim. Even during this period most do not react against village life, although some undoubtedly find prolonged visits dreary. Nevertheless, the periodic visits are for the majority not merely duty; they undoubtedly enjoy the experience, although some of the enjoyment is certainly the pleasure in being a figure of some importance on these occasions.

The town is essentially a place of activity. There one can work fruitfully during the height of one's powers. There also one can live fully when one has the energy to do so. But, as one begins to feel one's age, or as sickness brings warning signs of physical troubles, then one begins to think of retirement, in a very literal sense of the word, to the village. It is a place where the pace is appropriately slower, and where the old can receive more respect than they often do in the town. It is also closer to one's ancestors.

Yet the picture is not quite as simple as this. Even in the kind of cyclic, rural-urban-rural life described above, it is somewhat surprising to find that 56 per cent of urban respondents say they still have more good friends in the home village than in the town. There is little doubt that some migrants see too many dark shadows in the town for their own peace of mind, and some create whole philosophies, not unknown in the rural areas either, about how to behave when surrounded by enemies. Part of the problem is ethnic and linguistic, and these symptoms are found particularly commonly amongst those in the town originating from far-away areas from which few other persons have migrated. It is found most frequently too when the migrants have come from areas with a very different social and economic structure from that of the town.

Finally, what effect does rural-urban migration have on the town? The migrants are not a typical cross-section of the rural population, for they are largely self-selected in accordance with the various propensities to migrate that we have examined. Some of these propensities ensure that they are more akin in various characteristics to the urban population than is the average rural resident. Nevertheless, they are still a very distinctive addition to the towns.

The aggregate town population is essentially a product of two groups: those who have been born and reared within it and those who have migrated from outside. The effect is often to concentrate certain talents and skills, for two reasons. First, because of the pattern of government provision of educational facilities, because of the higher average income of urban residents, and because urban parents are aware that their children's earning power in the town will be very largely determined by their educational qualifications, the town-born are on average better educated than are the village-born. In 1960 it was found that 65 per cent of the children 6-14 years of age in Accra-Tema were currently in school, but the equivalent proportion in all urban areas was only 56 per cent and in villages with populations 2,000-5,000, 1,000-2,000, 500-999, 200-499, and under 200 it was 47, 41, 38, 32, and 21 per cent respectively. Second, because the village-educated are more disposed to migrate than the uneducated, such contrasts tend to become even more marked. Thus in 1960 the proportions of all persons over 6 years of age who had ever been to school were, for the centres named above, starting with Accra-Tema and working down to villages with fewer than 200 inhabitants, 52, 43, 31, 26, 22, 19, and 14 per cent respectively. It might be noted that the extra steepness that the second series shows over the first arises not merely from the movement of rural-urban migrants, but also from an historical association between education facilities and the number of inhabitants of a centre that has been even stronger in the past.

The degree of concentration of skills in the four towns, Accra-Tema, Kumasi, Sekondi-Takoradi, and Cape Coast, has been examined elsewhere (Caldwell 1968b: 12-15). Some of the noteworthy findings were that, although less than one-eighth of the whole population lived in these towns in 1960, seven-tenths of those with some university education were there and over half of those with some secondary education. This was admittedly a reflection of demand to a very considerable extent; for instance, 52 per cent of the employees in government service, and 74 per cent of those in the central government administration and defence services, large employers of persons with high qualifications, were to be found there.

Internal and external migration had resulted in other types of concentration. One-third of the foreign population in the country was enumerated in the four towns. It had raised the proportion of inhabitants in the main migrant age groups; in the country as a whole 43 per cent of persons were 15-44 years of age but in the four towns 51 per cent were.

The fundamental questions of rural-urban migration are closely related to these kinds of statistics, and most of them cannot yet be answered. Is this concentration of talent accelerating economic development? Will it make the growth of large-scale manufacturing possible? Or conversely, will the extension of schooling in the villages bring more educated migrants to the town than the urban employment structure can easily absorb? Over one-quarter of all the unemployed were in the four towns in 1960, but this may merely mean that unemployment is more easily defined in the town, and that rural-urban migration is often followed by a period of dislocation.

Not all the questions are economic; perhaps the most important are, in the long run, social. Can rural-urban migration continue to change so that the separation of husbands and wives and the breaking up of families for considerable periods will be made rarer? Can family migration become a common thing? Can migrants be absorbed into the towns without creating substandard shanty areas? The answer to the first two questions is probably 'yes'; the historical evidence is not strong, for the sex ratios of the population over 16 years of age (15 years in 1960) in the Accra Municipality rose from 122 males per 100 females in 1921 to 133 in 1948 and, as the result of much more massive rural-urban migration, had only fallen to 132 in 1960; however, the evidence around the latter date from census and survey on the migrant behaviour patterns of young adults strongly suggested that this male surplus would be slowly whittled down. Long-term migration is tending to supersede seasonal and other short-term migration, especially in the movements to the towns. Rural-urban migration appears to have worked towards creating nuclear families in the town, partly because all relatives have not migrated, partly because migration weakens some traditions, and partly because much of urban housing was not made for extended families (see also, on Nigeria, Ejiogu 1968). Spouses from some cultures tend to be housed together in the towns even though this was not the practice in the areas from which they came. It is probable that the immigrant quarters in the towns will become less conspicuous. This is likely to result partly from governmental rehousing schemes. But the ultimate solution will follow from the fact that the extension of literacy, schooling, and the cash economy into rural areas will reduce the differential in the towns between the newly arrived migrants and the town-born in manners, in skills, in suitability for jobs, and so in the ability to pay for accommodation.

Ultimately administrations are concerned with the kinds of findings presented here because they do raise questions of urban-rural balance. 'Balance' is used here merely in the sense that at any given time there is probably some ratio of urban to rural population and some level of rural-urban migration (although neither may be exactly definable), which maximises economic growth and the raising of individual living standards or which minimises urban unemployment or rural underemployment. It is clear that some administrative measures, short of physical control of movement, may well affect the volume of migration; for instance, expenditure on rural schooling could be manipulated so as to vary the flow over a decade. Decisions to implement such a policy will not be lightly taken, for rural schooling has many more implications for social change and economic development than the fashioning of the rural-urban migration stream. There may be real conflict, for instance, between raising the general level of skills in the workforce and ensuring that migrants do not move too rapidly into a few large cities which are ill-prepared to take all of them so quickly.

APPENDIX 1

Administrative and migration regions and survey locations

Key to Map

(a) Regions

No. on map	1960 administrative regions (employed by census)	1963 administrative regions (at the time of rural-urban migration survey)	1963 rural-urban migration survey (major migration regions)
1	Accra Capital District	Accra Capital District	(excluded from rural survey)
2	Eastern Region	Eastern Region	South
3	Western Region	Western Region	South
4	Western Region	Central Region	South
5	Volta Region	Volta Region	Volta
6	Ashanti Region	Ashanti Region	Ashanti
7	Brong-Ahafo Region	Brong-Ahafo Region	Ashanti
8	Northern Region	Northern Region	North
9	Northern Region	Upper Region	North

(b) Regional boundaries

——————— national

o o o o o o o 1960 administrative region

● ● ● ● ● ● ● 1963 administrative region

+ + + + + + + + + 1963 survey (major migration region)

Note: When boundaries coincide two or more marking systems are employed.

(c) Urban survey locations and other urban centres

▣ Urban survey centre, also used for descriptive purposes as 'a large town' in the rural survey

□ Urban survey centre, not usually used for descriptive purposes in the rural survey

O Other urban centres listed in Table 1:1 (i.e. as being amongst the eight largest in the country)

(d) Rural survey locations

● Locations in South, Volta, and Ashanti Major Migration Regions averaging around 400 persons per location

▲ Locations in North Major Migration Region averaging under 200 persons per location

(e) Other information

— — — — — Limits of areas with 1960 population density exceeding 50 persons per square mile (by local authority)

Arcs of radius 100 miles from Accra-Tema and Kumasi and 50 miles from Sekondi-Takoradi

Notes: The distribution of rural survey locations is related to the work on migration to Accra-Tema and Kumasi as well as to the interest in emigration from the Upper Region (mentioned in Chapter 1). However, the distribution pattern is, in most parts of the country, in keeping with the population distribution pattern (indicated on the map by the limits of the area exhibiting settlement densities in excess of 50 persons per square mile in 1960), and hence, as shown in Table 1:3, the number of respondents is approximately proportional to the total and rural populations of the major migration regions.

The rural survey locations have been named according to the largest centre in the area and in keeping with the orthography selected for the publication of the 1960 census findings (Vol. 1). This in no way implies identity with the census 'localities' for two reasons. At the time of the survey, the data for these localities were not available and hence identity would not have been possible. In any case, the names used here indicate a district in which centres of various sizes were chosen to approximate to the distribution of the population by locality size class. Sometimes this is shown by describing the district as 'Bolga' or 'Kongo', to show that a series of villages with this prefix were surveyed; sometimes a centre such as 'Kpandu' or 'Wa' is named, to show that a number of villages within a radius of the centre were included in the sample. In the North, two or three centres some distance apart were surveyed in some instances, although only one of the combination is shown on the map. The Accra Capital District was excluded from the rural survey.

APPENDIX 2

Percentage distribution of surveyed population by rural and urban surveys, and by sex, migration classification, major migration region, and age

(a) *Full distributions*

(i) Rural survey

Key to rural survey distributions:

	Primary division		Secondary division		Tertiary division
1	In rural area and has never migrated to the town	a	does not intend to do so	(i) (ii)	rarely visits the town often visits the town
		b	intends or hopes to do so	(i) (ii)	seasonally more permanently
2	In rural area and has returned to rural area after one or more migrations to the town	a	permanent return	(i) (ii)	after seasonal migration only after at least one period of more permanent migration
		b	intends or hopes to go again	(i) (ii)	seasonally more permanently
3	Away in the town	a	temporarily	(i) (ii)	visiting town seasonally
		b	more permanently	(i) (ii)	visits village at least once a year rarely or never visits village
4	Other		—		—
5	No entry		—		—

Notes: 'Surveyed population' means the total population formed by 'reconstituting' the village households, i.e. by obtaining information on all living persons who have ever formed part of the household and have resided with it; this excludes spouses and also children who were born to migrants after reaching the town and who have never resided with, as distinct from visited, the household. The rural survey was restricted to persons of Ghanaian origin. 'In rural areas' means in any rural areas at the time of the survey; 'often visits town' means at least once a year on average; 'seasonally' means for periods of less than one year, but either for more than three months or securing employment; 'more permanently' means indefinitely, or for more than one year; 'visiting' means for less than three months (providing no employment secured, other than as a household help for relatives or selling some things produced in the village or buying some goods for consumption or sale in the village); 'other' includes urban-rural migrants, especially teachers and other officials.

Percentage distributions: persons (total = 13,776)[a]

Major migration region	Rural-urban migration classification (see key)			Age 0-9	10-14	15-19	20-24	25-29	30-44	45-64	65+	All ages
All Regions	1	a	(i)	60	52	38	31	30	32	42	55	42
			(ii)	14	14	21	25	26	26	27	24	21
		b	(i)	7	8	6	4	3	2	2	0	5
			(ii)	5	8	10	5	4	3	1	0	4
	2	a	(i)	1	1	1	2	2	3	2	4	2
			(ii)	2	2	3	5	8	8	12	11	6
		b	(i)	1	2	3	4	5	4	2	1	3
			(ii)	3	3	3	5	3	3	2	1	3
	3	a	(i)	1	1	2	3	1	1	0	0	1
			(ii)	1	1	3	2	2	2	1	0	1
		b	(i)	1	3	7	9	10	10	5	1	7
			(ii)	1	1	2	2	2	3	2	1	2
	4			3	3	1	3	4	3	2	1	3
	5			0	1	0	0	0	0	0	1	0
Total				100	100	100	100	100	100	100	100	100

[a] In this and all other tables a small number of persons for whom there are no age data are excluded. This table includes 28 persons of unknown sex.

Percentage distributions: males (total = 6,964)

Major migration region	Rural-urban migration classification (see key)			Age 0-9	10-14	15-19	20-24	25-29	30-44	45-64	65+	All ages
All Regions	1	a	(i)	57	50	36	23	20	23	33	45	36
			(ii)	15	14	22	26	25	27	28	28	22
		b	(i)	8	8	7	4	4	3	2	0	5
			(ii)	5	10	11	7	5	3	1	0	5
	2	a	(i)	1	1	1	2	3	4	2	5	2
			(ii)	2	2	2	4	9	9	15	14	7
		b	(i)	2	2	2	5	7	4	3	2	3
			(ii)	3	2	2	4	4	3	3	2	3
	3	a	(i)	0	1	2	3	1	1	0	0	1
			(ii)	0	1	4	4	1	2	1	0	2
		b	(i)	2	3	8	13	14	13	7	0	8
			(ii)	2	2	2	3	2	5	3	2	3
	4			3	3	1	2	5	3	2	2	3
	5			0	1	0	0	0	0	0	0	0
Total				100	100	100	100	100	100	100	100	100

Percentage distributions: females (total = 6,784)

Major migration region	Rural-urban migration classification (see key)			Age								
				0-9	10-14	15-19	20-24	25-29	30-44	45-64	65+	All ages
All Regions	1	a	(i)	62	54	39	38	39	42	53	67	48
			(ii)	14	14	20	24	28	25	25	20	21
		b	(i)	6	8	5	4	3	2	1	0	4
			(ii)	4	6	10	4	3	2	0	0	4
	2	a	(i)	1	1	2	2	2	2	2	2	2
			(ii)	2	2	3	6	6	7	8	7	5
		b	(i)	1	2	3	3	3	3	1	1	2
			(ii)	3	3	3	5	2	3	2	0	3
	3	a	(i)	1	1	2	2	1	2	1	0	1
			(ii)	1	1	2	1	2	1	1	0	1
		b	(i)	1	4	6	6	7	6	3	1	5
			(ii)	1	1	2	2	1	3	1	1	2
	4			3	3	2	3	3	2	2	1	2
	5			0	0	1	0	0	0	0	0	0
Total				100	100	100	100	100	100	100	100	100

Percentage distributions: persons (total = 5,769)

Major migration region	Rural-urban migration classification (see key)			Age								
				0-9	10-14	15-19	20-24	25-29	30-44	45-64	65+	All ages
South	1	a	(i)	52	45	28	20	19	22	32	49	33
			(ii)	14	11	17	19	22	23	29	23	20
		b	(i)	12	13	9	6	4	2	2	0	6
			(ii)	3	9	14	7	6	4	2	0	5
	2	a	(i)	2	1	1	1	3	2	1	5	2
			(ii)	4	3	3	6	10	10	12	13	7
		b	(i)	2	3	3	5	6	4	3	2	3
			(ii)	3	4	4	8	4	3	3	3	3
	3	a	(i)	1	2	4	5	1	1	0	0	2
			(ii)	1	1	3	3	2	2	1	0	2
		b	(i)	2	4	12	16	17	17	9	1	11
			(ii)	1	1	1	2	2	6	4	2	3
	4			3	3	1	2	4	3	2	1	3
	5			0	0	0	0	0	1	0	1	0
Total				100	100	100	100	100	100	100	100	100

Percentage distributions: males (total = 2,874)

Major migration region	Rural-urban migration classification (see key)			Age								
				0-9	10-14	15-19	20-24	25-29	30-44	45-64	65+	All ages
South	1	a	(i)	48	41	27	16	12	16	25	26	27
			(ii)	15	12	15	16	17	19	27	30	18
		b	(i)	14	12	10	5	4	3	2	0	7
			(ii)	3	13	15	9	7	5	2	1	6
	2	a	(i)	2	2	1	1	3	2	1	6	2
			(ii)	4	3	2	5	13	11	14	21	8
		b	(i)	3	3	2	5	6	4	4	3	3
			(ii)	4	4	4	6	5	2	3	5	3
	3	a	(i)	1	2	4	5	2	1	0	0	2
			(ii)	0	1	2	5	2	3	1	0	2
		b	(i)	2	3	15	21	22	22	13	1	14
			(ii)	1	2	2	2	2	8	6	4	4
	4			3	2	1	4	5	4	2	2	4
	5			0	0	0	0	0	0	0	1	0
Total				100	100	100	100	100	100	100	100	100

Percentage distributions: females (total = 2,886)

Major migration region	Rural-urban migration classification (see key)			Age								
				0-9	10-14	15-19	20-24	25-29	30-44	45-64	65+	All ages
South	1	a	(i)	56	49	28	24	25	29	40	70	38
			(ii)	13	10	19	22	27	28	30	16	21
		b	(i)	11	14	7	6	4	2	2	0	6
			(ii)	3	5	13	5	5	3	1	0	4
	2	a	(i)	2	0	1	1	3	2	2	4	1
			(ii)	4	3	4	7	7	10	10	6	7
		b	(i)	1	3	5	6	5	4	2	1	3
			(ii)	3	4	4	10	3	3	3	0	4
	3	a	(i)	1	2	3	4	2	2	1	0	2
			(ii)	1	1	3	2	2	1	1	0	1
		b	(i)	2	5	10	10	13	11	5	2	8
			(ii)	0	0	2	2	2	4	1	0	2
	4			3	3	1	1	2	1	2	0	3
	5			0	1	0	0	0	0	0	1	0
Total				100	100	100	100	100	100	100	100	100

Percentage distributions: persons (total = 2,069)

Major migration region	Rural-urban migration classification (see key)			Age								
				0-9	10-14	15-19	20-24	25-29	30-44	45-64	65+	All ages
Volta	1	a	(i)	42	27	23	22	14	20	38	46	30
			(ii)	35	38	35	32	41	42	36	42	37
		b	(i)	0	1	2	1	3	1	1	0	1
			(ii)	12	20	17	7	4	3	1	0	9
	2	a	(i)	0	1	2	1	1	3	1	1	1
			(ii)	1	3	4	13	14	13	14	6	8
		b	(i)	0	0	1	3	3	1	0	0	1
			(ii)	1	0	3	3	2	3	1	0	2
	3	a	(i)	1	1	1	2	1	1	0	0	0
			(ii)	0	0	3	1	1	1	0	0	1
		b	(i)	1	3	6	8	9	5	4	0	4
			(ii)	3	1	2	4	2	3	0	1	2
	4			4	5	1	3	5	4	4	4	4
	5			0	0	0	0	0	0	0	0	0
Total				100	100	100	100	100	100	100	100	100

Percentage distributions: males (total = 1,012)

Major migration region	Rural-urban migration classification (see key)			Age								
				0-9	10-14	15-19	20-24	25-29	30-44	45-64	65+	All ages
Volta	1	a	(i)	41	26	21	9	9	18	29	48	27
			(ii)	35	35	32	36	28	42	37	40	36
		b	(i)	0	3	2	0	6	0	1	0	1
			(ii)	12	21	19	9	9	6	1	0	10
	2	a	(i)	0	2	3	1	2	3	1	2	2
			(ii)	1	4	6	11	14	15	17	5	8
		b	(i)	0	0	2	4	4	1	0	0	1
			(ii)	1	0	0	3	0	2	2	0	1
	3	a	(i)	0	0	1	1	1	1	1	0	1
			(ii)	0	1	5	3	0	1	1	0	1
		b	(i)	1	3	6	11	17	5	6	0	5
			(ii)	5	0	2	9	3	3	1	0	3
	4			4	4	1	3	7	3	3	5	4
	5			0	1	0	0	0	0	0	0	0
Total				100	100	100	100	100	100	100	100	100

Percentage distributions: females (total = 1,057)

Major migration region	Rural-urban migration classification (see key)			Age								
				0-9	10-14	15-19	20-24	25-29	30-44	45-64	65+	All ages
Volta	1	a	(i)	44	27	25	30	18	22	47	45	33
			(ii)	35	40	37	29	51	42	33	43	38
		b	(i)	0	0	3	2	1	1	0	0	1
			(ii)	11	18	16	6	1	1	1	0	7
	2	a	(i)	0	1	1	1	0	2	1	0	1
			(ii)	1	2	3	14	14	11	10	7	7
		b	(i)	1	1	0	2	1	1	0	0	1
			(ii)	2	0	5	3	4	5	0	0	3
	3	a	(i)	1	1	0	1	0	1	0	0	1
			(ii)	0	0	1	0	1	1	0	0	0
		b	(i)	0	4	5	6	4	6	3	0	3
			(ii)	2	1	2	2	1	2	0	2	1
	4			3	5	2	3	4	5	5	3	4
	5			0	0	0	1	0	0	0	0	0
Total				100	100	100	100	100	100	100	100	100

Percentage distributions: persons (total = 3,397)

Major migration region	Rural-urban migration classification (see key)			Age								
				0-9	10-14	15-19	20-24	25-29	30-44	45-64	65+	All ages
Ashanti	1	a	(i)	80	74	58	45	50	44	59	67	60
			(ii)	6	8	22	29	27	31	27	26	20
		b	(i)	4	5	2	1	2	2	1	0	3
			(ii)	4	6	6	4	3	2	0	0	3
	2	a	(i)	0	1	1	3	2	3	1	2	2
			(ii)	1	1	2	3	4	4	4	5	3
		b	(i)	0	2	1	2	2	2	1	0	1
			(ii)	3	0	2	5	3	4	2	0	3
	3	a	(i)	0	1	0	1	0	0	1	0	0
			(ii)	0	2	1	0	0	0	0	0	0
		b	(i)	1	0	4	4	4	5	2	0	3
			(ii)	0	0	0	1	2	1	1	0	1
	4			1	0	1	2	1	2	1	0	1
	5			0	0	0	0	0	0	0	0	0
Total				100	100	100	100	100	100	100	100	100

Percentage distributions: males (total = 1,676)

Major migration region	Rural-urban migration classification (see key)			Age 0-9	10-14	15-19	20-24	25-29	30-44	45-64	65+	All ages
Ashanti	1	a	(i)	80	72	52	39	37	30	44	56	53
			(ii)	5	10	26	35	27	36	36	34	24
		b	(i)	4	5	3	0	3	3	2	0	3
			(ii)	6	6	7	6	4	2	0	0	5
	2	a	(i)	1	1	1	3	4	5	1	4	2
			(ii)	1	1	1	4	6	5	6	6	3
		b	(i)	0	0	1	1	3	3	2	0	1
			(ii)	2	1	2	5	5	5	3	0	3
	3	a	(i)	0	0	1	1	1	0	1	0	0
			(ii)	0	0	1	0	0	0	0	0	0
		b	(i)	1	2	4	4	7	8	2	0	4
			(ii)	0	0	0	2	2	1	1	0	1
	4			0	1	1	0	1	2	2	0	1
	5			0	1	0	0	0	0	0	0	0
Total				100	100	100	100	100	100	100	100	100

Percentage distributions: females (total = 1,715)

Major migration region	Rural-urban migration classification (see key)			Age 0-9	10-14	15-19	20-24	25-29	30-44	45-64	65+	All ages
Ashanti	1	a	(i)	81	76	64	50	59	60	77	84	68
			(ii)	7	5	16	25	28	26	16	13	16
		b	(i)	5	4	1	2	2	2	1	0	3
			(ii)	2	4	5	2	2	1	0	0	2
	2	a	(i)	0	1	1	3	1	1	1	0	1
			(ii)	1	2	4	3	3	3	2	3	3
		b	(i)	0	2	1	2	1	1	0	0	1
			(ii)	3	3	2	4	2	3	1	0	3
	3	a	(i)	0	0	0	1	0	0	1	0	0
			(ii)	0	1	1	0	0	0	0	0	0
		b	(i)	0	2	4	4	2	2	1	0	2
			(ii)	0	0	0	1	0	0	0	0	0
	4			1	0	1	3	0	1	0	0	1
	5			0	0	0	0	0	0	0	0	0
Total				100	100	100	100	100	100	100	100	100

Percentage distributions: persons (total = 2,541)

Major migration region	Rural-urban migration classification (see key)			Age 0-9	10-14	15-19	20-24	25-29	30-44	45-64	65+	All ages
North	1	a	(i)	58	59	41	38	38	47	50	65	47
			(ii)	8	5	16	27	24	17	13	7	15
		b	(i)	9	9	10	7	5	4	2	0	7
			(ii)	0	0	2	1	1	0	0	0	1
	2	a	(i)	2	1	3	3	3	4	7	4	3
			(ii)	0	1	1	2	4	6	18	20	5
		b	(i)	3	3	5	5	7	6	5	3	5
			(ii)	3	4	2	1	1	2	2	0	2
	3	a	(i)	0	1	2	2	1	3	0	0	1
			(ii)	2	4	7	3	3	2	1	0	3
		b	(i)	3	3	3	6	6	4	0	0	4
			(ii)	3	5	5	2	2	2	1	1	3
	4			7	5	2	3	5	3	0	0	3
	5			2	0	1	0	0	0	1	0	1
Total				100	100	100	100	100	100	100	100	100

Percentage distributions: males (total = 1,402)

Major migration region	Rural-urban migration classification (see key)			Age 0-9	10-14	15-19	20-24	25-29	30-44	45-64	65+	All ages
North	1	a	(i)	55	61	42	23	20	32	42	64	39
			(ii)	8	4	18	30	33	22	16	9	18
		b	(i)	12	8	10	7	6	5	3	0	7
			(ii)	0	0	3	2	1	1	0	0	1
	2	a	(i)	1	2	2	4	2	4	6	5	3
			(ii)	1	0	1	1	4	7	23	18	7
		b	(i)	4	2	5	9	12	8	6	2	7
			(ii)	3	4	2	1	2	2	3	0	2
	3	a	(i)	0	0	1	3	1	2	0	0	1
			(ii)	2	4	8	6	3	4	0	0	3
		b	(i)	3	4	4	10	6	6	0	0	5
			(ii)	4	6	3	3	3	3	0	2	3
	4			5	5	0	1	6	4	0	0	3
	5			2	0	1	0	1	0	1	0	1
Total				100	100	100	100	100	100	100	100	100

Percentage distributions: females (total = 1,126)

Major migration region	Rural-urban migration classification (see key)	Age								
		0-9	10-14	15-19	20-24	25-29	30-44	45-64	65+	All ages
North	1 a (i)	62	56	40	51	52	65	68	71	57
	(ii)	8	7	13	24	17	10	6	0	12
	b (i)	6	10	10	6	4	3	1	0	5
	(ii)	0	0	0	1	0	0	0	0	0
	2 a (i)	2	1	5	1	3	4	8	0	3
	(ii)	1	1	2	3	4	4	9	23	4
	b (i)	2	3	4	2	3	3	2	6	3
	(ii)	3	6	3	1	1	2	2	0	2
	3 a (i)	0	1	2	0	2	3	1	0	2
	(ii)	2	4	5	1	3	1	1	0	2
	b (i)	2	1	1	3	6	1	0	0	3
	(ii)	3	4	8	1	1	1	2	0	2
	4	8	6	4	5	4	3	0	0	4
	5	1	0	3	1	0	0	0	0	1
Total		100	100	100	100	100	100	100	100	100

(ii) Urban survey

Key to urban survey distributions:

Primary division (birthplace)	Secondary division (migration status in town)	Tertiary division (rural-urban link)
1 Town of enumeration		
2 Other town in Ghana	a temporary visit	
	b seasonal migration	
	c more permanent migration	(i) visits home centre at least once a year
		(ii) visits home centre more rarely or never
3 Village in Ghana	a temporary visit	
	b seasonal migration	
	c more permanent migration	(i) visits home centre at least once a year
		(ii) visits home centre more rarely or never
4 Town outside Ghana	a temporary visit	
	b seasonal migration	
	c more permanent migration	(i) visits home centre at least once a year
		(ii) visits home centre more rarely or never
5 Village outside Ghana	a temporary visit	
	b seasonal migration	
	c more permanent migration	(i) visits home centre at least once a year
		(ii) visits home centre more rarely or never
6 No entry		

Notes: The urban survey was largely confined to predominantly immigrant suburbs and thus these figures cannot be taken to represent the composition of the whole urban population. Towns are centres with more than 10,000 inhabitants; these have been checked for Ghana, but not outside, where the percentages are probably overstated (see Chapter 2). Other terms are defined as for the rural survey.

Percentage distributions: persons (total = 3,167)

Rural-urban migration classification (see key)			Age								
			0-9	10-14	15-19	20-24	25-29	30-44	45-64	65+	All ages
1			55	29	25	22	19	17	21	36	28
2	a		1	1	1	0	0	1	0	0	1
	b		0	0	0	0	0	0	0	0	(0·2)[a]
	c	(i)	6	5	5	3	5	6	5	0	6
		(ii)	2	4	2	2	3	1	1	0	2
3	a		0	0	0	0	1	0	0	0	(0·1)
	b		0	0	0	0	0	0	0	0	1
	c	(i)	1	3	3	3	3	2	6	7	4
		(ii)	0	0	0	1	0	4	6	0	2
4	a		3	2	7	5	4	4	4	14	3
	b		1	1	5	3	2	2	2	0	2
	c	(i)	24	41	42	53	51	51	36	7	39
		(ii)	5	12	8	5	7	7	7	7	6
5	a		0	0	0	0	0	0	2	0	(0·3)
	b		0	0	0	0	1	0	0	0	(0·4)
	c	(i)	0	0	1	1	3	2	4	7	3
		(ii)	2	2	1	2	1	3	4	0	2
6			0	0	0	0	0	0	2	22	(0·3)
Total			100	100	100	100	100	100	100	100	100

[a] In the 'all ages' columns percentages which would otherwise have been rounded to zero, have been shown in parentheses to one place of decimals.

Percentage distributions: males (total = 1,716)

Rural-urban migration classification (see key)			Age								
			0-9	10-14	15-19	20-24	25-29	30-44	45-64	65+	All ages
1			57	30	21	21	15	11	13	37	25
2	a		1	1	2	0	0	1	0	0	1
	b		0	0	0	0	0	0	0	0	(0·3)
	c	(i)	7	4	2	2	3	6	5	0	5
		(ii)	2	6	1	1	4	0	1	0	2
3	a		0	0	0	0	1	0	0	0	(0·2)
	b		0	0	0	1	0	0	0	0	1
	c	(i)	2	3	3	4	4	3	6	13	4
		(ii)	1	0	0	0	0	4	9	0	2
4	a		3	3	7	5	4	3	1	25	3
	b		0	1	7	4	3	2	2	0	2
	c	(i)	21	41	48	54	51	57	40	13	41
		(ii)	5	8	7	5	7	8	11	12	6
5	a		0	1	0	0	1	0	2	0	(0·4)
	b		0	0	1	1	2	0	0	0	1
	c	(i)	0	0	0	1	4	2	6	0	4
		(ii)	1	2	1	1	1	3	4	0	2
6			0	0	0	0	0	0	0	0	0
Total			100	100	100	100	100	100	100	100	100

Percentage distributions: females (total = 1,443)

Rural-urban migration classification (see key)			Age								
			0-9	10-14	15-19	20-24	25-29	30-44	45-64	65+	All ages
1			54	28	30	23	23	27	38	33	32
2	a		0	1	1	0	1	1	0	0	(0·4)
	b		0	0	0	0	0	0	0	0	(0·1)
	c	(i)	7	5	8	5	6	6	7	0	6
		(ii)	2	2	1	3	2	1	0	0	2
3	a		0	0	0	0	0	0	0	0	0
	b		0	0	0	0	1	0	0	0	(0·1)
	c	(i)	1	3	3	2	1	1	6	0	3
		(ii)	0	0	1	3	1	4	2	0	2
4	a		2	2	7	4	4	7	9	0	3
	b		1	1	3	3	1	1	2	0	2
	c	(i)	27	41	36	50	50	41	27	0	37
		(ii)	5	16	7	5	8	6	2	0	6
5	a		0	0	0	0	0	1	1	0	2
	b		0	0	0	0	0	0	0	0	0
	c	(i)	0	0	2	0	1	2	0	17	3
		(ii)	1	1	1	2	1	2	2	0	2
6			0	0	0	0	0	0	4	50	0
Total			100	100	100	100	100	100	100	100	100

(b) *Condensed distributions*

(i) Rural survey

Key to rural survey condensed distributions:

Condensed distribution	Note	Full distribution classification
Never migrated	Includes those currently 'visiting' town, a few of whom may have been previous migrants	1 a (i), 1 a (ii), 1 b (i), 1 b (ii), 3 a (i)
Seasonal migrant	Includes those currently in the town and those in the village who intend to migrate again	2 b (i), 3 a (ii)
Permanent returnee	Those who have been either seasonal or long-term migrants but who do not intend to migrate again	2 a (i), 2 a (ii)
Long-term absentee	Includes the long-term absentees resident in the town whether in the town or temporarily visiting the village at the time of the survey	2 b (ii), 3 b (i), 3 b (ii)
Other; no entry	—	4, 5

Notes: These categories refer only to rural-urban migration; persons who have migrated only to other rural areas, whether in the village or not at the time of the survey, are classified as 'never migrated'.

Percentage distributions: persons (total = 13,776)

Major migration region	Condensed rural-urban migration classification (see key)	Age 0-9	10-14	15-19	20-24	25-29	30-44	45-64	65+	All ages
All regions	never migrated	87	83	77	68	64	64	72	79	73
	seasonal migrant	2	3	6	6	7	6	3	1	4
	permanent returnee	3	3	4	7	10	11	14	15	8
	long-term absentee	5	7	12	16	15	16	9	3	12
	other; no entry	3	4	1	3	4	3	2	2	3
Total		100	100	100	100	100	100	100	100	100

Percentage distribution: males (total = 6,964)

Major migration region	Condensed rural-urban migration classification (see key)	Age 0-9	10-14	15-19	20-24	25-29	30-44	45-64	65+	All ages
All regions	never migrated	85	83	78	63	55	57	64	73	69
	seasonal migrant	2	3	6	9	8	6	4	2	5
	permanent returnee	3	3	3	6	12	13	17	19	9
	long-term absentee	7	7	12	20	20	21	13	4	14
	other; no entry	3	4	1	2	5	3	2	2	3
Total		100	100	100	100	100	100	100	100	100

Percentage distributions: females (total = 6,784)

Major migration region	Condensed rural-urban migration classification (see key)	Age 0-9	10-14	15-19	20-24	25-29	30-44	45-64	65+	All ages
All regions	never migrated	87	83	76	72	74	73	80	87	78
	seasonal migrant	2	3	5	4	5	4	2	1	3
	permanent returnee	3	3	5	8	8	9	10	9	7
	long-term absentee	5	8	11	13	10	12	6	2	10
	other; no entry	3	3	3	3	3	2	2	1	2
Total		100	100	100	100	100	100	100	100	100

Percentage distributions: persons (total = 5,769)

Major migration region	Condensed rural-urban migration classification (see key)	Age 0-9	10-14	15-19	20-24	25-29	30-44	45-64	65+	All ages
South	never migrated	82	80	72	57	52	52	65	72	66
	seasonal migrant	3	4	6	8	8	6	4	2	5
	permanent returnee	6	4	4	7	13	12	13	18	9
	long-term absentee	6	9	17	26	23	26	16	6	17
	other; no entry	3	3	1	2	4	4	2	2	3
Total		100	100	100	100	100	100	100	100	100

Percentage distributions: males (total = 2,874)

Major migration region	Condensed rural-urban migration classification (see key)	Age 0-9	10-14	15-19	20-24	25-29	30-44	45-64	65+	All ages
South	never migrated	81	80	71	51	42	44	56	57	60
	seasonal migrant	3	4	4	10	8	7	5	3	5
	permanent returnee	6	5	3	6	16	13	15	27	10
	long-term absentee	7	9	21	29	29	32	22	10	21
	other; no entry	3	2	1	4	5	4	2	3	4
Total		100	100	100	100	100	100	100	100	100

Percentage distributions: females (total = 2,886)

Major migration region	Condensed rural-urban migration classification (see key)	Age 0-9	10-14	15-19	20-24	25-29	30-44	45-64	65+	All ages
South	never migrated	84	80	70	61	63	64	74	86	71
	seasonal migrant	2	4	8	8	7	5	3	1	4
	permanent returnee	6	3	5	8	10	12	12	10	8
	long-term absentee	5	9	16	22	18	18	9	2	14
	other; no entry	3	4	1	1	2	1	2	1	3
Total		100	100	100	100	100	100	100	100	100

Percentage distributions: persons (total = 2,069)

Major migration region	Condensed rural-urban migration classification (see key)	Age 0-9	10-14	15-19	20-24	25-29	30-44	45-64	65+	All ages
Volta	never migrated	90	87	78	64	63	67	76	88	77
	seasonal migrant	0	0	4	4	4	2	0	0	2
	permanent returnee	1	4	6	14	15	16	15	7	9
	long-term absentee	5	4	11	15	13	11	5	1	8
	other; no entry	4	5	1	3	5	4	4	4	4
Total		100	100	100	100	100	100	100	100	100

Percentage distributions: males (total = 1,012)

Major migration region	Condensed rural-urban migration classification (see key)	Age 0-9	10-14	15-19	20-24	25-29	30-44	45-64	65+	All ages
Volta	never migrated	88	85	75	55	53	67	69	88	75
	seasonal migrant	0	1	7	7	4	2	1	0	2
	permanent returnee	1	6	9	12	16	18	18	7	10
	long-term absentee	7	3	8	23	20	10	9	0	9
	other; no entry	4	5	1	3	7	3	3	5	4
Total		100	100	100	100	100	100	100	100	100

Percentage distributions: females (total = 1,057)

Major migration region	Condensed rural-urban migration classification (see key)	Age 0-9	10-14	15-19	20-24	25-29	30-44	45-64	65+	All ages
Volta	never migrated	91	86	81	68	71	67	81	88	80
	seasonal migrant	1	1	1	2	2	2	0	0	1
	permanent returnee	1	3	4	15	14	13	11	7	8
	long-term absentee	4	5	12	11	9	13	3	2	7
	other; no entry	3	5	2	4	4	5	5	3	4
Total		100	100	100	100	100	100	100	100	100

Percentage distributions: persons (total = 3,397)

Major migration region	Condensed rural-urban migration classification (see key)	Age 0-9	10-14	15-19	20-24	25-29	30-44	45-64	65+	All ages
Ashanti	never migrated	94	94	88	80	82	79	88	93	86
	seasonal migrant	0	4	2	2	2	2	1	0	1
	permanent returnee	1	2	3	6	6	7	5	7	5
	long-term absentee	4	0	6	10	9	10	5	0	7
	other; no entry	1	0	1	2	1	2	1	0	1
Total		100	100	100	100	100	100	100	100	100

Percentage distributions: males (total = 1,676)

Major migration region	Condensed rural-urban migration classification (see key)	Age 0-9	10-14	15-19	20-24	25-29	30-44	45-64	65+	All ages
Ashanti	never migrated	95	93	89	81	72	71	83	90	85
	seasonal migrant	0	0	2	1	3	3	2	0	1
	permanent returnee	2	2	2	7	10	10	7	10	5
	long-term absentee	3	3	6	11	14	14	6	0	8
	other; no entry	0	2	1	0	1	2	2	0	1
Total		100	100	100	100	100	100	100	100	100

Percentage distributions: females (total = 1,715)

Major migration region	Condensed rural-urban migration classification (see key)	Age 0-9	10-14	15-19	20-24	25-29	30-44	45-64	65+	All ages
Ashanti	never migrated	95	89	86	80	91	89	95	97	89
	seasonal migrant	0	3	2	2	1	1	0	0	1
	permanent returnee	1	3	5	6	4	4	3	3	4
	long-term absentee	3	5	6	9	4	5	2	0	5
	other; no entry	1	0	1	3	0	1	0	0	1
Total		100	100	100	100	100	100	100	100	100

Percentage distributions: persons (total = 2,541)

Major migration region	Condensed rural-urban migration classification (see key)	Age								
		0-9	10-14	15-19	20-24	25-29	30-44	45-64	65+	All ages
North	never migrated	75	74	71	75	69	71	65	72	71
	seasonal migrant	5	7	12	8	10	8	6	3	8
	permanent returnee	2	2	4	5	7	10	25	24	8
	long-term absentee	9	12	10	9	9	8	3	1	9
	other; no entry	9	5	3	3	5	3	1	0	4
Total		100	100	100	100	100	100	100	100	100

Percentage distributions: males (total = 1,402)

Major migration region	Condensed rural-urban migration classification (see key)	Age								
		0-9	10-14	15-19	20-24	25-29	30-44	45-64	65+	All ages
North	never migrated	75	73	74	65	61	62	61	73	66
	seasonal migrant	6	6	13	15	15	12	6	2	10
	permanent returnee	2	2	3	5	6	11	29	23	10
	long-term absentee	10	14	9	14	11	11	3	2	10
	other; no entry	7	5	1	1	7	4	1	0	4
Total		100	100	100	100	100	100	100	100	100

Percentage distributions: females (total = 1,126)

Major migration region	Condensed rural-urban migration classification (see key)	Age								
		0-9	10-14	15-19	20-24	25-29	30-44	45-64	65+	All ages
North	never migrated	76	74	65	82	75	81	76	71	76
	seasonal migrant	4	7	9	3	6	4	3	6	5
	permanent returnee	3	2	7	4	7	8	17	23	7
	long-term absentee	8	11	12	5	8	4	4	0	7
	other; no entry	9	6	7	6	4	3	0	0	5
Total		100	100	100	100	100	100	100	100	100

(ii) Urban survey

Key to urban survey condensed distributions:

Condensation	Condensed distribution	Note	Full distribution classification
Birthplace condensation	urban	i.e. in towns as defined in the urban survey distribution key	1, 2 a, 2 b, 2 c (i), 2 c (ii), 3 a, 3 b, 3 c (i), 3 c (ii).
	rural		4 a, 4 b, 4 c (i), 4 c (ii), 5 a, 5 b, 5 c (i), 5 c (ii).
	no entry		6
Migration status condensation	local	born in centre of enumeration	1
	long-term		2 c (i), 2 c (ii), 3 c (i), 3 c (ii), 4 c (i), 4 c (ii), 5 c (i), 5 c (ii).
	seasonal		2 b, 3 b, 4 b, 5 b.
	temporary	includes visiting	2 a, 3 a, 4 a, 5 a.
	no entry		18

Notes: There are few old persons, especially old females, in the migrant suburbs of the towns. Hence the failure to secure birthplace data about a small number of women over 60 years of age has given a high percentage response in the 'no entry' category for that age in both the persons and females groupings.

Percentage distributions: persons (total = 3,167)

Condensation	Condensed distribution (see key)	Age								
		0-9	10-14	15-19	20-24	25-29	30-44	45-64	65+	All ages
Birthplace condensation	urban	65	42	36	31	31	31	39	43	44
	rural	35	58	64	69	69	69	59	35	56
	no entry	0	0	0	0	0	0	2	22	0
Total		100	100	100	100	100	100	100	100	100

Percentage distributions: males (total = 1,716)

Condensation	Condensed distribution (see key)	Age								
		0-9	10-14	15-19	20-24	25-29	30-44	45-64	65+	All ages
Birthplace condensation	urban	70	44	29	29	27	25	34	50	41
	rural	30	56	71	71	73	75	66	50	59
	no entry	0	0	0	0	0	0	0	0	0
Total		100	100	100	100	100	100	100	100	100

Percentage distributions: females (total = 1,443)

Condensation	Condensed distribution (see key)	Age								
		0-9	10-14	15-19	20-24	25-29	30-44	45-64	65+	All ages
Birthplace condensation	urban	64	39	44	36	35	40	53	33	45
	rural	36	61	56	64	65	60	43	17	55
	no entry	0	0	0	0	0	0	4	50	0
Total		100	100	100	100	100	100	100	100	100

Percentage distributions: persons (total = 3,167)

Condensation	Condensed distribution (see key)	Age								
		0-9	10-14	15-19	20-24	25-29	30-44	45-64	65+	All ages
Migration status condensation	local	55	29	25	22	19	17	21	36	28
	long-term	40	67	62	70	73	76	69	28	64
	seasonal	1	1	5	3	3	2	2	0	4
	temporary	4	3	8	5	5	5	6	14	4
	no entry	0	0	0	0	0	0	2	22	0
Total		100	100	100	100	100	100	100	100	100

Percentage distributions: males (total = 1,716)

Condensation	Condensed distribution (see key)	Age								
		0-9	10-14	15-19	20-24	25-29	30-44	45-64	65+	All ages
Migration status condensation	local	57	30	21	21	15	11	13	37	25
	long-term	40	64	62	68	74	83	82	38	66
	seasonal	0	1	8	6	5	2	2	0	4
	temporary	3	5	9	5	6	4	3	25	5
	no entry	0	0	0	0	0	0	0	0	0
Total		100	100	100	100	100	100	100	100	100

Percentage distributions: females (total = 1,443)

Condensation	Condensed distribution (see key)	Age								
		0-9	10-14	15-19	20-24	25-29	30-44	45-64	65+	All ages
Migration status condensation	local	54	28	30	23	23	27	38	33	32
	long-term	43	68	59	70	70	62	46	17	61
	seasonal	1	1	3	3	2	2	2	0	2
	temporary	2	3	8	4	5	9	10	0	5
	no entry	0	0	0	0	0	0	4	50	0
Total		100	100	100	100	100	100	100	100	100

(c) *Diagrams of condensed distributions*

Fig. 1 Distribution of rural survey population by condensed migration classification and age, subdivided by major migration region and sex

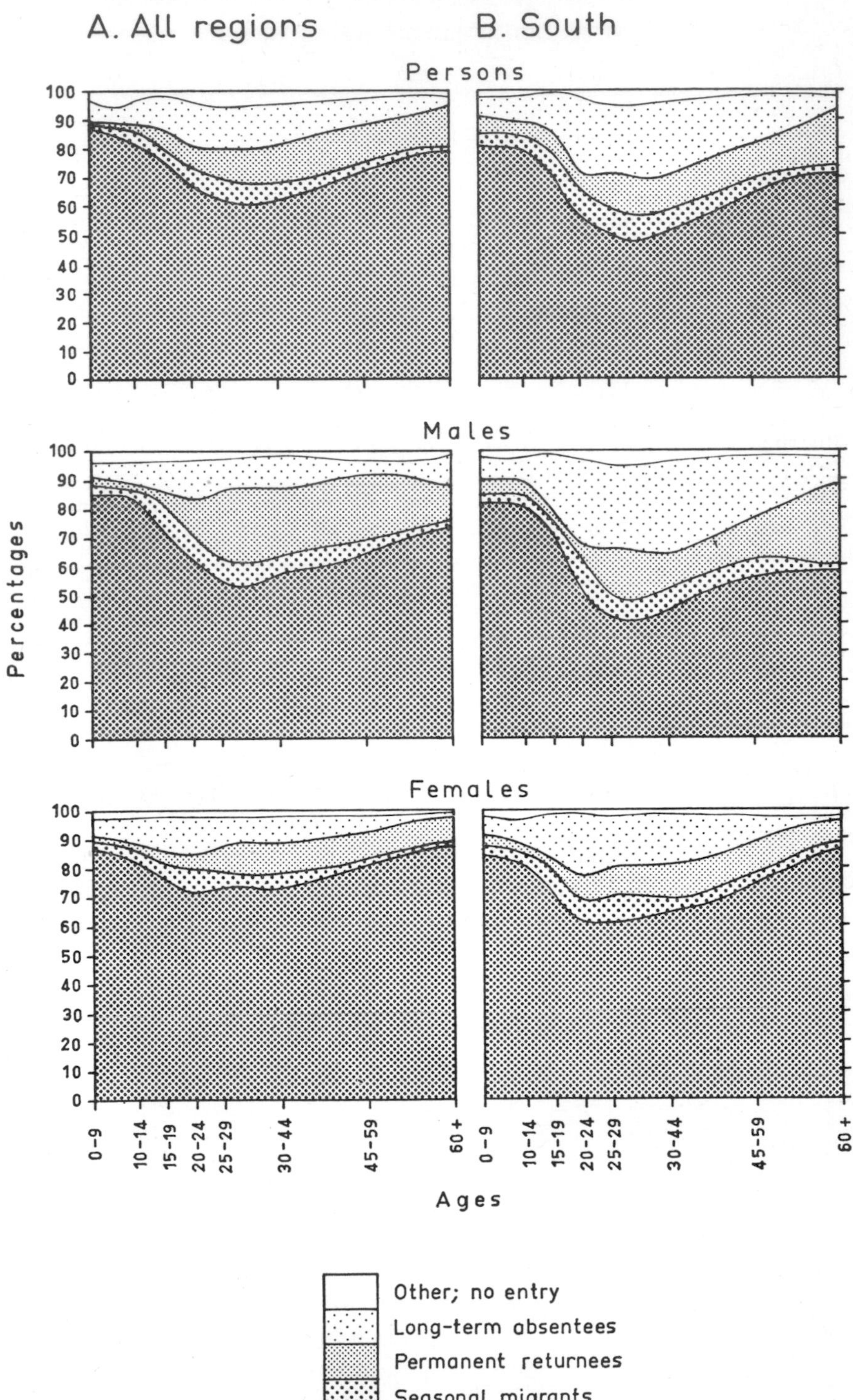

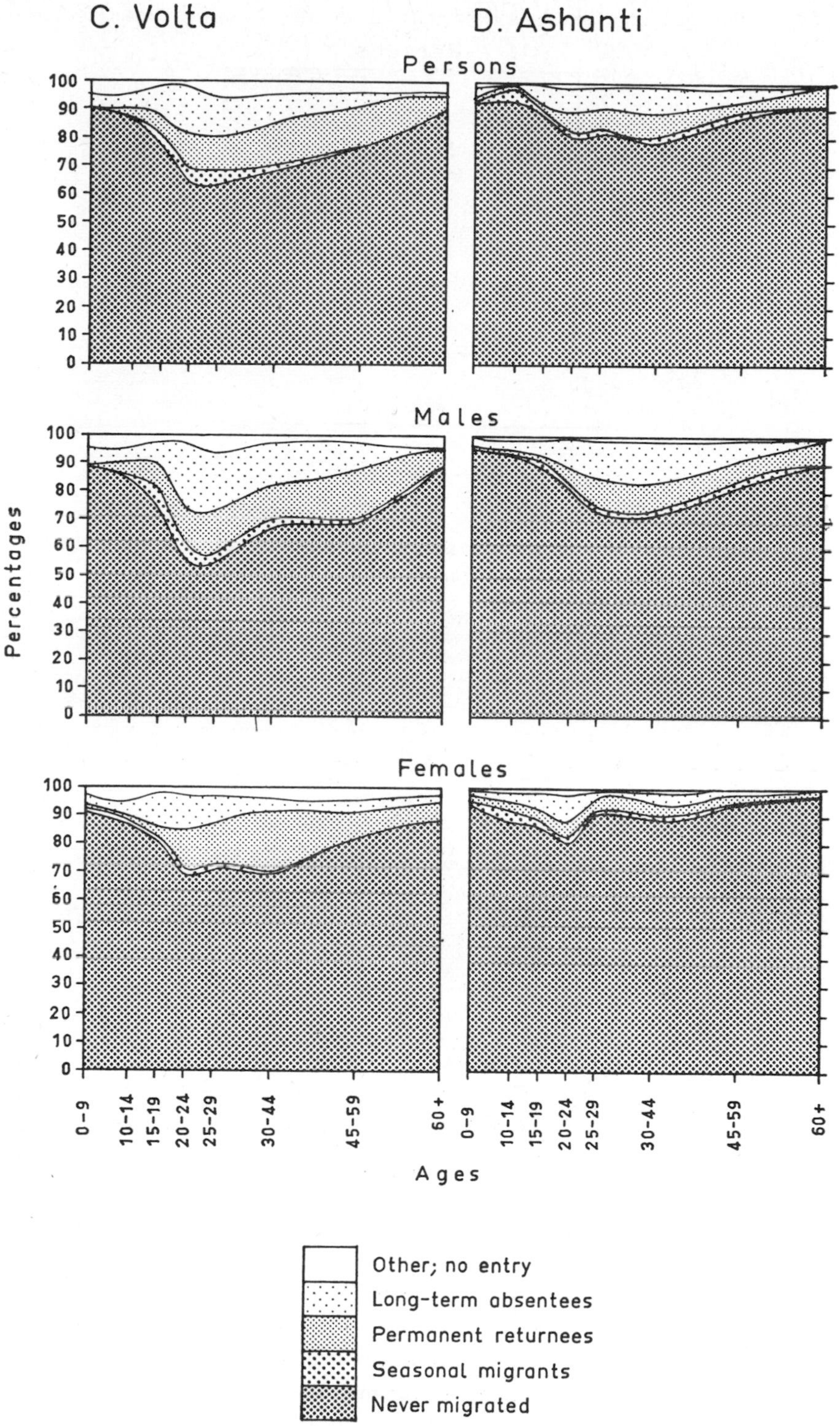

C. Volta

D. Ashanti

Persons

Males

Females

Percentages

100 90 80 70 60 50 40 30 20 10 0

0–9 10–14 15–19 20–24 25–29 30–44 45–59 60+

Ages

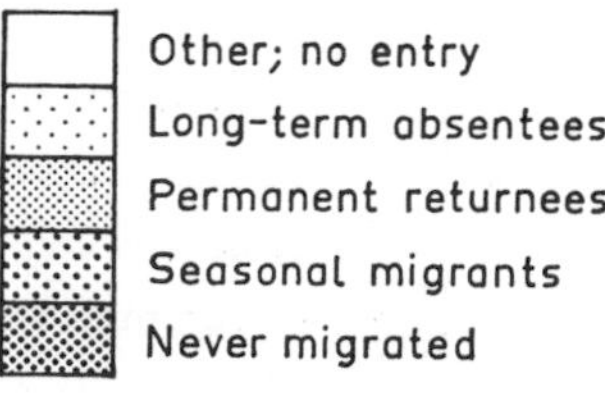

E. North

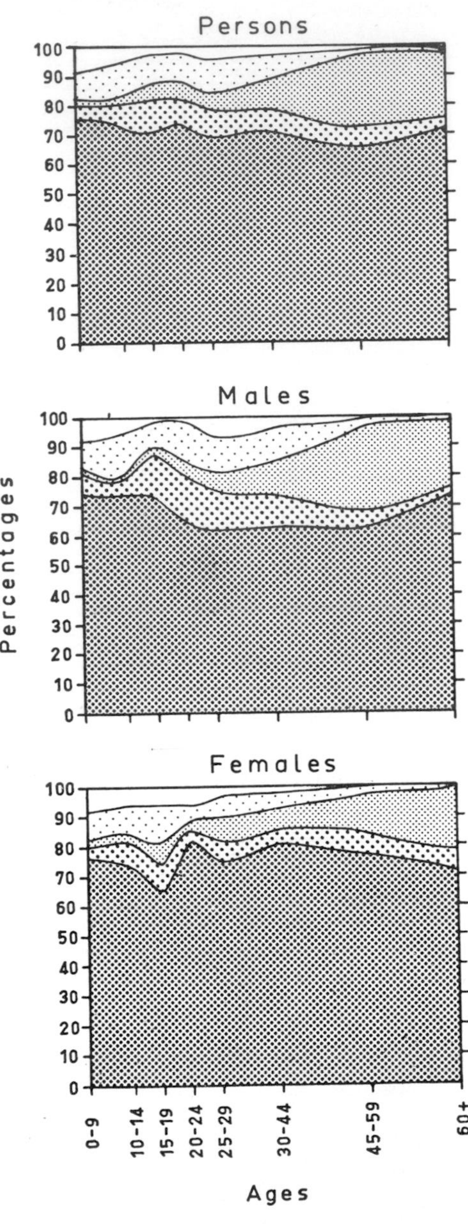
Persons
Males
Females
Percentages
100
90
80
70
60
50
40
30
20
10
0
0-9
10-14
15-19
20-24
25-29
30-44
45-59
60+
Ages

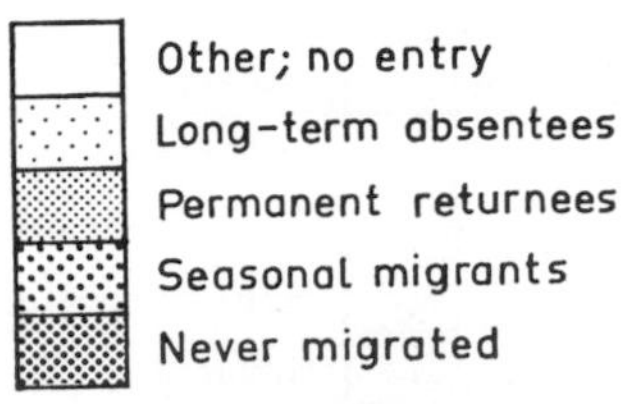
Other; no entry
Long-term absentees
Permanent returnees
Seasonal migrants
Never migrated

Fig. 2 Distribution of urban survey population by condensed migration classification and age, subdivided by sex

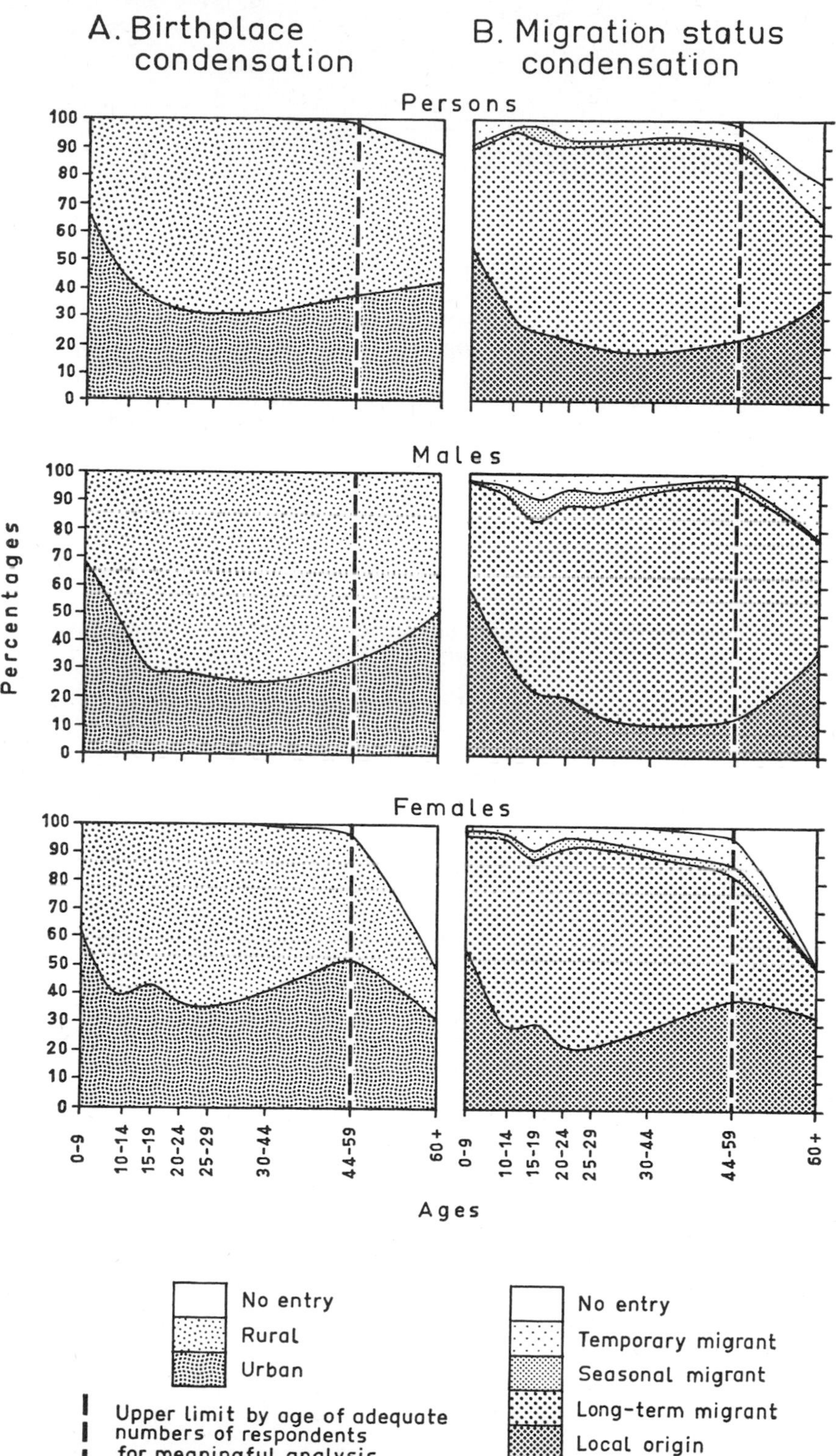

References Cited

Acquah, Ioné (1958). *Accra Survey*, London.

Addo, Nelson Otu (1966). 'Demographic Aspects of Urban Development in Ghana in the Twentieth Century', paper presented to the First African Population Conference, Ibadan, 3-7 January.

Aldous, Joan (1962). 'Urbanization, the Extended Family, and Kinship Ties in West Africa', in Pierre L. van den Berghe (ed.), *Africa: Social Problems of Change and Conflict*, San Francisco, 1966, 107-16 (reprinted from *Social Forces*, Vol. 41, 1962, 6-12).

Apter, David E. (1955). *The Gold Coast in Transition*, Princeton.

Austin, Dennis (1964). *Politics in Ghana, 1946-1960*, London.

Bascom, William (1962). 'Some Aspects of Yoruba Urbanism', *American Anthropoligist*, Vol. LXIV, 1962, 699-709.

Berg, Elliott J. (1965). 'The Economics of the Migrant Labour System', in Hilda Kuper (ed.), *Urbanization and Migration in West Africa*, 160-84.

Birmingham, Walter, Neustadt, I., and Omaboe, E. N. (eds.) (1966, 1967). *A Study of Contemporary Ghana*, Vol. I, *The Economy of Ghana*, 1966; Vol. II, *Some Aspects of Social Structure*, 1967, London and Chicago.

Brokensha, David (1966). *Social Change at Larteh, Ghana*, Oxford.

Caldwell, J. C., (1965). 'Extended Family Obligations and Education: A Study of an Aspect of Demographic Transition amongst Ghanaian University Students', *Population Studies*, Vol. XIX, No. 2, 183-99.

——— (1966). 'The Erosion of the Family: A Study of the Fate of the Family in Ghana', *Population Studies*, Vol. XX, No. 1, 8-26.

——— (1967a). 'Population: General Characteristics', 'Population Change', 'Migration and Urbanization', and 'Population Prospects and Policy', in Walter Birmingham, I. Neustadt, and E. N. Omaboe (eds.), *A Study of Contemporary Ghana*, Vol. II, *Some Aspects of Social Structure*, London and Chicago, 17-200.

——— (1967b). 'Fertility Attitudes in Three Economically Contrasting Regions of Ghana', *Economic Development and Cultural Change*, Vol. XV, No. 2, 217-38.

——— (1967c). 'Fertility Differentials as Evidence of Incipient Fertility Decline in a Developing Country: the Case of Ghana', *Population Studies*, Vol. XXI, No. 1, 5-21.

——— (1968a). 'The Determinants of Rural-urban Migration in Ghana', *Population Studies*, Vol. XXII, No. 3, 361-77.

——— (1968b). *Population Growth and Family Change in Africa: The New Urban Elite in Ghana*, Canberra.

———and Chukuka Okonjo (eds.) (1968). *The Population of Tropical Africa*, London and New York.

Census (1921). *1921 Population Census of the Gold Coast Report*, Accra.

——— (1931). *1931 Population Census of the Gold Coast Report*, Accra.

——— (1948). *1948 Population Census of the Gold Coast Report*, Accra.

——— (1960). *1960 Population Census of Ghana*, Accra.

Individual volumes are shown as follows:

Vol. I. *The Gazetteer, Alphabetical List of Localities*, Accra, 1962.

Vol. II. *Statistics of Localities and Enumeration Areas*, Accra, 1962.

Advance Report. Advance Report of Volumes III and IV, Accra, 1962.

Vol. III. *Demographic Characteristics*, Accra, 1964.

Vol. IV. *Economic Characteristics of Local Authorities, Regions and Total Country*, Accra, 1964.

Special Report A. Statistics of Large Towns, Accra, 1964.

Special Report E. Tribes in Ghana: Demographic, Economic and Social Characteristics, Accra, 1964.

Atlas. Atlas of Population Characteristics, Accra, 1964.

Church, R. J. Harrison (1957). *West Africa: A Study of the Environment and of Man's Use of It*, London.

Davis, Kingsley and Golden, Hilda Hertz (1954-5). 'Urbanization and the Development of Pre-industrial Areas', *Economic Development and Cultural Change*, Vol. III, 6-26.

Davison, R. B. (1955). *Migrant Labour in the Gold Coast*, Accra.

——— (1957). 'Labour Relations in Ghana', *The Annals*, Vol. CCX, March, 133-41.

E.C.A. (Economic Commission for Africa) (1962). 'Demographic Factors Related to Social and Economic Development in Africa', *Economic Bulletin for Africa*, Vol. II, No. 2, 59-81.

——— (1965). 'Recent Demographic Levels and Trends in Africa', *Economic Bulletin for Africa*, Vol. V, 30-79.

——— (1966). 'The Demographic Situation in West Africa', a report to a Sub-regional Meeting on Economic Co-operation in West Africa, Niamey, 10-22 October.

Ejiogu, C. N. (1968). 'African Rural-urban Migrants in the Main Migrant Areas of the Federal Territory of Lagos', in J. C. Caldwell and Chukuka Okonjo (eds.), *The Population of Tropical Africa*, London, 320-30.

Elkan, Walter (1959). 'Migrant Labour in Africa: An Economist's Approach', *American Economic Review*, Vol. XLIX, No. 2, 188-97.

Gil, B. (1967). 'Immigration into Ghana and its Contribution in Skill', paper presented to the United Nations World Population Conference, Belgrade, 1965, and printed in United Nations, *World Population Conference, 1965*, Vol. IV, New York, 1967.

——— and Omaboe, E. N. (1963). 'Appendix to the Paper on "Internal Migration Differentials from Conventional Census Questionnaire Items—Ghana" ' (see Gil and Omaboe 1966), appendix to paper presented to the 1963 session of the International Statistical Institute, Ottawa.

——— and ——— (1966). 'Internal Migration Differentials from Conventional Census Questionnaire Items in Ghana', *Proceedings of the 1963 Session of the International Statistical Institute.*

Hailey, Lord (1957). *An African Survey, Revised 1956: A Study of Problems arising in Africa South of the Sahara.* London.

Hill, Polly (1961). 'The Migrant Cocoa Farmers of Southern Ghana', *Africa*, Vol. XXXI, No. 3, 209-30.

——— (1963). *The Migrant Cocoa-farmers of Southern Ghana: A Study in Rural Capitalism*, Cambridge.

Hilton, T. E. (1968). 'Population Growth and Distribution in the Upper Region of Ghana', in John C. Caldwell and Chukuka Okonjo (eds.), *The Population of Tropical Africa*, London, 278-90.

Hoyt, Michael P. E. (1962). *Migratory Labour in West Africa*, Department of State, Foreign Service Institute, Washington.

Hurd, G. E. (1967). 'Education', in Walter Birmingham, I. Neustadt, and E. N. Omaboe (eds.), *A Study of Contemporary Ghana*, Vol. II, *Some Aspects of Social Structure*, London and Chicago, 217-39.

I.L.O. (International Labour Office) (1960). *Why Labour Leaves the Land: A Comparative Study of the Movement of Labour out of Agriculture*, Geneva.

International African Institute (1956). *Social Implications of Industralization and Urbanization in Africa South of the Sahara*, UNESCO.

I.U.S.S.P. (International Union for the Scientific Study of Population) (1960). *Problems in African Demography*, Paris.

Killick, Tony (1966). 'Labour: A General Survey', in Walter Birmingham, I. Neustadt, and E. N. Omaboe (eds.), *A Study of Contemporary Ghana*, Vol. I, *The Economy of Ghana*, London and Chicago, 121-53.

Kimble, George H. T. (1962). *Tropical Africa*, Vol. I, *Land and Livelihood*, New York.

Kuper, Hilda (ed.) (1965). *Urbanization and Migration in West Africa*, Berkeley.

Little, Kenneth (1957). 'The Role of Voluntary Associations in West African Urbanization', *American Anthropologist*, Vol. LIX, 579-96.

——— (1965). *West African Urbanization: A Study of Voluntary Associations in Social Change*, Cambridge.

Lorimer, Frank (1961). *Demographic Information on Tropical Africa*, Boston.

——— and Karp, Mark (1960). *Population in Africa*, Boston.

McCall, Daniel (1955). 'Dynamics of Urbanization in Africa', *The Annals*, Vol. CCIIC, March, 151-60.

Miner, Horace M. (1965). 'Urban Influences on Rural Hausa', in Hilda Kuper (ed.), *Urbanization and Migration in West Africa*, Berkeley, 110-30.

Okigbo, Pius (1956). 'Social Consequences of Economic Development in West Africa', *Annals of the American Academy of Political and Social Science*, Vol. XXXV, May, 125-33.

Omaboe, E. N. (1967). 'An Introductory Survey', in Walter Birmingham, I. Neustadt, and E. N. Omaboe (eds.), *A Study of Contemporary Ghana*, Vol. I, *The Economy of Ghana*, London and Chicago, 17-33.

Pool, D. I. (1968). 'The Number and Type of Conjugal Unions as Correlates of Levels of Fertility and Attitudes to Family Limitation in Ghana', paper presented to the Annual Meeting of the Population Association of America, Boston, 18-20 April.

Prothero, R. Mansell (1957). 'Migratory Labour from North-western Nigeria', *Africa*, Vol. XXVII, No. 3, 251-61.

——— (1958). *Migrant Labour from Sokoto Province, Northern Nigeria*, Government Printer, Northern Region of Nigeria.

——— (1965). *Migrants and Malaria*, London.

——— (1968). 'Migration in Africa', in J. C. Caldwell and Chukuka Okonjo (eds.), *The Population of Tropical Africa*, London and New York, 250-63.

Rouch, Jean (1954). 'Notes on Migrations into the Gold Coast: First Report of the Mission carried out in the Gold Coast from March to December, 1954', Accra, 73 pp., mimeographed.

——— (1956). 'Migrations au Ghana (Gold Coast), enquête 1953-55', *Journal de la Société des Africanistes*, Vol. XXVI, Nos. 1 and 2, 33-164.

——— (1961a). Report in *Study of Migrations in West Africa, Joint Project*, No. 3, Symposium, Niamey, 13-25 February.

——— (1961b). 'Second Generation Migrants in Ghana and the Ivory Coast', in Aidan Southall (ed.), *Social Change in Modern Africa*, Oxford, 300-4.

Skinner, Elliott P. (1960). 'Labour Migration and its Relationship to Socio-cultural Change in Mossi Society', *Africa*, Vol. XXX, No. 4, 375-99.

——— (1965). 'Labour Migration Amongst the Mossi of the Upper Volta', in Hilda Kuper (ed.), *Urbanization and Migration in West Africa*, Berkeley, 60-84.

Szereszewski, Robert (1966). 'The Macroeconomic Structure', in Walter Birmingham, I. Neustadt, and E. N. Omaboe (eds.), *A Study of Contemporary Ghana*, Vol. I, *The Economy of Ghana*, London, 37-117.

Tetteh, P. A. (1967). 'Marriage, Family and Household', in Walter Birmingham, I. Neustadt, and E. N. Omaboe (eds.), *A Study of Contemporary Ghana*, Vol. II, *Some Aspects of Social Structure*, London and *Chicago*, 201-16.

United Nations (1957). 'Urbanization in Africa South of the Sahara', in *Report on the World Social Situation*, New York, 144-69.

van den Berghe, Pierre L. (1965). *Africa: Social Problems of Change and Conflict*, San Francisco.

van de Walle, E. (1968). 'Population Change and Economic Development in Tropical Africa', in J. C. Caldwell and Chukuka Okonjo (eds.), *The Population of Tropical Africa*, London and New York, 360-7.

Wallerstein, Immanuel (1965). 'Migration in West Africa: The Political Perspective', in Hilda Kuper (ed.), *Urbanization and Migration in West Africa*, Berkeley, 148-50.

Index

Dr John C. Caldwell, now Professor of Demography, University of Ife, Nigeria, is Regional Director for Africa in the Demographic Division of the Population Council, New York. He is a graduate of the University of New England and of the Australian National University. In 1962-4, while Associate Professor of Sociology at the University of Ghana, he organised a large demographic research program in that country, and it was during this period that the research for this book was undertaken.

Dr Caldwell is the author of *Population Growth and Family Change in Africa*, and co-editor of *The Population of Tropical Africa*.

Set in 10 Point Linotype Times New Roman, one point leaded, and printed on 85 gsm Burnie English Finish paper by Brown Prior Anderson Pty Ltd. Melbourne.